"EACH MAN CRIED OUT TO HIS GOD"

The Specialized Religion
of Canaanite and Phoenician Seafarers

HARVARD SEMITIC MUSEUM PUBLICATIONS

Lawrence E. Stager, General Editor
Michael D. Coogan, Director of Publications

HARVARD SEMITIC MONOGRAPHS

edited by
Peter Machinist

Number 58
"EACH MAN CRIED OUT TO HIS GOD"
The Specialized Religion
of Canaanite and Phoenician Seafarers

by
Aaron Jed Brody

Aaron Jed Brody

"EACH MAN CRIED OUT TO HIS GOD"

The Specialized Religion of Canaanite and Phoenician Seafarers

Scholars Press
Atlanta, Georgia

"EACH MAN CRIED OUT TO HIS GOD"

The Specialized Religion of Canaanite and Phoenician Seafarers

by
Aaron Jed Brody

Copyright © 1998 by The President and Fellows of Harvard College

All rights reserved. No part of this work may be reproduced or transmitted in any form or by any means, electronic or mechanical, including photocopying and recording, or by means of any information storage or retrieval system, except as may be expressly permitted by the 1976 Copyright Act or in writing from the publisher. Requests for permission should be addressed in writing to the Rights and Permissions Office, Scholars Press, P.O. Box 15399, Atlanta, GA 30333-0399, USA.

Library of Congress Cataloging in Publication Data
Brody, Aaron Jed.
    "Each man cried out to his God" ; the specialized religion of Canaanite and Phoenician seafarers / Aaron Jed Brody.
        p.   cm. — (Harvard Semitic museum publications) (Harvard Semitic monographs ; no. 58)
      Includes bibliographical references.
      ISBN 0-7885-0466-5 (hardcover : alk. paper)
      1. Sailors—Religious life—Phoenicia. 2. Sailors—Religious life—Palestine. 3. Seafaring life—Religious aspects. 4. Gods, Phoenician—Cult—Lebanon. 5. Gods, Canaanite—Cult—Palestine. 6. Excavation (Archaeology)—Mediterranean Region. 7. Mediterranean Region—Antiquities. 8. Lebanon—Religion. 9. Palestine—Religion. 10. Mediterranean Region—Religion.   I. Title. II. Series. III. Series: Harvard Semitic monographs ; no. 58.
BL1665.S24B76   1998
299'.26—dc21   98-18411
                                    CIP

Printed in the United States of America
on acid-free paper

DEDICATION

I would like to dedicate this work to my family and friends, whose support, encouragement, patience, and love has seen me through the project from its inception to completion: Richard, Marjorie, Gordon, Deborah, David, and Bill; John and Gail, Ron, Malcolm, Ezra, Jack, Anna, Judy, John and Ute, Michael, Benjamin, Peter, Jeff, Haddon, Glenda, Liz, Ann, Eric, and especially Chrissy. Thanks goes out to all of you.

CONTENTS

Acknowledgements...viii
Abbreviations..ix
Introduction...1
CHAPTER 1 The Patron Deities of Canaanite and
            Phoenician Seafarers...9
CHAPTER 2 Seaside Temples and Shrines....................................39
CHAPTER 3 Sacred Space Aboard Ship...63
CHAPTER 4 Religious Ceremonies Performed by
            Levantine Sailors 73
CHAPTER 5 Maritime Mortuary Ritual and
            Burial Practices...87
Conclusions..95
Bibliography...105
List of Figures...125
Figures 129
Index 173

ACKNOWLEDGEMENTS

My academic interest in sea trade and interconnections between ancient societies began my first year at Berkeley, during a lecture by William Collins on early links between Southeast Asia and the Middle East. This interest was further developed under the guidance and friendship of Ezra Marcus and Michal Artzy in Haifa, who introduced me to Near Eastern and maritime archaeology, the pleasures of fieldwork on land and underwater, and planted the seeds which eventually lead me to my present research. It is Mark Mancall whom I blame for getting me over to Israel in the first place, and inspiring me to learn languages, both living and dead.

As this work is a revision of my doctoral dissertation, I would like to thank the members of my thesis committee, Lawrence Stager, Frank Moore Cross, Irene Winter, and Jo Ann Hackett, whose careful attention to both detail and structure can be seen throughout the work. My advisor Lawrence Stager's influences permeate my research whether in method or theory, taking archaeology not just as a study of material culture but as an approach to understanding ancient societies. Thanks also to the editors of the monograph series, Michael Coogan, Peter Machinist, and Lawrence Stager, for their thoughtful comments and corrections.

I must also thank Dr. Stager for making me part of the excavation team at Tel Ashkelon. My fieldwork at Ashkelon benefitted under the tutelage of Liz Bloch-Smith and Egon Lass, and from interactions with my fellow supervisors and volunteers, who I learn from every season.

The staff and fellows at the Albright Institute, especially Sy Gitin and Edna Sachar, must also be acknowledged for their continuing intellectual and moral support. I would like to thank the American Schools of Oriental Research, the Dorot Foundation, the United States Information Agency, and the Brody family whose financial support has made this research possible.

While back in California I learned a whole new set of archaeological issues working with the Muwekma-Ohlone nation. Thanks go out to Laura Jones, Alan Leventhal, Rosemary Cambra, Norma Sanchez, and to the Muwekma, Esselen, and Amah-Mudson people for introducing me to the past in my own backyard and teaching me the possibilities of bridging the gap between native peoples, archaeology, and archaeologists.

ABBREVIATIONS

AJA	*American Journal of Archaeology*
Akk.	Akkadian
ANEP	J. B. Pritchard, ed., *The Ancient Near East in Pictures Relating to the Old Testament*
ANET	J. B. Pritchard, ed., *Ancient Near Eastern Texts Relating to the Old Testament*
Arab.	Arabic
BA	*Biblical Archaeologist*
BASOR	*Bulletin of the American Schools of Oriental Research*
BCH	*Bulletin du Correspondance Hellénique*
BDB	F. Brown, S. R. Driver, and C. A. Briggs, *A Hebrew and English Lexicon of the Old Testament*
CIS	*Corpus Inscriptionum Semiticarum*
CTA	A. Herdner, *Corpus des tablettes en cunéiformes alphabétiques*
Eg.	Egyptian
EI	*Eretz-Israel*
Eth.	Ethiopic
GGM	C. Müller, *Geographici Graeci Minores*
Gk.	Greek
Heb.	Hebrew
ID	F. Durrbach, *Inscriptions de Délos*
IEJ	*Israel Exploration Journal*
JAOS	*Journal of the American Oriental Society*
JNES	*Journal of Near Eastern Studies*
KAI	H. Donner and W. Röllig, *Kanaanäische und Aramäische Inschriften*
KTU	M. Dietrich, O. Loretz, and J. Sanmartin, *Die keilalphabetischen Texte aus Ugarit*
KUB	Staatliche Museen zu Berlin, Vorderasiatische Abteilung. *Keilschrifturkunden aus Boghazköi.* Berlin: 1921-.
MUSJ	*Mélanges de l'Université Saint-Joseph*
PEQ	*Palestine Exploration Quarterly*
Phoen.	Phoenician
Praep. Evang.	Eusebius, *Praeparatio Evangelica*

QDAP	*Quarterly of the Department of Antiquities in Palestine*
RSF	*Rivista di studi fenici*
StudPhoen	*Studia Phoenicia*
UF	*Ugarit-Forschungen*
Ug.	Ugaritic

INTRODUCTION

Sailors crossing the waters of the Mediterranean from prehistoric times to the present have shared similar concerns caused by the winds, tides, and uncertainties of navigating at sea. Though the water has always had great potential for opening up avenues of contact and communication between Mediterranean cultures, it also poses both a physical and a psychological boundary for humans more familiar with terrestrial surroundings. In response to the unique set of issues generated by the sea, seafarers have developed specialized religious beliefs and practices. Though past works have touched upon facets of the maritime religions of Near Eastern cultures, the topic has yet to be fully addressed with regard to the Bronze Age seafaring Canaanites and their descendants the Phoenicians.[1]

The present study draws on a framework derived from research on seafaring and religion in the classical Mediterranean world and on anthropological studies of the religion of traditional seafaring communities. Despite differences in geographical region, time period, and culture from the Canaanites and Phoenicians, I have found that the similarity of concerns posed by the sea and the dangers of sailing allows

[1] The terms Canaanite and Phoenician are the West Semitic and Greek names for the same people. This is especially apparent in the fact that individuals called Phoenician or Punic by authors writing in Greek and Latin refer to themselves as Canaanites; see D. Harden, *The Phoenicians* (Harmondsworth, England: Penguin Books, 1971), pp. 19-20; and W. F. Albright, "The Role of the Canaanites in the History of Civilization," in *The Bible and the Ancient Near East*, ed. G. E. Wright (Garden City, NY: Doubleday, 1961), p. 328, n. 1. Following the work on ethnicity by the social anthropologist F. Barth, the way that a group refers to itself is one category for defining an ethnic group; see Introduction to *Ethnic Groups and Boundaries: The Social Organization of Culture Difference*, ed. F. Barth (Boston: Little, Brown, 1969), pp. 9-38. Therefore, following Albright, I shall use the term "Canaanite" to refer to the culture of western Syria-Palestine before the end of the Late Bronze Age, and "Phoenician" for the same group, which also spread throughout the Mediterranean, for the Iron Age and later periods when they are called Phoenician in Greek texts; see Albright, "The Role of the Canaanites," p. 328.

me to adapt this work, with appropriate modifications, in order to develop a model for investigating possible Canaanite-Phoenician maritime religion.[2]

Classical studies vary in their treatment of the religion of seafarers; most focus on a single aspect of the subject. Semple's work, for instance, details the sacred significance of promontories to Mediterranean mariners.[3] She relies primarily on Greek textual evidence, but does not overlook references to promontories sacred to Phoenician sailors mentioned in classical works.[4] Svoronos's research into ships' sacred symbols collects and interprets the numerous emblems depicted on vessels on classical coinage.[5] His study, like Semple's, focuses primarily on the Greek evidence, but does not ignore the data from Phoenician coins. Aegean model ships are catalogued in Johnston's work, which includes interpretive sections describing models discovered in sacred contexts which are votive, that is, offered in response to a vow.[6] Aegean artifacts with sacral significance which have been found underwater are the subject of Kapitän's research.[7] Objects recovered from the sea such as portable altars, libation vessels, lead-filled bulls' horns, and anchor stocks with cultic motifs or inscriptions parallel the textual evidence of Greek maritime ritual. The importance of anchors found on land in sacred contexts on Crete is the subject of Davaras's study.[8] He also discusses the dedication of votive anchors in sanctuaries found in classical texts, and comparative archaeological evidence for sacred anchors discovered at Greek, Roman, and Canaanite sites.

---

[2]The impulses behind the religious needs created by venturing at sea appear to be universal. The response to these universal impulses, however, varies according to localized beliefs and practices. This shall be considered when examining the similarities and differences between classical, traditional, and Canaanite-Phoenician seafarers' religion.
[3]E. C. Semple, "The Templed Promontories of the Ancient Mediterranean," *The Geographical Review* 17/3 (1927), 353-86.
[4]*Ibid.*, especially p. 366.
[5]J. N. Svoronos, "Stylides, ancres hierae, aphlasta, stoloi, ackrostrolia, embola, proembola et totems marins," *Journal international d'archéologie numismatique* 16 (1914), 81-152.
[6]P. F. Johnston, *Ship and Boat Models in Ancient Greece* (Annapolis, MD: Naval Institute Press, 1985). Definition of votive taken from *The Oxford English Dictionary*, XIX (Oxford: Clarendon, 1989), 769.
[7]G. Kapitän, "Archaeological Evidence for Rituals and Customs on Ancient Ships," in *Tropis I: 1st International Symposium on Ship Construction in Antiquities*, ed. H. Tzalas (Piraeus: Hellenic Institute for the Preservation of Nautical Tradition, 1985), pp. 147-62.
[8]C. Davaras, "Une ancre minoenne sacrée?" *BCH* 104 (1980), 47-71.

More comprehensive studies on classical maritime religion are found in only two sources. Wachsmuth's examination of the cultic practices of Greek seafarers, ΠΟΜΠΙΜΟΣ Ο ΔΑΙΜΩΝ: Untersuchung zu den Antiken Sakralhandlungen bei Seereisen, is perhaps the most thorough look at ancient maritime religion.[9] Wachsmuth draws primarily on classical textual sources to detail maritime ceremonies, rites, omens, divination, taboos, sacrifices, offerings, and prayers, as well as religious attitudes towards the sea and ships, and deities important to sailors. He includes a wealth of comparative material from other ancient cultures and modern, anthropological studies, too. His study utilizes a few examples of Canaanite and Phoenician maritime religion, but it is limited by depending on secondary references for the Canaanite material and by drawing only on Phoenician evidence which is mentioned in classical sources.[10]

Rougé devotes a small chapter in his book *La marine dans l'Antiquité* to "La religion des navigateurs."[11] While Wachsmuth's study focuses primarily on ancient Greece and Crete, Rougé's details many different facets of the religion of Roman seafarers. He organizes the evidence into four broad categories which allow for a well-rounded view of the maritime aspects of Roman religion: the sacred qualities of Roman ships, divinities helpful to seafarers, sanctuaries important to sailors, and religious ceremonies during different parts of the voyage.

Anthropological and folkloristic studies, like classical works, deal with many different aspects of the religion of traditional seafarers. The research of Hornell, Rivers, and Göttlicher concentrates on the sacred character of ships and the special religious ceremonies connected with vessels.[12] Hornell focuses on South Asian ships and Rivers on those of the South Pacific, but both authors bring in numerous examples from other cultures around the world. Göttlicher's work is more comprehensive, including chapters on cultic ships in ancient Egypt, Mesopotamia, and classical lands; however he does not include a chapter on Canaanite or Phoenician vessels. In a further study on the

---

[9]D. Wachsmuth, ΠΟΜΠΙΜΟΣ Ο ΔΑΙΜΩΝ: Untersuchung zu den Antiken Sakralhandlungen bei Seereisen (Berlin: Ernst-Reuter-Gesellschaft, 1967).
[10]*Ibid.*, pp. 345, 395-96, for Canaanite material; pp. 120, 254, and 381, for Phoenician examples.
[11]J. Rougé, *La marine dans l'Antiquité* (Vendome: Presses Universitaires de France, 1975), pp. 206-10.
[12]J. Hornell, "The Prow of the Ship: Sanctuary of the Tutelary Deity," *Man* 43 (1943), 121-28; W. H. R. Rivers, "Ships and Boats," *The Encyclopaedia of Religion and Ethics*, vol. XI, eds. J. Hastings *et al.* (New York: Charles Scribner's Sons, 1921), pp. 471-74; and A. Göttlicher, *Kultschiffe und Schiffskulte im Altertum* (Berlin: Gebr. Mann, 1992).

apotropaic eye found on vessels' prows, placed there in order to ward off or avert bad luck, Hornell uses illustrations from both ancient and modern seafaring peoples, including the Phoenicians.[13] The use of both ancient and modern evidence is also found in Canney's paper on ship models and their offering as votives in sacred spaces.[14]

Works which offer a more comprehensive view of the religious beliefs, practices, taboos, and superstitions of sailors are those by Bassett, Sébillot, and Lethbridge.[15] These studies present diverse ethnographic and folkloristic data from throughout the modern world, and utilize ancient sources, as well. Bassett even includes Phoenician and Punic examples mentioned in classical texts.[16] These cross-cultural and multiperiod data show that the specialized religion of sailors and fishermen is a phenomenon which occurs among seafaring cultures, regardless of geographical region or historical period.

The classical and anthropological studies on nautical religion suggest a four-part classification scheme for clarifying and connecting evidence of the religious beliefs and practices of seafarers: 1. deities with special maritime, celestial, or meteorological attributes important to the well-being of the sailors; 2. seaside sanctuaries and temples with special associations for sailors; 3. the concept of the ship itself possessing a divine spirit; and 4. religious ceremonies or acts performed by seafarers regarding the safety of the voyage.[17] I have added another category, 5. mortuary ritual and funereal practices with connections to the sea, because burials provide insight into a culture's religious acts associated with death and because the presence of nautical symbols in Canaanite and Phoenician burials suggests specialized, maritime funereal rites. This classification scheme gives us

---

[13]"The Cult of the Oculus," in *Water Transport: Origins & Early Evolution* (Cambridge: Cambridge University Press, 1946), pp. 285-89. Definition of apotropaic taken from *The Oxford English Dictionary*, I, 560.

[14]M. A. Canney, "Boats and Ships in Temples and Tombs," in *Occident and Orient: Gaster Anniversary Volume*, eds. B. Schindler & A. Marmorstein (London: Taylor's Foreign Press, 1936), pp. 50-57.

[15]F. Bassett, *Legends and Superstitions of the Sea and of Sailors* (1885; reprinted, Detroit: Singing Tree Press, 1971); P. Sébillot, *Le folk-lore des pêcheurs* (Paris: G.-P. Maisonneuve & Larose, 1968); T.C. Lethbridge, "Superstition and Ritual," in *Boats and Boatmen* (London: Thames and Hudson, 1952), pp. 63-92.

[16]Bassett, *Legends and Superstitions of the Sea*, pp. 13-14, 39, 57-59, 380, 384, 463.

[17]These four categories are used most specifically to organize the chapter "La Religion des Navigateurs," in Rougé, *La marine dans l'Antiquité*, pp. 206-10, but can be found, together with maritime legends, superstitions, and taboos, in any of the more comprehensive works by Wachsmuth, Bassett, Sébillot, or Lethbridge.

a framework which can be adapted to illuminate Canaanite-Phoenician maritime religion.

Previous studies on Canaanite and Phoenician culture have touched on several of these categories of maritime religion. Canaanite and Phoenician deities with links to the sea or seafarers are the subjects of several works. Fantar's monograph *Le dieu de la mer chez les Phéniciens et les Puniques* looks at the presence of Poseidon in Phoenicia and Carthage and tries to solve the puzzle of the Semitic identification of this sea god.[18] While the study is commendable for bringing together information from diverse sources, such as Ugaritic and classical texts, Phoenician coinage, and Punic inscriptions, Fantar's conclusion that *Ba‘l Ḥamōn* was the Phoenician sea god is based on questionable evidence from secondary literature.[19] Redford's study focuses on Canaanite-Phoenician goddesses connected with the sea, detailing the primacy of female deities in the mythic battle against the deified sea in the southern Levantine coast.[20] Hours-Miedan's work on the iconography of Punic sacrificial stelae includes a section on maritime motifs, such as ships, anchors, and steering rudders attributed to the goddess Tinnit.[21] Other works by Dussaud, Eissfeldt, Hvidberg-Hansen, and Katzenstein focus on maritime or storm aspects of Canaanite-Phoenician gods and goddesses, but it is Albright who really recognizes their importance to sailors.[22] In his study on *Ba‘l Ṣapōn*,

---

[18] M. Fantar, "Le dieu de la mer chez les Phéniciens et les Puniques," *Studi semitici* 48 (1977), 1-133.

[19] *Ibid.*, p. 130. Fantar relies almost entirely on French studies of Phoenician religion for his arguments, and accepts many misconceptions from the secondary literature regarding the attributes of gods like Milqart and *Ba‘l Ḥamōn*, to be discussed in ch. 1.

[20] D. B. Redford, "The Sea and the Goddess," in *Studies in Egyptology Presented to Miriam Lichtheim*, vol. 2, ed. S. Israelit-Groll (Jerusalem: Magnes, 1990), pp. 824-35.

[21] M. Hours-Miedan, "Les représentations figurées sur les stèles de Carthage," *Cahiers de Byrsa* 1 (1950), 65-68. I have opted to vocalize the goddess *Tnt*'s name as Tinnit rather than the traditional "Tanit", because it is a better representation of the transliteration of her name preserved in Greek (*Thinith, Thenneith*), *KAI*, vol. 2, p. 90. F. M. Cross has argued that the name derives from the standard pattern of *tannīn* plus a feminine ending appropriate to the goddess: **tannit< *tannittu< *tannintu;* Tinnit thus reflects vowel harmony, which appears in late Phoenician: *tinnit< *tannit*, like *Šipṭi-bi‘l< Šipṭi-ba‘l*, or *mutun< matton<mantan;* see *Canaanite Myth and Hebrew Epic* (Cambridge, MA: Harvard University Press, 1973), pp. 32-33.

[22] R. Dussaud, "Astarté, Pontos et Ba‘al," *Comptes rendus de l'Académie des inscriptions et belles-lettres* (1947), 201-24; O. Eissfeldt, *Baal Zaphon, Zeus Kasios und der Durchzug der Israeliten durchs Meer* (Halle: Max Niemeyer, 1932); O. Hvidberg-Hansen, "Ba‘al-Malagê dans le traité entre Asarhaddon et le

Albright calls the storm god the "*par excellence* patron(s) of ships and seafaring men" because Ba'l controls the winds which could bring favor or disaster to a voyage.[23]

Stone anchors found in stratified contexts on land, from Canaanite harbor sites, have been the subject of H. Frost's research.[24] Through her studies on stone anchors found underwater, Frost was able to recognize the significance of those found on land, incorporated into religious buildings at the Canaanite sites of Byblos and Ugarit. She explains the significance of the anchors found in sacred contexts as offerings placed there by sailors, but does not support her contentions with additional evidence of religious beliefs or cultic practices of Canaanite mariners.

Despite the number of works illustrating individual features of Canaanite-Phoenician maritime religion, no one has discussed the topic in a comprehensive fashion, using all of the available resources. I propose to survey the historical, archaeological, and pictorial records of Canaanite-Phoenician maritime civilization, using the aforementioned five-point model, in order to present convergent evidence for the specialized religious beliefs and practices of its seafaring population.[25]

roi de Tyr," *Acta orientalia* 35 (1973), 57-81; H. J. Katzenstein, "Some Reflections on the Phoenician Deities Mentioned in the Treaty Between Esarhaddon King of Assyria and Baal King of Tyre," in *Atti del II congresso internazionale di studi fenici e punici*, I (Rome: Consiglio Nazionale delle Ricerche, 1991), 373-77; W. F. Albright, "Baal-Zephon," in *Festschrift Alfred Bertholet*, ed. W. Baumgartner et al. (Tübingen: J. C. B. Mohr, 1950), pp. 1-14.

[23]*Ibid.*, p. 12. Albright reiterates this same claim in his later work *Yahweh and the Gods of Canaan* (New York: Doubleday, 1968), pp. 127-28.

[24]H. Frost, "The Stone-Anchors of Byblos," *MUSJ* 45 (1969), 425-42; "The Stone-Anchors of Ugarit," *Ugaritica* VI (1969), 235-45; and "Anchors Sacred and Profane: Ugarit-Ras Shamra, 1986; the Stone Anchors Revised and Compared," in *Ras Shamra-Ougarit*, vol. VI, *Arts et industries de la pierre*, ed. M. Yon (Paris: ERC, 1991), 355-410.

[25]See L. White, *Medieval Technology and Social Change* (London: Oxford University Press, 1962), p. v; and K. C. Chang, *Early Chinese Civilization: Anthropological Perspectives*, vol. 23, *Harvard-Yenching Institute Monograph Series* (Cambridge, MA: Harvard University Press, 1976), pp. v-xi, for an historian's and an anthropological archaeologist's call for the use of all resources available in the study of the past. For similar approaches used in modern social sciences see D. T. Campbell, "Convergent and Discriminant Validation by the Multitrait-Multimethod Matrix," in *Methodology and Epistemology for Social Science* (Chicago: University of Chicago Press, 1988), pp. 37-61. The difficulties of identifying ethnicity in the material cultural record are recognized, see K. A. Kamp and N. Yoffee, "Ethnicity in Ancient Western Asia During the Early Second Millennium B.C.: Archaeological and Ethnoarchaeological Perspectives," *BASOR* 237 (1980), 94-97; M. C. S. Kelly and R. E. Kelly, "Approaches to Ethnic Identification in Historical Archaeology," in *Archaeological Perspectives on*

Introduction   7

The fullest understanding of a religion, and its development over time, is possible through studying a complement of different classes of data.[26] This has been addressed, in part, by Renfrew in his work *The Archaeology of Cult*, where he proposes four categories of data for the study of modern or ancient religion:

> 1. Verbal testimony, whether oral or written, relating to the religious activities of the community, or elucidating the meaning ascribed by it to its religious practices.
>
> 2. Direct observation of cult practices, involving the use of expressive action, of vocal utterances and of symbolic objects and materials.
>
> 3. Study of non-verbal records, mainly depictions, which document either (a) the beliefs themselves, e.g. portraying deities or mythical events; or (b) the cult practices carried out in the community.
>
> 4. Study of the material remains of cult practices, including structures and symbolic objects and materials.[27]

Ethnicity in America, vol. 1, *Baywood Monographs in Archaeology*, ed. R. L. Schuyler (Farmingdale, NY: Baywood Publishing, 1980), pp. 133-43; R. H. McGuire, "The Study of Ethnicity in Historical Archaeology," *Journal of Anthropological Archaeology* 1 (1982), 159-78; S. Shennan, ed. *Archaeological Approaches to Cultural Identity* (London: Unwin Hyman, 1989); and S. Jones, *The Archaeology of Ethnicity: Constructing Identities in the Past and Present* (London: Routledge, 1997). I have evaluated whether or not data are to be considered products of Canaanite or Phoenician culture before including them as evidence in my study.

[26] For a defense of the diachronic study of cultural traditions see I. Hodder, *Reading the Past* (Cambridge: Cambridge University Press, 1991), pp. 10-11, and "The Contribution of the Long Term," in *Archaeology as Long-Term History*, ed. I. Hodder (Cambridge: Cambridge University Press, 1987), pp. 1-8. Hodder states that identifying cultural continuities over the long term, and how traditions change and transform over time, is one of archaeology's basic goals, *Reading the Past*, p. 11. This also applies to the *Annales* school's view of the *longue durée* of history; see F. Braudel, *The Mediterranean and the Mediterranean World in the Age of Philip II*, trans. S. Reynolds, 2 vols. (New York: Harper & Row, 1972). For the application of the *Annales* paradigm to archaeological method and theory see J. Bintliff, ed., *The Annales School and Archaeology* (Leicester: Leicester University Press, 1991); A. B. Knapp ed., *Archaeology, Annales, and Ethnohistory* (Cambridge: Cambridge University Press, 1992); A. B. Knapp, *Society and Polity at Bronze Age Pella: An Annales Perspective*, vol. 6, *JSOT/ASOR Monograph Series* (Sheffield: Sheffield Academic Press, 1993), pp. 3-20; and T. E. Levy and A. F. C. Holl, "Social Change and the Archaeology of the Holy Land," in *The Archaeology of Society in the Holy Land*, ed. T. E. Levy (New York: Facts on File, 1995) pp. 2-8.

[27] C. Renfrew, *The Archaeology of Cult: The Sanctuary at Phylakopi* (London: The British School of Archaeology at Athens, 1985), p. 12. For further works on

As Renfrew details, only categories (3) and (4) are available for his study of religion in preliterate Cycladic society, giving a limited view of Cycladic religion.[28] Fortunately both the Canaanites and the Phoenicians left written records illustrating aspects of their religion, which would fall under (1), and contemporary neighboring cultures, such as the Egyptians, Assyrians, Greeks, and Romans, have also left texts with some details of Canaanite-Phoenician religious practices (2). This written evidence from both internal and external sources, when combined with pictorial (3) and archaeological (4) data, gives a fuller presentation of Canaanite-Phoenician religion than would a study which focuses on any one of the different classes.[29]

When presented together, the textual, archaeological, and pictorial data demonstrate that a specialized religion existed among Canaanite and Phoenician sailors. This maritime religion was a subset of Canaanite-Phoenician general religious beliefs and practices, which stemmed from the particular dangers and uncertainties of life and travel at sea.

---

the study of archaeology and religion see J. A. Alexander, "The Archaeological Recognition of Religion: The Examples of Islam in Africa and 'Urnfields' in Europe," in *Space, Hierarchy and Society: Interdisciplinary Studies in Social Area Analysis*, vol. 59, *B. A. R. International Series*, eds. B. C. Burnham and J. Kingsbury (Great Britain: B. A. R., 1979), pp. 215-28; P. Garwood et al., eds. *Sacred and Profane: Proceedings of a Conference on Archaeology, Ritual and Religion*, vol. 32, *Oxford University Committee for Archaeology Monograph* (Oxford: Oxford University Committee for Archaeology, 1991); Ø. Johansen, "Religion and Archaeology: Revelation or Empirical Research?" in *Words and Objects: Towards a Dialogue Between Archaeology and History of Religion*, ed. G. Steinsland (Oslo, Denmark: Norwegian University Press, 1986), pp. 67-77; J. Marcus and K. V. Flannery, "Ancient Zapotec Ritual and Religion: An Application of the Direct Historical Approach," in *The Ancient Mind: Elements of Cognitive Archaeology*, eds. C. Renfrew and E. B. W. Zubrow (Cambridge: Cambridge University Press, 1994), pp. 55-74; and C. Renfrew, "The Archaeology of Religion," in *The Ancient Mind: Elements of Cognitive Archaeology*, eds. C. Renfrew and E. B. W. Zubrow (Cambridge: Cambridge University Press, 1994), pp. 47-54.

[28]Renfrew, *The Archaeology of Cult*, p. 13.

[29]For a critique of the narrowness of past studies on Canaanite religion, which tend to focus on only one category of data, see W. G. Dever, "The Contribution of Archaeology to the Study of Canaanite and Early Israelite Religion," in *Ancient Israelite Religion*, eds. P. D. Miller et al. (Philadelphia: Fortress, 1987), pp. 209-48.

Chapter 1
THE PATRON DEITIES OF CANAANITE AND PHOENICIAN SEAFARERS

Because of the unusual dangers of sailing, mariners took on patron gods and goddesses to help them safely through a voyage. The sea posed the biggest threat and created the greatest trepidation for sailors; therefore it was critical to the seafarer to be protected from the depths and its guardian spirits. The tutelary deities of the mariner, as well as the physical presence of the ship, guarded him from the uncertainties of the water.

Two types of deities were of utmost importance to classical and modern traditional sailors: those gods who controlled the winds or storms, because of their abilities to power the sails of a ship with a favorable wind, and to raise or calm tempests; and the gods whose attributes aided in safe and successful navigation:

> And for them (mariners preparing a boat to sail) the son of Oeagrus touched his lyre and sang in rhythmical song of Artemis, savior of ships, . . . who has in her keeping those peaks by the sea, and the land of Iolcos.[1]
>
> But when he in his turn, as he passed over the wine-dark sea in the hollow ships, reached in swift course the steep height of Malea,

---

[1] Apollonius Rhodius, *The Argonautica*, I.570-72. Trans. R.C. Seaton, *The Loeb Classical Library* (Cambridge: Harvard University Press, 1988), p. 43. For further evidence see Pausanias, *Description of Greece*, I.1.3. Bassett, *Legends and Superstitions of the Sea*, pp. 36-52; G. Foucart, "Storm, Storm-Gods," *The Encyclopaedia of Religion and Ethics*, vol. XI, pp. 882-3; F. Queyrel, "Aphrodite et les marins," in *Tropis II: 2nd International Symposium on Ship Construction in Antiquities*, ed. H. Tzalas (Delphi: Hellenic Institute for the Preservation of Nautical Tradition, 1987), pp. 283-85; and Semple, "Templed Promontories," 365-69.

then verily Zeus, whose voice is borne afar, planned him a hateful path and poured upon him the blasts of shrill winds, and the waves were swollen to huge size, like unto mountains.[2]

I shall demonstrate that deities with similar attributes were the main patrons of Canaanite and Phoenician mariners.

Storm Gods

Perhaps the god of chief importance for Canaanite and Phoenician seafarers was the storm god, Baʿl-Haddu.[3] In addition to Baʿl-Haddu's importance on land as the god who brought storms necessary for growing crops dependant on rain, it was he who controlled the winds which could either benefit or devastate a voyage at sea.[4] The threat which storm gods posed to ships is vividly demonstrated in the seventh century B. C. E. treaty between Esarhaddon, the ruler of Assyria, and Baʿl, the king of Tyre.[5]

The Esarhaddon/Baʿl of Tyre treaty confirms Assyrian hegemony over Phoenicia and aspects of Phoenician commerce in the eastern Mediterranean. The treaty specifically stipulates that goods from any ship wrecked along the Levantine coast rightfully belong to the king of Assyria, and details Baʿl of Tyre's rights over maritime trade in the region (Rev.III.15'-21'). Given the nautical nature of the agreement, it is not surprising that the curses against breaking the treaty include the invocation of three Phoenician storm gods (Rev.IV.10'-13'): *Baʿl Šamêm* (Akk. ^{d}*ba-al sa-me-me*), *Baʿl Malagê* (Akk. ^{d}*ba-al ma-la-ge-e*), and *Baʿl*

---

[2]Homer, *The Odyssey*, III.287-90. Trans. A.T. Murray, vol. 1, *The Loeb Classical Library* (Cambridge: Harvard University Press, 1984), p. 89.

[3]Especially *Baʿl Ṣapōn*, see Albright, "Baal-Zephon," 1-14. Albright reiterates his view that *Baʿl Ṣapōn* was the "marine storm-god *par excellence*" and patron of seafarers in his *Yahweh and the Gods of Canaan*, pp. 127-28. I have vocalized Haddu's epithet as Baʿl, and shall accordingly change the standard King James transcription, Baal, in quotations from other scholars for the sake of uniformity. Titles including the older transcription will remain unaltered.

[4]For the critical role that winds play in sailing and in a sailor's mentality see D. Logan, "The Known and Unknown Wind," *Parabola* 20/1 (1995), 34-39.

[5]For editions of the text and translations see R. Borger, "Die Inschriften Asarhaddons Königs von Assyrien." *Archiv für Orientforschung*, Beiheft 9 (1956), 107-9; and more recently S. Parpola and K. Watanabe, *Neo-Assyrian Treaties and Loyalty Oaths* (Helsinki: Helsinki University Press, 1988), pp. 24-27. Other translations without the text include E. Reiner's in *ANET*, pp. 533-4, and R. Borger's "Der Vertrag Asarhaddons mit Baal von Tyrus," in *Texte aus der Umwelt des Alten Testaments*, vol. I/2, eds. R. Borger et al. (Gütersloh: G. Mohn, 1983), pp. 158-59.

Ṣapōn (Akk. ᵈba-al ṣa-pu-nu) are called upon to destroy the Tyrian king's fleet if he breaks his vow to his Assyrian overlord. The three gods would accomplish this by causing an "evil wind" (Akk. šāru lemnu) to rise up against the ships.⁶ This wind would damage the boats, and would churn up a "strong wave" (Akk. edu dannu), a "violent tide" (Akk. šamru agu), which would sink the vessels.

Baʿl Šamêm

The Esarhaddon/Baʿl of Tyre treaty provides the only evidence linking Baʿl Šamêm to marine storms or ships. Baʿl Šamêm continues to function in the Phoenician pantheon as a storm god, but we have no other examples, besides the Assyrian treaty, of his connection to the welfare of mariners.⁷

Baʿl Malagê

Baʿl Malagê remains somewhat mysterious because his only mention is in the Assyrian vassal treaty. Numerous studies have attempted to reveal more about this god through looking at the

---

⁶The verb lušatba, which relates the three storm gods' action of creating the storm wind, is a 3rd m. s. precative of the causative, or Š stem, of the verb "to arise, rise up; to occur" (Akk. tebû). This masculine singular treatment of the verb may connote that the three gods are viewed as different aspects of the same individual storm god, which is in agreement with J. Teixidor, The Pagan God (Princeton, NJ: Princeton University Press, 1977), p. 32. The 3rd m. s. use of the verb may also be distributive, and therefore the three gods are viewed as separate deities merely combined into a single unit because of their similar powers over marine tempests, see M. L. Barré, The God-List in the Treaty Between Hannibal and Philip V of Macedonia (Baltimore: The Johns Hopkins University Press, 1983), p. 55.

⁷A possible exception to this is found in Jonah 1:9. After Yahweh has raised a storm to sink the vessel carrying Jonah, the non-Israelite (likely Phoenician) sailors beseech him through prayer to calm the storm. Here Yahweh is called "god of the heavens" by Jonah, Heb. ʾĕlōhê haš-šāmayīm, an epithet taken from Baʿl Šamêm, see B. Mazar's "The Philistines and the Rise of Israel and Tyre," in The Early Biblical Period (Jerusalem: Israel Exploration Society, 1986), pp. 80-81. For recent treatments of Baʿl Šamêm demonstrating his function as a storm god in the Phoenician pantheon see H. Niehr, Der höchste Gott: Alttestamentlicher JHWH-Glaube in Kontext syrisch-kanaanäischer Religion des 1. Jahrtausend v. Chr., Beihefte zur Zeitschrift für die alttestamentiche Wissenschaft, vol. 190 (Berlin & New York: Walter de Gruyter, 1990), pp. 17-29; D. Chase, "Baʿl Šamêm: A Study of the Early Epigraphic Sources," Diss. Harvard University, 1994; and K. Engelken, "Baʿalšamem: Eine Auseinandersetzung mit der Monographie von H. Niehr," parts I and II, Zeitschrift für die alttestamentliche Wissenschaft 108. no. 2 (1996), 233-48; no. 3 (1996), 391-407.

etymology of his name, with special attention paid to the nautical sense of his power and his importance to sailors.

Eissfeldt was the first to posit that the Assyrian scribe had made an error, and that the name should read *Baʿl Malāḫu*, or "Baʿl der Schiffer", based on the Akkadian *malāḫu*, "sailor".[8] *Malaḥ*, with a similar meaning, is attested in Phoenician and other West Semitic languages, which makes it a possible *Vorlage* for the Akkadian transcription of the Phoenician name of the god.[9] The *ḫ>g* shift necessary for *malāḫu>malagê* has been attested in other Akkadian words, which lends credence to Eissfeldt's suggestion but by no means proves his alternative reading.[10] Albright initially viewed *Malagê* as a proper name, but later changed his mind and wanted to emend the middle *la* sign in *ma-la-ge-e* to *ad*, in order to read *Baʿl Madgê* or the "Lord of fishing".[11] This emendation seems forced, however, since the reading of the *la* sign in the text has never been in question.[12] R. Du Mesnil du Buisson translates the name as "le baʿl du port" based on the suggestion by Caquot that *Malagê* is a substantive related to the Arabic root *ljʾ*, "to take refuge".[13] However, the elision of the aleph necessary to lengthen the vowel (*gaʾ>gā>gē*) never takes place with an Akkadian ʾ1, which renders moot this suggestion.[14] S. Moscati proposes that *Baʿl Malagê* is identical to Zeus Meilichios, mentioned by Philo of Byblos, whom he terms the "lord of sailors".[15] Moscati does not explain this identification; presumably it is based on reading

---

[8]Eissfeldt, *Baal Zaphon, Zeus Kasios*, p. 7, n. 4.

[9]For the comparative West Semitic evidence see R. S. Tomback, *A Comparative Semitic Lexicon of the Phoenician and Punic Languages* (Missoula, MT: Scholars Press, 1978), p. 179.

[10]For evidence backing the posited *ḫ>g* shift see the summary in Hvidberg-Hansen, "Baʿal-Malagê," 59, n. 17, as well as E. E. Knudsen, "Spirantization of Velars in Akkadian," in *lišān mitḫurti: Festschrift Wolfram Freiherr von Soden*, vol. 1, *Alter Orient und Altes Testament*, eds. M. Dietrich and W. Röllig (Neukirchen-Vluyn: Butzon & Bercker Kevelaer, 1969), pp. 147-55.

[11]"Baal-Zephon," 9, n. 2, and *Yahweh and the Gods of Canaan*, pp. 227-28.

[12]See Borger, "Die Inschriften Asarhaddons," 109, and Parpola and Watanabe, *Neo-Assyrian Treaties and Loyalty Oaths*, p. 27.

[13]First put forth in R. Du Mesnil du Buisson, "Origine et évolution du panthéon de Tyr," *Revue de l'histoire des religions* 164 (1963), 147, and repeated in the author's *Nouvelles études sur les dieux et les mythes de Canaan* (Leiden: E. J. Brill, 1973), p. 48. Arabic *j* is the equivalent to *g* in Akkadian.

[14]W. von Soden, *Grundriss der Akkadischen Grammatik*, vol. 33/47, *Analecta orientalia* (Rome: Pontificium Institutum Biblicum, 1969), §24, pp. 25-26. Originally critiqued by Hvidberg-Hansen, "Baʿal-Malagê," 60-61.

[15]*The World of the Phoenicians* (New York: Frederick A. Praeger, 1968), p. 35; Philo is quoted by Eusebeus in *Praep. Evang.*, 1.10.11.

meilichios as a Greek transcription of the West Semitic *mlḥ*. However, Gk. *meilichios*, "gentle", is a common epithet of several Greek gods, including Zeus in both Argolis and Athens, and in this case is used by Philo to describe the Phoenician craftsman god (Gk. *Chousōr*= *Hephaistos*, Ug. *Kôṯar*) and not a storm god.[16]

These investigations into the etymology of the word *Malagê* present ingenious methods of trying to learn more about the nature of the god.[17] Yet, all have their shortcomings. Until we have further data relating to *Malagê*, it is safest merely to posit that he is one of the numerous aspects of the Phoenician storm god, clearly important to seafarers because of his potential to damage ships, as is described in the Esarhaddon/Baʿl of Tyre treaty.

Baʿl Ṣapōn

There is further evidence outside of the Esarhaddon/Baʿl of Tyre treaty which connects *Baʿl Ṣapōn* with specialized maritime worship. This evidence demonstrates that *Baʿl Ṣapōn* was one of the patron deities of Canaanite sailors.[18]

The home of the storm god, *Baʿl Ṣapōn*, was on the mountain from which he took his name, Ug. *Ṣapān* = Heb. *Ṣapōn*, which is known from numerous attestations in Ugaritic myths and administrative lists, as well as in Assyrian royal inscriptions and Hittite texts.[19] Mt. *Ṣapōn* is

---

[16] For *meilichios* see H. G. Liddell, R. Scott, and H. S. Jones, *A Greek-English Lexicon* (Oxford: Clarendon, 1968), p. 1093a. Barré, following Moscati's suggestion, would use the *Baʿl Malagê*=Zeus Meilichios equation to posit that *Malagê* is the Phoenician craftsman god *Kôṯar*, *The God-List*, pp. 85-86. Despite the creative path Barré follows to demonstrate that *Malagê*=*Kôṯar*, he seems to disregard the different functions of these two gods, storm god and divine craftsman, which nullifies any link.

[17] Unlike other studies, Hvidberg-Hansen rejects the maritime interpretation of *Malagê*. He prefers to translate *Baʿl Malagê* as the "Baʿl de l'abondance", based on the semitic root *mlg* which has a variety of meanings including ripened produce, animal's milk, and a dowry, see "Baʿal-Malagê," 67. From there he posits that the "lord of abundance" is an epithet of the Phoenician grain god Dagnu, 71-81. This identification of *Baʿl Malagê* as Dagnu should be disregarded on the basis of the functions of the two deities: the Esarhaddon/Baʿl of Tyre treaty clearly demonstrates that *Malagê* acts as a storm god, while we know from Philo of Byblos that Dagnu is the god of grain (*Praep. Evang.*, 1.10.16 & 25), and from the Ugaritic corpus that he is the father of the storm god (*KTU* 1.2.19,35,37; 1.14.II.25; 1.14 .IV.7; these are a few of numerous instances where Baʿl [Haddu] is called *binu Dagni*).

[18] See n. 4 above.

[19] Surveys of the material are quite numerous. See especially Eissfeldt, *Baal*

identified with modern Jebel el-ʾAqraʿ, located forty km. north of Ras Shamra on the Syrian coast, which rises to a peak over 1700 m. high.[20] This height means that Mt. Ṣapōn is visible from a great distance out to sea, and was likely utilized as a navigational aid for ships coming into or leaving Ugarit's port at Minet el-Beida.[21]

Back at the site of Ugarit, it is clear that Canaanite sailors were dedicating stone anchors as votive offerings at one of the two temples on the acropolis of the city [figs. 41 and 43].[22] Though we have no textual references to add further detail to this cultic practice, the clustering of these anchors around one temple and their complete absence from the second, neighboring temple shows a deliberate preference of sailors in their maritime rituals.[23] The temple with the anchor votives also contained a stela, found in the excavations of the building, which is inscribed with a dedication to Baʿl Ṣapōn, thus it is apparent that the storm god was worshipped in this monumental structure which has been identified as the Temple of Baʿl at Ugarit.[24] The presence of both a stela offered to Baʿl Ṣapōn and votive anchors in the same temple suggests another sacral link between the storm god and Canaanite mariners.

Unfortunately, no other type of maritime votive was uncovered in the Temple of Baʿl at Ugarit. There is Late Bronze Age textual

---

Zaphon, Zeus Kasios, pp. 1-30; Albright, "Baal-Zephon," 1-14; G. Saadé, "Légendes et histoire d'une montagne syrienne," Levante 15 (1968), 5-22; R. J. Clifford, The Cosmic Mountain in Canaan and the Old Testament (Cambridge, MA: Harvard University Press, 1972), pp. 57-79; M. Astour, "Place Names," in Ras Shamra Parallels, vol. II, ed. L. R. Fisher (Rome: Pontificum Institutum Biblicum, 1975), pp. 318-24; P. N. Hunt, "Mount Saphon in Myth and Fact," in StudPhoen, vol. XI, Phoenicia and the Bible, ed. E. Lepinski (Leuven: Uitgeverij Peeters, 1991), pp. 103-15.
[20]See Eissfeldt, Baal Zaphon, Zeus Kasios, p. 4, for the earliest identification of Mt. Ṣapōn with Jebel el-ʾAqraʿ. This has been accepted by most following studies.
[21]Albright, "Baal-Zephon," 11, and Hunt, "Mount Saphon in Myth and Fact," 111-12.
[22]Frost, "The Stone-Anchors of Ugarit," 235-45. Frost's early work is updated in her "Anchors Sacred and Profane," 355-410.
[23]For the lack of textual references to the cultic use of anchors see J. M. de Tarragon, La culte à Ugarit, vol. 19, Cahiers de la Revue biblique (Paris: Gabalda, 1980), p. 182. For the clustering of anchors around one acropolis temple and not the other see Frost, "Anchors Sacred and Profane," 395.
[24]The stela was dedicated by an Egyptian official at Ugarit named Mami, and has the name Baʿl Ṣapōn transliterated in hieroglyphs. See C. F. A. Schaeffer, "Les fouilles de Minet-el-Beida et de Ras Shamra, deuxième campagne (printemps 1930)," Syria 12 (1931), 10. For a recent overview of the stela and its find spot within the temple see M. Yon, "Stèles de pierre," in Ras Shamra-Ougarit, vol. VI, Arts et industries de la pierre, ed. M. Yon (Paris: ERC, 1991), pp. 284-88.

evidence, however, which shows that Mt. Ṣapōn and Baʿl Ṣapōn were represented, and likely worshipped, in the form of a ship. This is not an uncommon phenomenon among traditional seafaring societies, given the general belief that a vessel is imbued with the spirit of a divine guardian; therefore the ship itself, or a representation of the ship, becomes a symbol of its protective deity.[25]

In the Ugaritic epic poem of Kirta we find evidence that the storm god Baʿl's sacred mountain, Ṣapōn, is compared to a "ship" (Ug. any).[26] The setting for this reference in the epic is a dirge sung by mourning women lamenting the death of king Kirta. They sing out to the deified Mt. Ṣapōn (KTU 1.16.I.6-9, 1.16.II.44-47):

tbkyk ab ǵr bʿl	tabkiyuka ʾabī ǵūru baʿli	Baʿl's mountain weeps for you father,
ṣpn ḥlm qdš	ṣapānu, ḥēlu-mi qadušu	Ṣapōn, the holy fortification
any ḥlm adr	ʾanyu, ḥēlu-mi ʾaduru[27]	The ship, the mighty fortification
ḥl rḥb mknpt	ḥēlu raḥabu mvknvpati	The fortification wide of span

This stichometric arrangement follows that of Ginsberg's study, which has been accepted in most subsequent commentaries.[28] The subject of the first line, ǵr bʿl, the mountain of the storm god, is paralleled in the second line with the mountain's name, ṣpn.[29] I read the last three lines of the lament as a tricolon with repetitive parallelism describing Mt. Ṣapōn. Thus ṣpn, the sacred mountain of Baʿl-Haddu, is the subject of the first part of the tricolon and is paralleled in the second with the noun any, "ship".[30] Both ṣpn and any are described as a ḥl, a

---

[25]See ch. 3, below.
[26]KTU 1.16. I. 8, 1.16. II.46.
[27]For the vocalization and translation of Ugaritic adr see J. Huehnergard, Ugaritic Vocabulary in Syllabic Transcriptions (Atlanta, GA: Scholars Press), p. 104.
[28]H. L. Ginsberg, "The Legend of King Keret," BASOR Supplementary Studies 2-3 (1946), 26; J. Gray, The KRT Text in the Literature of Ras Shamra (Leiden: E. J. Brill, 1964), p. 22; M. Pope, "Marginalia to M. Dahood's Ugaritic-Hebrew Philology," Journal of Biblical Literature 85 (1966), 460-62; and A. Caquot et al., Textes Ougaritiques, vol. I (Paris: Les Éditions du Cerf, 1974), p. 550.
[29]Pope, "Marginalia," 461.
[30]See Albright, "Baal-Zephon," 3-5, especially 4, n. 3. P. Bordreuil has argued that the word in question does not begin with a, but rather n, whose signs in the Ugaritic alphabet are only one stroke in difference, see "La citadelle sainte du

fortification.³¹ The ḫl is then placed as the subject of the third verse of the tricolon, a poetic repetitiveness which is typical of Ugaritic and Hebrew poetry, and called literally "wide of wing," which is better read "wide of span."³² This reference to *knpt* may be an allusion to the metaphor of the oars or steering rudders of a ship which appeared wing-like to ancient writers, as is shown by parallel uses in the Hebrew Bible and the Odyssey.³³ Most other translations, except Albright's,

Mont Nanou," *Syria* 66 (1989), 275-79. Thus *any* would read *nny*, the name of a mountain near Mt. Ṣapōn known from Hittite documents. He goes to great lengths to establish this emendation and even provides a photograph of the original tablets (*KTU* 1.16.I.8, 1.16.II.46) to back his case, *ibid.*, 276. From this photograph, however, it is clear that the letter in question is *a*, with two horizontal strokes, and not *n*, so the reading should remain *any*.

³¹Caquot *et al.*, *Textes Ougaritiques*, vol. I, p. 550. My reading of Ug. ḫl as "fortification", rather than the more common "fortress", is based on biblical parallels where Heb. ḥel, or ḥêl represents the outermost ring of fortification of a walled city, BDB, p. 298. The ḥêl is typically mentioned in conjunction with the ḥômāh, the second or inner wall of a fortified city, see Isa 26:1; Lam 2:8; Nah 3:8. This textual evidence describes defensive networks excavated at Syro-Palestinian sites which have dual walls ringing the city, the outer ḥêl and inner ḥômāh, see R. de Vaux, *Ancient Israel, Its Life and Institutions*, trans. J. McHugh (London: Darton, Longman, and Todd, 1961), p. 233; G. R. H. Wright, *Ancient Building in South Syria and Palestine*, vol. I (Leiden: E. J. Brill, 1985), pp. 186-87; and the fine example from Lachish, Levels IV-III, D. Ussishkin, "Lachish," in *The New Encyclopedia of Archaeological Excavations in the Holy Land*, vol. 3, ed. E. Stern (New York: Simon and Schuster, 1993), pp. 906-908. More important for the nautical sense in our translation of this Ugaritic passage, and supporting the reading of Ug. *any* as "ship", is the use of both ḥêl and ḥômāh in the metaphoric description of the Phoenician city of Tyre as a ship (Heb. ʾŏnîyāh= Ug. *any*), Ezek 27:3,10, 11. In v. 10 ḥēlēk has been traditionally translated as "your (Tyre's) army," and some read it in v. 11 as "Helech," the supposed name of a city near Arwad, see H. J. Van Dijk, *Ezekiel's Prophecy on Tyre*, vol. 20, *Biblica et orientalia* (Rome: Pontifical Biblical Institute, 1968), pp. 72-73; and W. Zimmerli, *Ezekiel 2*, trans. J. D. Martin (Philadelphia: Fortress, 1983), pp. 45-46, 59-60. Given the presence of ḥômāh in v. 11, it is preferable to translate ḥēlēk as "your (Tyre's) outer fortification wall," which is paired with the ḥômāh, the inner wall. For an Assyrian depiction of the walled city of Tyre, with shields hanging on its outer wall as is described in v. 10, see R. D. Barnett, "Ezekiel and Tyre," *EI* 9 (1969), 6, pl. 1, fig. 1. This same Assyrian relief shows Phoenician warships and merchant vessels with shields hanging from their sides, which adds to the metaphoric image in the text of the city as a ship. I would like to thank Prof. L. Stager for pointing this out to me.

³²For a brief discussion of the use of the tricolon and repetitiveness in Ugaritic and Hebrew poetry see Albright, *Yahweh and the Gods of Canaan*, pp. 4-10.

³³Isa 18:1 and *Odyssey* XI.125, see Albright, "Baal-Zephon," 3, n. 4. The ṣilṣal kənāpāyīm mentioned in Isa 18:1 is traditionally translated as "rustling of wings," but has been reinterpreted by G. R. Driver as "sailing boats," see "Isaiah I-XXXIX: Textual and Linguistic Problems," *Journal of Semitic Studies* 13 (1968), 45.

take *any* as a verb form related to Heb. *ʾny*, "to mourn".³⁴ This fits with the sense of the passage as a dirge; however, it breaks up the tricolon which preserves a more poetic reading for the text, and ignores the following evidence from Egypt.

Baʿl Ṣapōn, like his deified mountain, is described with the West Semitic term *ʾany*, "ship", in an Egyptian papyrus which enumerates both local and foreign gods near the city of Memphis. Papyrus Sallier IV, whose thirteenth century B. C. E. date is only slightly later than the Ugaritic corpus, lists a triad of Canaanite deities: "*n B-ʿ-al-ta n Qdš(t) n ʾi-na-yat B-ʿ-al-(?) ḏa-pu-na*," "to Baʿlat, to Qudšu, to the ship of Baʿl Ṣapōn."³⁵ The identification of *ʾi-na-yat* with West Semitic *ʾany*, "ship", was first put forth by Albright but has gained acceptance among some Egyptologists.³⁶ Others would not translate *ʾi-na-yat*, but prefer

---

Driver bases his argument on the root *ṣlṣl²* in Aramaic, but one could also turn to Heb. *ṣll²* (BDB, p. 853) which has the meaning "launch" or "float" from Akk. and Eth. cognates. Therefore *ṣilṣāl* can be translated as a "launch" or a "boat." This is paralleled in Isa 18:2 by another type of Egyptian boat, the *kəlê gōmeʾ*, or "reed vessels" commonly found sailing on the Nile. The translation of *ṣilṣāl* as "boat" also fits the sense of *ṣilṣal dāgîm* in Jb 40:31b, which is traditionally translated as "fish-spear, harpoon," (BDB, p. 852) but better reads "fishing boat," In both Isa 18:1 and Jb 40:26b(=31b) the Septuagint translates *ṣilṣāl* as *ploion*, "ship." There is another nautical allusion which parallels *ṣilṣal dāgîm* in Jb 40:31a which has been mistranslated: *śukkôt* should read "ship," rather than "barbs, spears," (BDB, p. 968). The Septuagint reads *plōton*, "ship," which assumes a different Hebrew *Vorlage* for the Greek. Based on Eg. *śk.ty* and the equivalent Ug. *ṯkt*, both meaning "ship," the *Vorlage* may have been *škyt*, singular **śəkît*, see Albright, "Baal-Zephon," 4, n. 3; and T. O. Lambdin, "Egyptian Loan Words in the Old Testament," *JAOS* 73 (1953), 154-55, for a similar reading of *śəkîyôt* in Isa 2:16. Thus Jb 40:31, *hatmallēʾ başukkôt ʿôrô, ûbaṣilṣal dāgîm rōšô*, should be translated "Can you fill a ship with his (Leviathan's) skin, a fishing boat with his head," which better preserves the nautical sense of Jb 40:25-32. I disagree with Driver's reading of *kənāpayīm* as "sails", since as Driver has noted ancient ships did not have more than one sail prior to the Roman period, *ibid.*, 45, yet the Hebrew is in the dual form. Rather the symbol of either the double steering rudders of ancient merchantmen or the banks of oars on both sides of warships seem a more likely reminder of a pair of wings for a vessel. Therefore I would translate *ṣilṣal kənāpayīm* as "oared boat". I would like to thank Prof. L. Stager for pointing this out to me.

³⁴Ginsberg, "The Legend of King Keret," 44; Gray, *The KRT Text*, p. 65; Pope, "Marginalia," 461; Caquot *et al.*, *Textes Ougaritiques*, vol. I, p. 550; and Margalit, "Studies in *Krt* and *Aqht*," 150.

³⁵Papyrus Sallier IV, verso I, 6. For the hieroglyphic text see A. H. Gardiner, *Late Egyptian Miscellanies*, vol. VII, *Bibliotheca Aegyptiaca* (Leiden: E. J. Brill, 1937), p. 89. For the transliteration and translation see Albright, "Baal-Zephon," 6-8; a similar translation is in R. A. Caminos, *Late-Egyptian Miscellanies* (London: Oxford University Press, 1954), pp. 333.

merely to vocalize the word as *Anyt*, and take *Anyt* as the name of a fourth Canaanite god in the list.[37] This, however, would posit a god otherwise unattested in Canaan, while the comparison of *Baʿl Ṣapōn*'s mountain with a ship has been shown in the Ugaritic epic of Kirta, and is reasonable given the storm god's demonstrated importance to the safety of ships and mariners.

On the way from the Egyptian delta to southern Canaan is a harbor site called *Baʿal Ṣəpôn* (Heb.), known to us by its West Semitic name only from sources from the Hebrew Bible.[38] The fact that a port was named after *Baʿl Ṣapōn* is not surprising given the practice of classical sailors to dedicate their havens to their patron divinities.[39] Thus this may be taken as another example of the nature of *Baʿl Ṣapōn* as a guardian of Canaanite seafarers.

Given the amalgamation of maritime evidence, E. Porada has interpreted the depiction of the weather god on a Canaanite cylinder seal found at Tell el-Dabʿa in the Nile delta as representing *Baʿl Ṣapōn*.[40] The seal, found in a 13th Dynasty level at the site, depicts the Canaanite storm god striding across two mountains, with typical helmet, curled hair, and weapons in each hand [fig. 10].[41] Behind the storm god is a bull, a totem animal of the deity, while a snake and lion lie below. In front of the weather god and animals is a boat, which Porada views as under the protection of the striding god; thus she tentatively identifies the deity as *Baʿl Ṣapōn*.[42] I agree with Porada's identification of *Baʿl Ṣapōn*, but believe he is not the only patron deity shown on the seal. The serpent and lion are emblems of another

---

[36]"Baal-Zephon," 7; Albright is followed by R. Stadelmann, *Syrisch-Palästinensische Gottheiten in Ägypten* (Leiden: E. J. Brill, 1967), p. 36, and W. Helck, "Ein Indiz Früher Handelsfahrten Syrischer Kaufleute," *UF* 2 (1970), 35.
[37]J. Černy, *Ancient Egyptian Religion* (London: Hutchinson House, 1952), p. 127, and Caminos, *Late-Egyptian Miscellanies*, pp. 333, 338.
[38]Ex 14:2,9, and Num 33:7.
[39]Pausanias, *Description of Greece*, I.1.3. R. Garland, *The Piraeus* (Ithaca, NY: Cornell University Press, 1987), pp. 101-38; Semple, "Templed Promontories," 353-86.
[40]"The Cylinder Seal from Tell el-Dabʿa," *AJA* 88 (1984), 485-88. For further comments on the seal and Porada's article see M. Dijkstra, "The Weather-God on Two Mountains," *UF* 23 (1991), 127-40.
[41]For the date of the seal see Porada, "Cylinder Seal from Dabʿa," 485. For the iconography of the weather god see *ibid.*, 485-85; Dijkstra, "The Weather-God on Two Mountains," 129-31; and A. Vanel, *L'iconographie du dieu de l'orage*, vol. 3, *Cahiers de la Revue biblique* (Paris: Gabalda, 1965), pp. 69-110.
[42]*Ibid.*, 487. This identification of *Baʿl Ṣapōn* is backed by Dijkstra, "The Weather-God on Two Mountains," 137.

divinity who is a protector of sailors, which I shall discuss in greater detail below.

The Hellenized equivalent of *Baʿl Ṣapōn*, Zeus Kasios, is a patron god of sailors. Kasios is honored for saving a merchant from a storm with an offering of a stone carving of the ship which the god protected.[43] Further evidence for Kasios's guardianship of mariners is found on anchor stocks which were inscribed with the god's name in order to insure Kasios's protection when the anchors were dropped during a storm.[44]

In connection with *Baʿl Ṣapōn*'s importance to mariners, it must also be mentioned that we possess the Ugaritic mythic cycle which describes Baʿl-Haddu's struggle with the god of the deified waters, Yamm.[45] The text never refers to the storm god specifically as *Baʿl Ṣapōn*, but does relate that Baʿl-Haddu is given permission to build his palace on Mt. Ṣapōn.[46] Thus he is clearly the local god referred to elsewhere at Ugarit as *Baʿl Ṣapōn*. We have no direct evidence of the myth's relevance to seafarers. However, it must be reiterated that sailors fear the water and praise those deities who protect them from the harm of the sea. Thus Baʿl-Haddu's defeat of Yamm, whose name literally means "Sea" in Ugaritic, may have been an inspiring tale for Canaanite sailors who sought protection and divine intervention from their storm god against the constant dangers of the waters of the Mediterranean sea.[47]

---

[43]Procopius, *De Bello Gothico*, IV:22. For general studies on Zeus Kasios see A. Salač, "ΖΕΥΣ ΚΑΣΙΟΣ," *BCH* 46 (1922), 160-89; A. B. Cook, *Zeus, A Study in Ancient Religion*, vol. II (New York: Biblo and Tannen, 1965), pp. 981-87; and W. Fauth, "Das Kasion-Gebirge und Zeus Kasios," *UF* 22 (1990), 105-18. For the equation of *Baʿl Ṣapōn* with Zeus Kasios see Eissfeldt, *Baal Zaphon, Zeus Kasios*, pp. 1-48; and Albright, "Baal-Zephon," 11-12.

[44]Wachsmuth, ΠΟΜΠΙΜΟΣ Ο ΔΑΙΜΩΝ, p. 396. More commonly these anchor stocks were dedicated to Zeus Soter, or Zeus the Savior, see Svoronos, "Stylides," 105-110.

[45]*KTU* 1.1 and 1.2.

[46]*KTU* 1.4.V.51-57.

[47]L. E. Toombs views this section of the Baʿl cycle as a metaphor for the separation of the land from sea, "Baal, Lord of the Earth: The Ugaritic Baal Epic," in *The Word of the Lord Shall Go Forth*, eds. C. L. Meyers and M. O'Connor (Winona Lake, IN: Eisenbrauns, 1983), pp. 613-23. The tale establishes Baʿl's rule over the land, while Yamm's dominion is the sea: "Human beings may venture upon the sea, but it is not their home. The seafarer is an alien in a strange environment, subject to the whims and threatened by the unpredictable moods of Yam(m)," *ibid.*, p. 618.

Libyan Ammon

Besides the three epithets of the storm god enumerated in the Esarhaddon/Baʿl of Tyre treaty, we have further examples of aspects of the storm god important to Phoenician sailors. From a Roman text, detailing the Punic wars, comes evidence that Libyan Ammon was the tutelary deity of a Carthaginian warship.[48] Ammon is specifically called the "deity of the vessel" (Latin *numen carinae*), and a statue of the god was placed at the stern of the ship:

> Ammon, the native god of Libya, . . . sat there (at the stern) looking over the sea, wearing the horns on his brow.[49]

A Punic warrior, Sabratha, prays to this statue for help during a battle with the Romans.[50] With the impending destruction of the ship, her navigator, Bato, sacrifices himself to the god. He makes a vow to Ammon, stabs himself, collects blood in his own hands, and pours it between the horns on the head of the statue.[51]

The question remains as to which Phoenician god was equated with Libyan Ammon. Our answer comes earlier in Silius's account, where the Carthaginian Bostar sets sail for Libya to consult the oracles of the horned god Ammon.[52] At the scene of his return, Bostar brings the response from the Libyan shrine, but the same god is called by his Latin name, *Iovis*, the thunder god.[53] Later the god's ability to control all the elements of the storm is vividly described, under Jove's epithet Jupiter, *Iuppiter*:

> Jupiter . . . stirred up all his armory--winds and clouds and angry hail, thunder and lightning and black rain storms. A deluge of rain came down, mingled with pitchy hurricanes and black storms.[54]

Thus Libyan Ammon, a patron god to Carthaginian warships, is clearly an aspect of the Phoenician storm god. He should not be confused with *Baʿl Ḥamōn*, the patriarchal deity of Carthage, who is identified with *Saturnus* in Latin.[55]

---

[48] Silius Italicus, *Punica*, XIV.436-39.
[49] *Ibid.*, XIV.438. Trans. J. D. Duff, vol. 2, *The Loeb Classical Library* (Cambridge: Harvard University Press, 1989), p. 305.
[50] *Ibid.*, XIV.440-41.
[51] *Ibid.*, XIV. 458-61.
[52] *Ibid.*, III.6-11.
[53] *Ibid.*, III.647-49.
[54] *Ibid.*, XII.605-22. Trans. J. D. Duff, vol. 2, *The Loeb Classical Library* (Cambridge: Harvard University Press, 1989), p. 193.

Baʿl Rōʾš

A final epithet of the storm god must be mentioned, though we have no direct evidence connecting him to specialized religious beliefs or practices of Phoenician seafarers. This is the "Lord of the promontory", or *Baʿl Rōʾš*, who is known to us from Assyrian, Egyptian, Punic, Phoenician, and Talmudic sources.[56]

Despite the diversity of these attestations, almost nothing is known about the nature of the god. It is clear from the Annals of Shalmaneser III that a mountain, or promontory, near Tyre was named after *Baʿl Rōʾš* (Akk. ^{KUR}Ba-ʾ-li-ra-ʾ-si).[57] This same geographical location near Tyre is called *Rōʾšu Qudši* (r-š q-d-š), or "the sacred promontory", in several Egyptian lists dating from the New Kingdom.[58] Our other sources which mention *Baʿl Rōʾš*, a Punic grave stela from Sousse on the Tunisian coast, an inscription in Greek from Byblos, and a passage from the Jerusalem Talmud, show that his presence was not limited to the environs of Tyre, but they reveal little else with regard to the function of the deity or the nature of his cult.[59] It must be noted, however, that promontory gods were of special

---

[55]Cross, *Canaanite Myth and Hebrew Epic*, pp. 24-28, 35-36; and P. Xella, *Baal Hammon*, vol. 32, *Collezione di studi fenici* (Rome: Consiglio nazionale delle ricerche, 1991), pp. 145-46.

[56]For a summary of the evidence see E. Lipinski, "Note de topographie historique: *Baʿli-Raʾši* et *Raʾšu Qudšu*," *Revue biblique* 78 (1971), 84-92. Lipinski overlooked the Punic mention, but it appears in Fantar, "Le dieu de la mer." 120-26. *Rōʾš* literally means "head", or in geographic terms "headland" or "cape," and is still in use in both modern Arabic and Hebrew (e.g. Arab. *Rās en-Nāqūra*, Heb. *Rōʾš han- Niqra*).

[57]See rev. IV.8 in F. Safar's "A Further Text of Shalmaneser III from Assur," *Sumer* 7 (1951), 11.

[58]J. Simons, *Handbook for the Study of Egyptian Topographical Lists Relating to Western Asia* (Leiden: E. J. Brill, 1937), list I.48, XXIII.1, and XXVII.108. These lists date to the reigns of Thutmosis III, Rameses II, and Rameses III, respectively. For a note on the vocalization of the Canaanite toponym r-š q-d-š see A. Rainey, review of *Canaanite Toponyms in Ancient Egyptian Documents*, by S. Ahituv, *JAOS* 107 (1987), 537.

[59]The Punic stela was first published in P. Cintas, "Le sanctuaire punique de Sousse," *Revue africaine* 91 (1947), 39, fig. 65. However, Cintas mistakingly read *bʿl rš* as an abbreviated form of Baʿl Resh(ef). This was corrected by J. Février's reading of *bʿl rš* as *Baʿl Rōʾš*, "Les inscriptions puniques de Sousse," *Bulletin archéologique du comité des travaux historiques et scientifiques* (1946-49), 561. The Greek inscription was discovered on an altar found near Byblos, R. Du Mesnil du Buisson & R. Mouterde, "Dédicace au Zeus de Resa," *MUSJ* 7 (1914-21), 390-94. Our final source is the Talmudic passage in *ʿAbōdā zārā*, III.43a bottom. This mention of *Baʿl Rōʾš* was first identified by Lipinski, "*Baʿli-Raʾši* et *Raʾšu Qudšu*," 87.

importance to Greek seafarers, who venerated their patron deities by erecting shrines and temples in port or on the gods' sacred headlands:

> And if we ever reach Ithaca, our native land, we will straightway build a rich temple to Helios Hyperion, and put therein many goodly offerings. And if haply he be wroth at all . . . and be minded to destroy our ship . . . rather would I lose my life once for all with a gulp at the wave, than pine slowly away in a desert isle.[60]

> Of the Hellenes, on the other hand, the first to sail over were some Chalcidians from Euboea who settled Naxos with Thucles as founder, and built an altar in honor of Apollo Archegetes. This is now outside of the city, and on it the sacred deputies, when they sail from Sicily, first offer sacrifice.[61]

Canaanite and Phoenician sailors had similar practices, demonstrated by the anchors dedicated to *Baʿl Ṣapōn* in his temple at Ugarit and by a temple set up on a promontory for the Phoenician "Poseidon," but we do not have the evidence connecting any coastal sanctuaries to *Baʿl Rōʾš*.[62] However, the fact that Canaanites and Phoenicians held this cape near Tyre as sacred, shown by the appellation *Rōʾšu Qudši*, is reason enough to conjecture that the "lord of the promontory" was a protector of those who sailed within sight of his headland. This promontory could have served as a landmark and navigational reference, much like Mt. Ṣapōn farther to the north.

Marine deities

Two marine deities of the Phoenicians shall be discussed in light of their patronage of seafarers. It must be noted that these two deities, "Poseidon" and the god riding on a winged seahorse, have marine affiliations which aided sailors, but are not to be taken as late manifestations of the deified sea, Yamm.[63]

---

[60] Homer, *The Odyssey*, XII.345-51. Trans. A.T. Murray, vol. 1, *The Loeb Classical Library* (Cambridge: Harvard University Press, 1984), p. 457.
[61] Thucydides, *History of the Peloponnesian War*, VI.3.1-2. Trans. C. F. Smith, vol. 3, *The Loeb Classical Library* (Cambridge: Harvard University Press, 1992), p. 187. For further references see Pausanias, *Description of Greece*, I.1.3; and Semple, "Templed Promontories," 353-86.
[62] The dedication of a temple to "Poseidon" is described in the periplus of the Carthaginian voyager, Hanno. See *GGM*, vol.I, p. 13.
[63] M. Pope has identified "Poseidon" with Yamm based on the analogy of a Homeric myth of the division of the three parts of the world between Kronos's sons with the parallel tale from Ugarit. Zeus, Hades, and Poseidon each receive their appropriate domain much as Baʿl-Haddu, Môt, and Yamm do in the West

"Poseidon"

Though we are not sure of his Semitic identity, it is clear from a number of sources that "Poseidon" was worshiped by the Phoenicians.[64] I place the name "Poseidon" in quotation marks because it comes down to us as a translation in Greek of the equivalent Phoenician god; unfortunately we possess no bilinguals which allow us to know for sure which Semitic deity the Greek authors identified with their god of marine winds and earthquakes, whose abode was the sea.[65] Greek Poseidon was feared and revered by Aegean sailors, and

---

Semitic world view; see *El in the Ugaritic Texts. Vetus Testamentum Supplement* 2 (Leiden: E. J. Brill, 1955), p. 29. However, Philo of Byblos's pantheon seems to prove otherwise, for he lists "Poseidon" as a son of Pontos (Gk. "Sea"= Ug. Yamm, "Sea"), *Praep. Evang.*, 1.10.26-27. The identification of Pontos=Yamm is further backed by Philo's story of the slaying of Pontos by Demarous, *Praep. Evang.*, 1.10.28, 35, which parallels Yamm's death at the hands of Baʿl-Haddu in the Ugaritic corpus; see Dussaud, "Astarté, Pontos et Baʿal," 206-207, and L. R. Clapham, "Sanchuniathon: The First Two Cycles," Diss. Harvard University, 1969, pp. 147-49. Dussaud identified the god on the winged seahorse as a syncretism between Yamm and Baʿl-Haddu, manifested in the deity Milqart, "Astarté, Pontos et Baʿal," 215, and "Melqart," *Syria* 25 (1946-48), 205-30. This identification is totally unfounded, the link to Yamm being posited merely on the god's association with the sea, which he rides over on his mythic beast, see J. W. Betlyon, *The Coinage and Mints of Phoenicia* (Chico, CA: Scholars Press, 1980), p. 46.

[64]*Praep. Evang.*, 1.10.27 & 35; Polybius VII.9.2; Diodorus V.58.2, XI.21.4, XIII.86.3; Periplus of Hanno, *GGM*, vol.I, p. 13; Periplus of Pseudo-Scylax, *GGM*, vol 1, p 93. Epigraphic material includes an inscription from the environs of Berytus, R. du Mesnil du Buisson & R. Mouterde, "Dédicace à Baalmarqod et à Poséidon," *MUSJ* 7 (1914-21), 387-90, and dedications to the god by Ashkelonites [*ID* 1720, 1721], Tyrians [*ID* 1519], and Berytians [*ID* 1520, 1722-96, 2323-27, 2611] found on the Aegean island of Delos; see P. Bruneau, *Recherches sur les cultes de Délos à l'époque hellénistique et à l'époque impériale* (Paris: E. de Boccard, 1970), pp. 257-67, 622-30. For a survey of most of this material and a review of the problems of identifying the Phoenician "Poseidon" see Fantar, "Le dieu de la mer," 1-133.

[65]The one bilingual inscription which mentions Poseidon is in Palmyrene Aramaic and not Phoenician; see J. Cantineau, "Un Poseidôn palmyrénien," *Syria* 19 (1938), 78-79. The text, inscribed on a stone altar, equates Poseidon, written in Greek, with ʾĒl qōne raʿ, an Aramaic epithet meaning "god, possessor of earth". The same epithet is used to describe Baʿl Šamêm in an Aramaic inscription from Hatra: Baʿ(l) Šamōn qoneh dî raʿh (*KAI* 244.3). This Aramaic material is derivative of the Phoenician and Hebrew evidence for ʾĒl qōnê ʾarṣ, "ʾĒl creator of earth" (*KAI* 26 A III.18; 129.1; and Gen 14:19). For the most recent review of this material see J. Teixidor, *The Pantheon of Palmyra* (Leiden: E. J. Brill, 1979), pp. 25-28. This is a possible clue that the Palmyrenes viewed Baʿl Šamêm and "Poseidon" as the heavenly and maritime aspects of the same storm god. The Phoenicians, however, clearly had two separate gods, "Poseidon" and Baʿl Šamêm. This is seen in the pantheons of Philo of Byblos and Hannibal,

from the following evidence we can extrapolate similar beliefs among Phoenician seafarers.[66]

During a colonizing sea voyage in the fifth-fourth century B. C. E., the Punic captain, Hanno, erected a temple to "Poseidon" on a seaside promontory.[67] This act, clearly undertaken to thank the god and ensure the safety of the fleet, demonstrates that "Poseidon" was a guardian of Phoenician mariners. A later Punic account, recorded in the periplus of Pseudo-Scylax, reports an altar consecrated to "Poseidon" on the same cape, showing the continued importance of the god and the promontory to Punic seafarers.[68]

Diodorus provides us with further evidence which shows that the Semitic "Poseidon" was a patron of the Carthaginian navy, in a fifth century B. C. E. campaign against the Greeks.[69] While the fleet was harbored at Panormus (Palermo, Sicily), the Punic commander, Hamilcar, prepared a huge sacrifice in honor of the god. It is not clear from the text whether this sacrifice was meant to thank "Poseidon" for the safety of the voyage from Carthage, or to appeal to the god for protection in the ensuing battle with the Greeks, or both.[70] Hamilcar was set upon by his Greek enemies, who had slipped into the naval camp while he was occupied with his sacrifice to "Poseidon". He was either killed or took his own life by throwing himself on the sacrificial fire, and the rites he was performing to honor the god "Poseidon" are not detailed.[71]

---

which list "Poseidon" and the storm god as distinct deities (Baʻl-Haddu is translated as Zeus or Demarous by Philo, *Praep. Evang.*, 1.10.31; Zeus by Polybius, VII.9.2. Each author's reference to "Poseidon", distinct from the storm god, is listed in the above note). On the nature of the Greek Poseidon see L. R. Farnell, *The Cults of the Greek States*, vol. IV (Oxford: Clarendon, 1907), pp. 1-97.

[66]Herodotus, *The Persian Wars*, VII.192. For further classical references see Farnell, *Cults of the Greek States*, vol. IV, pp. 4-5, 13, 26; Semple, "Templed Promontories," 365-69.

[67]The original Phoenician text of Hanno's Periplus was carved on a dedicatory stela placed in the temple of Saturn (*Baʻl Ḥamōn*) at the successful return of the voyage to Carthage; D. Harden, *The Phoenicians*, p. 162, and S. Moscati, *The World of the Phoenicians*, trans. A. Hamilton (New York: Frederick A. Praeger, 1968), p. 182. The stela, however, is lost. The text comes down to us in fragmentary form in Greek translation presented in *GGM*, vol.I, pp. 1-14; for Hanno's dedication of the temple to Poseidon see p. 13.

[68]*Ibid.*, p. 93.

[69]XI.21.4.

[70]D. Baramki, *Phoenicia and the Phoenicians* (Beirut: Khayats, 1961), p. 38, believes the sacrifice is in preparation for battle.

[71]In Diodorus XI.22.1 Hamilcar is killed; in Herodotus, *The Persian Wars*, VII.167 he takes his own life.

The final piece of evidence linking "Poseidon" with Phoenician sailors comes down to us in the form of a Greek myth.[72] Cadmus, the legendary Phoenician prince attributed with the founding of Thebes, was said to have been crossing the Mediterranean in search of the abducted Europa, when his ship was besieged by several storms. He is reported as having prayed to "Poseidon" for protection from the tempests. When he reached safe ground at the island of Rhodes, Cadmus founded a temple in honor of "Poseidon" and left Phoenicians from the ship to manage the holy precinct as fulfillment of his vows made at sea.

The god riding on a winged seahorse

From the coins of Tyre and two Punic plaques come the representation of a second marine god, holding a bow, riding over the waves of the Mediterranean on the back of a mythic beast [fig. 23].[73] This beast, known to the Greeks as the hippokamp, has the body and tail of a sea serpent, the head and front legs of a horse, and the wings of a bird.[74] In Greek iconography this composite animal is associated with several different maritime gods, including Poseidon, and Fantar has suggested that the Phoenician representation of the god riding on the hippokamp is the Semitic "Poseidon."[75] Betlyon, whom I follow, cautions against any firm identification of this god and refers to him merely as a "marine" deity.[76]

---

[72]Diodorus, V.58.2.
[73]For further coins see Betlyon, *The Coinage and Mints of Phoenicia*, pl. 5. I have chosen in general to refer to Phoenician coins presented by Betlyon because of the availability of the publication. Most of the coin types are of similar issue, and thus are also found in the other standard works, such as G. F. Hill, *Catalogue of the Greek Coins of Phoenicia* (London: British Museum, 1910), and E. Babelon, *Monnaies Grecques et Romaines*, vol. II, part 2 (Paris: E. Leroux, 1910). For the terra-cotta plaques see Fantar, "Le dieu de la mer," pl. IV.1 & VII.2.
[74]H. Lamer has a summary of the classical evidence, "Hippokampus," in *Real-Encyclopädie der classischen Altertumswissenschaft*, vol. 8, eds. A. Pauly et al. (Stuttgart: J. B. Metzler, 1913), cols. 1748-72.
[75]"Le dieu de la mer," 43-94. For the seahorse as companion to different Greek deities see Lamer, *ibid.*, and the sources summarized in Betlyon, *The Coinage and Mints of Phoenicia*, p. 128, n. 31.
[76]Betlyon, *The Coinage and Mints of Phoenicia*, p. 46. Earlier identifications of the "marine" god with both Milqart and Baʿl Šamêm is rightfully questioned by Betlyon, *ibid.*, pp. 67-69, n. 44-45. The description of Yahweh's storm theophany in Hab 3:8-15 shows many parallels to the Phoenician iconography of the "marine" storm god riding his composite beast: Yahweh treads over Sea (Heb. *Yam*), in a chariot pulled by horses, shooting arrows from his bow. The Tyrian coins show the "marine" god holding a bow, mounted on a horse-headed

This "marine" deity is clearly a protector of seafarers because his totem animal, the winged seahorse, is depicted riding below ships on the coins of Byblos and Aradus [figs. 21 and 22].[77] It is more accurate to say that the ships are shown riding on top of the winged seahorse, which is reminiscent of the common feature in Near Eastern iconography of the gods, and symbols of the gods, riding on their totem animals.[78] Thus I would interpret these coins as displaying Phoenician ships under the guidance or protection of the winged seahorse and the "marine" god.[79]

Horse-head prows are commonly depicted on Phoenician ships [figs. 22, 63, and 64]. This type of vessel is also known to us from its mention in classical sources, where they are called *hippoi*, literally "horses."[80] I take this prow figure as a representation of an abbreviated form of the winged seahorse, whose spirit is imbued in the vessel.[81] Thus the hippokamp's companion deity is watching over these horse-headed ships and their crew, since the composite creature represented in the prow is a symbol of its "marine" god rider.

Goddesses as protectors of sailors

Two goddesses from the Canaanite and Phoenician pantheons exhibit connections to the world of seafarers. Like the previous gods described whose control of winds or marine storms made them important to mariners, it shall be suggested that both ᵓ*Ašerah*'s and Tinnit's celestial connections were believed to have influence over the weather which was crucial for safety at sea.

ᵓ*Ašerah*

The highest ranking goddess in the Canaanite pantheon, ᵓ*Ašerah*, has clear marine attributes. She is called ᵓ*Ašerah* of the Sea (ᵓ*Aṯiratu*

---

creature, riding over the waves of the sea.
[77]*Ibid.*, pl. 6.5 & 9.2.
[78]*ANEP*, figs. 470-74, 486, 500, 501, 522-23, 531, 534, & 537.
[79]Betlyon believes that the seahorse on the Aradus coin is the attendant of the fish-tailed god on the obverse of the coin, *ibid.*, p. 84. I, however, take the seahorse to be the totem of the anthropomorphic deity riding on its back on the coins of Tyre.
[80]The classical citations are gathered by C. Torr, *Ancient Ships*, (1895; Reprinted, with additional material edited by A. J. Podlecki, Chicago: Argonaut, 1964) pp. 113-14.
[81]Perhaps the hull of the ship was likened to the creature's sea serpent body, and the oars or dual steering rudders to its wings. See above n. 36. The concept of divine spirits residing in ships shall be discussed below, in ch. 3.

yammi) in the Ugaritic texts, and her divine helper is called Fisherman (*Daggay ʾAṯirati*).[82] These nautical qualities are intriguing, but it appears to have been ʾAšerah's celestial links which made her important to early navigators.

The goddess ʾAšerah is shown on Canaanite gold pendants, standing on a crescent moon or with crescents in her headdress, and she is portrayed on Egyptian stelae with a crescent-and-disk on her headdress [figs. 1, 2, and 6].[83] These same lunar symbols, the crescent and the crescent-and-disk, are found mounted on poles placed at the stern of Phoenician ships [fig. 66].[84] ʾAšerah should not be misconstrued, however, as the deified moon itself. Yariḫ, whose name literally means moon, was the lunar deity of the pantheon at Ugarit and a male god.[85] The goddess is only linked to one of many aspects of the moon, the crescent moon.

The placement of ʾAšerah's crescent or crescent-and-disk symbol at the stern of the ship shows that her presence was being invoked especially for aid in steering or navigation. The stern of Phoenician ships was the place where the twin rudders, which expert pilots used to guide the vessel, were mounted.[86] Though we know little about

---

[82]Occurrences of these appellations in the Ugaritic corpus are summarized in R. E. Whitaker, *A Concordance of the Ugaritic Literature* (Cambridge, MA: Harvard University Press, 1972), p. 43, which lists twenty-two instances of ʾAšerah's marine epithet and three of her fisherman helper, *ibid.*, p. 179.

[83]Cross, *Canaanite Myth and Hebrew Epic*, pp. 31-35. The identification of the goddess Qudšu, who rides on the back of the lion, as an epithet of ʾAšerah is based on a carving in the Winchester collection which names the three Canaanite goddesses, "*Qudšu-ᶜAštart-ᶜAnat*"; see I. E. S. Edwards, "A Relief of Qudshu-Astarte-Anath in the Winchester College Collection," *JNES* 14 (1955), 49-51. Thus Qudšu is taken to be the equivalent of ʾAšerah. The Egyptian Qudšu stelae are further illustrated in C. Boreaux, "La stèle C. 86 du Musée du Louvre et les stèles similaires," *Mélanges syriens offerts a Monsieur René Dussaud*, vol. 2 (Paris: Librarie orientaliste Paul Geuthner, 1939), pp. 673-87, figs. 2, 3, and pl. following p. 698. The equating of Qudšu with ʾAšerah has been questioned recently by S. A. Wiggins, "The Myth of Asherah: Lion Lady and Serpent Goddess," *UF* 23 (1991), 383-94; and I. Cornelius, "Anat and Qudshu as the 'Mistress of Animals,' Aspects of the Iconography of the Canaanite Goddesses," *Studi epigrafici e linguistici* 10 (1993), 21-45. See below n. 97

[84]Svoronos, "Stylides," 86. Svoronos calls these lunar emblems symbols of ᶜAštart-Selene, conflating the Phoenician and Greek goddesses. Betlyon emends the goddess to ʾAšerah-ʾĒlat, *The Coinage and Mints of Phoenicia*, p. 30, n. 37, adding that these stylides represent the goddess "in her role as protectress of ships at sea," *ibid*.

[85]*KTU* 1.39.14, 1.43.14.

[86]P. Bartoloni, "Ships and Navigation," in *The Phoenicians*, ed. S. Moscati (Milan: Bompiani, 1988), pp. 72-77.

Phoenician navigational practices, the moon and its light are crucial for sailing in the darkness of night.[87]

In order to explain the link between the crescent, or crescent-and-disk, and navigation, one must interpret the symbol as a representation of the new moon. This lunar aspect of ʾAšerah is important nautically because both ancient and modern seafarers considered different appearances of the new moon to portend a variety of weather conditions at sea, which were crucial to the well being of the crew, the safety of the ship, and proper navigation during its voyage:

> Soon as the moon gathers her returning fires, if she encloses a dark mist within dim horns, a heavy rain is awaiting farmers and seamen. But if over her face she spreads a maiden blush, there will be wind; as wind rises, golden Phoebe ever blushes. But if at her fourth rising--for that is our surest guide--she pass through the sky clear and with undimmed horns, then all that day, and the days born of it to the month's end, shall be free from rain and wind; and sailors, safe in port, shall pay their vows on the shore to Glaucus, and to Panopea, and to Melicerta, Ino's son.[88]

Reading future meteorological conditions from the appearance of the new moon must have been of upmost importance for travel at sea. Thus, much like the patron gods already discussed, I would postulate that ʾAšerah had influence over certain elements at sea which were crucial to the well-being of Canaanite and Phoenician navigators.

Further evidence is found in an Egyptian coffin text and a Canaanite cylinder seal. Middle Kingdom coffin text no. 61 equates the goddess Ḥatḥor with the Canaanite Lady of Byblos (ʾAšerah), who is said to "hold the steering oars of . . . (funerary) barks."[89] An unprovenienced Canaanite cylinder seal from the same period, the Middle Bronze IIA, depicts a Ḥatḥor head right above the steering oars of two opposed ships [fig. 7].[90] A sailor and the pilot of the left-hand

---

[87]The Phoenicians' ability to sail at night, especially following the Little Bear, is detailed by Silius Italicus, *Punica*, III.663-65, XIV.457.

[88]Virgil, *Georgics*, I.424-37. Trans. H. R. Fairclough, vol. 1, *The Loeb Classical Library* (Cambridge: Harvard University Press, 1986), p. 111. For another classical example see Apuleius, *The Golden Ass*, XI.1-7; for cross-cultural examples demonstrating the importance of the moon to seafarers see Bassett, *Legends and Superstitions of the Sea*, pp. 45-52.

[89]P. Barguet, *Les textes des sarcophages égyptiens du Moyen Empire* (Paris: Les éditions du Cerf, 1986), p. 200; and R. O. Faulkner, *The Ancient Egyptian Coffin Texts*, vol. 1, *Spells 1-354* (Warminster, England: Aris & Phillips, 1973), p. 56. For the original hieroglyphic text see A. de Buck, *The Egyptian Coffin Texts*, vol. I, *Texts of Spells 1-75* (Chicago: The University of Chicago Press, 1935), pp. 256-64. For the equasion of the Lady of Byblos with ʾAšerah see W.A. Maier, *ʾAšerah: Extrabiblical Evidence* (Atlanta, GA: Scholars Press, 1986), pp. 88-96.

vessel face the goddess, whom I would interpret as representing ʾAšerah, as she is depicted in later representations as resembling Ḥatḫor [figs. 1-6].

ʾAšerah's importance to mariners is also demonstrated in the dedication of a harbor to the goddess, just as the port of Baʿal Ṣapôn was consecrated to the storm god. ʾĒlat, a port city on the Red Sea, is the proper name of the goddess familiar from the texts of Ugarit.[91] A late coin minted in Tyre depicts a goddess standing in a galley, representing the ship's divine guardian. Her name, inscribed in Phoenician, reads ʾIlat Ṣur, "ʾĒlat of Tyre".[92]

I have already mentioned the cylinder seal from Tell el-Dabʿa and its important representation of Baʿl Ṣapōn as protector of a ship. Underneath the depiction of the striding storm god and his bull totem is a register with two other sacred animals, which are also positioned to guard over the ship [fig. 10].[93] These animals, the snake and the lion, are symbols of the goddess ʾAšerah. She is often depicted holding snakes in one or both hands, riding on the back of a lion, and is even called Labiʾt, "Lioness", in Ugaritic [figs. 2-6, and 8].[94] The prow

---

[90]B. Teissier, *Egyptian Iconography on Syro-Palestinian Cylinder Seals of the Middle Bronze Age*, vol. 11, *Orbis Biblicus et Orientalis, Series Archaeologica* (Fribourg, Switzerland: University Press, 1996), pp. 102, 104 fig. 206. Teissier links Egyptian Ḥatḫor with the patronage of seafaring, travel, and border areas, *ibid*. p. 184; see also Stadelmann, *Syrisch-Palästinensische Gottheiten in Ägypten*, p. 10-11, 143.

[91]Deut 2:8; II Kings 14:22, 16:6; see KTU 1.14.IV. 35, 39 for examples of the numerous occurrences of ʾIlat in Ugaritic.

[92]H. Hamburger, "A Hoard of Syrian Tetradrachms and Tyrian Bronze Coins from Gush Halav," *IEJ* 4 (1954), 224, no. 137. Hamburger translates the inscription as "The goddess of Tyre"; Cross, however, would emend this to "'ʾĒlat of Tyre", *Canaanite Myth and Hebrew Epic*, p. 31.

[93]Porada, "Cylinder Seal from Dabʿa," 486, ill. 1.

[94]See *CTA* 5.1.14 for Labiʾt (the corresponding text in *KTU* 1.5.I.14 has lbim not lbit). The lion is identified with ʾAšerah by Cross, *Canaanite Myth and Hebrew Epic*, p. 34. The goddess's feline title is also part of a name inscribed on several arrowheads from the El-Khaḍr hoard: ʿAbd-labiʾt, "servant of the Lioness", F. M. Cross, "The Origin and Early Evolution of the Alphabet," *EI* 8 (1967), 13*, n. 31-33. The link between Qudšu and ʾAšerah, and therefore the identification of ʾAšerah with the symbol of the lion, has been challenged by Wiggins, "The Myth of Asherah," 383-94; and Cornelius, "Anat and Qudshu," 21-45. These authors, however, ignore the later, Iron Age iconography on a pithos from Kuntillet ʿAjrûd which depicts a palm tree, a motif clearly representing ʾAšerah, flanked by ibexes, riding on the back of a lion [fig. 9], see R. Hestrin, "The Lachish Ewer and the ʾAsherah," *IEJ* 37 (1987), 220-21; and S. M. Olyan, *Asherah and the Cult of Yahweh in Israel*, vol. 34, *Society of Biblical Literature Monograph Series* (Atlanta, GA: Scholars Press, 1988), p. 60. This

figure on some ships shown on Byblian coins is the head of a lion [fig. 21].⁹⁵ This further illustrates ʾAšerah's role as guardian over vessels, represented by the placement of the goddess's totem animal as the protective spirit of the Byblian warship.⁹⁶

Tinnit⁹⁷

In Phoenician-Punic sources the goddess Tinnit has similar lunar and maritime qualities to the goddess ʾAšerah, which strengthens the argument equating the the two goddesses.⁹⁸ Tinnit, like ʾAšerah, is

same pithos is inscribed with a dedication "to Yahweh of Samaria and his ʾašerah," (Heb. *lyhwh.šmrn.wlʾšrth*); following Hestrin I view the drawing of the palm tree as a representation of the mentioned cult symbol, Yahweh's ʾašerah, *ibid.*, 221; for a review of the numerous past treatments of the inscription see Olyan, *Asherah and the Cult of Yahweh*, pp. 25-34. Similar imagery of a tree flanked by ibexes, flanked by two lionesses is found modeled in the round on two cult stands from Iron Age Taʿanach, one of which also includes a register depicting a nude goddess in a frontal pose flanked by two lionesses which is very close to the earlier *Qudšu* iconography, see Hestrin, *ibid.*, p. 220; and R. Hestrin, "The Cult Stand from Taʿanach and its Religious Background," in *StudPhoen*, vol. V, *Phoenicia and the Eastern Mediterranean in the First Millennium B.C.*, ed. E. Lepinski (Leuven: Uitgeverij Peeters, 1987), pp. 60-77. These Iron Age representations are parallel to the Bronze Age *Qudšu* reliefs, with the tree sometimes substituting for the anthropomorphic depiction of the goddess riding on, or flanked by, her companion animal, the lion/lioness.

⁹⁵The Egyptian ships depicted in battle against invading Sea Peoples, at Rameses III's mortuary temple at Medinet Habu, also have lioness-headed prows; see H. H. Nelson, "The Naval Battle Pictured at Medinet Habu," *JNES* 2 (1943), 44. It is possible that this prow figure represented *Qudšu-ʾAšerah* to Egyptian sailors, but it is more likely that the lioness was a depiction of the Egyptian goddess Sekhmet, a war-goddess, *ibid*. The Egyptian vessels are warships and the each lioness prow figure grasps the head of an Asiatic in her mouth, which fits Sekhmet's role as a destructive deity.

⁹⁶In the case of the lion prow figure it is possible that the totem animal represents another patron deity of sailors. Both Milqart and Baʿl have been associated with a companion lion in secondary literature based on iconographic representations of a male, warrior god riding on the back of a lion, depicted on stelae and engraved seals, see R. Dussaud, "Melqart," *Syria* 25 (1946-48), 222-24; Y. Yadin, "New Gleanings on Reshef from Ugarit," in *Biblical and Related Studies Presented to Samuel Iwry*, eds. A. Kort and S. Morschauser (Winona Lake, IN: Eisenbrauns, 1985), pp. 266-68; and I. Cornelius, *The Iconography of the Canaanite Gods Reshef and Baʿal*, Orbis Biblicus et Orientalis, vol. 140 (Fribourg, Switzerland: University Press, 1994), pp. 195-208. I consider the evidence linking Milqart with the god on the lion stronger than that for Baʿl, and shall demonstrate below that Milqart was a protector of mariners.

⁹⁷The reasoning behind this vocalization of the goddess's name is explained above, p. 5, n. 21.

symbolized by the crescent, or new moon.[99] The crescent-and-disk motif appears frequently on sacrificial stelae dedicated to the goddess Tinnit and her consort, Ba‛l Ḥamōn [figs. 13, 15, 67a, and 67b].[100] There is some debate over which god is represented by the crescent-and-disk, since both are mentioned on stelae with the symbol.[101] Hours-Mieden points out that the crescent-and-disk is found on a majority of stelae consecrated to both the god and the goddess, yet there are some with the symbol which are dedicated only to Ba‛l Ḥamōn, or his later Neo-Punic equivalent, Saturn.[102] This, however, does not necessitate Ba‛l Ḥamōn's link to the motif since the inscriptions on the stelae do not necessarily parallel or illustrate their symbols. Yadin takes the crescent-and-disk as a representation of Ba‛l Ḥamōn.[103] He argues that the crescent-and-disk must symbolize the god because the other two main motifs on the stelae, the sign of Tinnit and the caduceus, represent the goddess. Yadin's assumption, however, ignores the earlier, Canaanite evidence linking the crescent-and-disk to ʾAšerah, who is equated with Tinnit.

I view the crescent-and-disk as a continuation of the earlier motif found on Qudšu's/ʾAšerah's headdress and on poles at stern of galleys

---

[98]Cross, Canaanite Myth and Hebrew Epic, pp. 31-35; Maier, ʾAšerah: Extrabiblical Evidence, pp. 96-118; Olyan, Asherah and the Cult of Yahweh, pp. 53-61.
[99]S. Gsell, Histoire ancienne de l'Afrique du nord, vol. IV (Paris: Librairie Hachette, 1920), pp. 247-50, 360-62, and Y. Yadin, "Symbols of Deities at Zinjirli, Carthage and Hazor," in Near Eastern Archaeology in the Twentieth Century, ed. J. A. Sanders (Garden City, NY: Doubleday, 1970), pp. 217-20. Yadin largely follows Gsell's argument, based on a Greek-Phoenician bilingual inscription from Athens, KAI 53. The text equates the personal name Artemidōros (Gk.) with ‛Abdi-Tinnit (Phoen.), therefore Artemis=Tinnit, since dōros=‛Abdi ["servant"]. It is not clear, however, that Artemis's lunar characteristic is really that prominent, though she is sometimes linked with the goddess Selene, the deified moon; see R. C. T. Parker, "Selene," in The Oxford Classical Dictionary, 3rd ed., eds. S. Hornblower and A. Spawforth (Oxford: Oxford University Press, 1996), pp. 1379-80. Artemis was also associated with another lunar deity, Hekate, and representations depict her with the crescent moon on her forehead, Farnell, Cults of the Greek States, vol. II, p. 457-61. Stronger evidence of Tinnit's lunar aspect comes from the crescentic symbols on funerary stelae from Carthage; see Gsell, ibid., pp. 249-50, 360-62.
[100]Hours-Miedan, "Les stèles de Carthage," pl. XIII. F. Bertrandy and M. Sznycer, Les stèles puniques de Constantine (Paris: Ministère de la Culture et de la Communication, 1987), pp. 62-63.
[101]Brown reviews the different opinions, but does not come to any definite conclusion regarding the identity of the god symbolized by the crescent and disk, Late Carthaginian Child Sacrifice, pp. 136-37, 144-45.
[102]"Les stèles de Carthage," 38.
[103]Yadin, "Symbols of Deities," 205.

depicted on Phoenician coins [figs. 2, 6, and 66]. Thus I equate later illustrations of this lunar symbol with the goddess Tinnit as the equivalent goddess to ʾAšerah, and do not view the symbol in any connection with Baʿl Ḥamōn. This is supported by the appearance of the crescent-and-disk on a Carthaginian coin, placed below the back of the head of a bust of a goddess with kernels of grain in her braided hair [fig. 11]. The same bust is portrayed on another coin from Carthage, with two dolphins facing the goddess and the sign of Tinnit positioned where the crescent-and-disk was on the preceding coin [fig. 11]. Therefore the sign of Tinnit and the symbol of the new moon appear to be interchangeable hallmarks of the goddess Tinnit. The link between these two symbols is further illustrated on Carthaginian sacrificial stelae which depict a motif which combines the sign of Tinnit with the crescent-and-disk, which shows how closely the goddess and the crescent-and-disk are related [fig. 13].

The same stylized symbol, the sign of Tinnit, is also portrayed on Punic funeral stelae with dolphins and fish, and on a clay pellet with a dolphin [figs. 12, 14, and 15].[104] Dolphins are important omens to ancient and modern sailors who believe that their presence around a ship foretells an impending storm or change in sea conditions:

> I like not the tossing of the trees or the beat of the waves on the shore; or when the dolphin with changing course challenges the sea to rise . . . I like not these signs . . . With these words he unmoored his boat and spread his canvas to the winds.[105]

It is therefore telling that dolphins are often depicted along side the sign of Tinnit.

The goddess has further maritime attributes, more directly related to sailors.[106] Tinnit's protection of ships is nicely illustrated by the

---

[104] Brown has recently summarized the different interpretations of the sign of Tinnit, and concludes that the sign is a representation of the goddess, *Late Carthaginian Child Sacrifice*, pp. 123-31.

[105] Lucan, *The Civil War*, V.552-60. Trans. J. D. Duff, *The Loeb Classical Library* (Cambridge: Harvard University Press, 1988), p. 281. For further classical references see Artemidorus Daldianus, *Onirocritica*, I.16; and Isidorus, *Origines*, XVII.6, 11. For cross-cultural evidence see Bassett, *Legends and Superstitions of the Sea and of Sailors*, pp. 132-34, 245.

[106] A number of terra-cotta, female figurines have been recovered from the sea near Shave-Ziyyon and Tyre on the Syro-Palestinian coast, E. Linder, "A Cargo of Phoenicio-Punic Figurines," *Archaeology* 26/3 (1973), 182-87; and W. Culican, "A Votive Model from the Sea," *PEQ* 108 (1976), 119. Some of these figurines are stamped with the sign of Tinnit and are clearly representations of the goddess. Following Linder, the quantity of figurines discovered at Shave-Ziyyon without other finds or remnants of ship's hull suggest jettisoned cargo. Culican

presence of her sign on a ship, mounted on standards placed both fore and aft, as depicted on a stela from Carthage [fig. 16].[107] Other representations of ships and sacred parts of ships, such as the prow or stern of the vessel, are found on stelae with and without the sign of Tinnit [figs. 18, 19, 67a, 67b, and 70].[108] Ba‘l Ḥamōn, the other god to whom the stelae are consecrated, has no maritime attributes.[109] Therefore, I would suggest that these nautical images were dedicated to Tinnit, in her role as a guardian of seafarers.

Further nautical symbols are portrayed on sacrificial stelae, together with the sign of Tinnit. Sacred anchors, like the earlier stone anchors dedicated in the Temple of Ba‘l at Ugarit mentioned above, may symbolize the goddess's protection of sailors from storms [figs. 17 67a, and 67b]. Images of steering rudders on stelae attest to Tinnit's importance to the safe guidance or proper navigation of ships [figs. 20 67a, and 67b].[110]

Milqart, a different type of nautical guardian

Classical texts record promontories, islands, and ports dedicated by Phoenicians to "Herakles," who we know is equated with the Tyrian god Milqart.[111] Based on this geographic evidence and the presence of Milqart sanctuaries on headlands and in ports stretching from Tyre to the Atlantic coast of the Iberian peninsula, Semple has proposed that Milqart was a tutelary deity of Phoenician sailors.[112] I agree with Semple, and will add further data to support her claim.

Arrian, in his description of Alexander the Great's conquest of Tyre, mentions a Tyrian ship consecrated to Herakles-Milqart.[113]

---

posits that the Tinnit figurines may have been thrown in the sea to "secure protection from reefs," which is an intriguing suggestion, *ibid.*

[107]Fig. 16 is a detailed drawing. For a photograph of the stela itself see P. Bartoloni, "Le figurazioni di carattere marino rappresentate sulle più tarde stele di Cartagine II. Le imbarcazioni minori," *RSF* 7/2 (1979), pl. LIV.1.

[108]*Ibid.*, pls. LIV-LIX.

[109]Cross, *Canaanite Myth and Hebrew Epic*, pp. 24-28, 35-36; and Xella, *Baal Hammon*, pp. 106-40.

[110]See also Bertrandy and Sznycer, *Les stèles puniques de Constantine*, no. 40 & 75.

[111]These geographical references are gathered together by Gsell, *Histoire*, vol. IV, p. 307, n. 2. A Phoenician and Greek inscription from Malta is one of several bilinguals identifying Milqart with Herakles, *KAI* 47. Philo of Byblos makes the same equation, *Praep. Evang.*, 1.10.27.

[112]Strabo, *Geography*, III.1.4. Semple, "Templed Promontories," 366.

[113]"*kai tēn naun tēn Tyrian tēn hieran tou Herakleos*," Arrian, *Anabasis of Alexander*, II.24.6.

Similarly, a war ship painted on the wall of a Carthaginian tomb at Kef el-Blida depicts a figure of a god on its prow [fig. 24]. This prow figure, of the Phoenician type called the "smiting god," holds an axe with his raised hand and a shield with the lowered one, wears a conical cap, and is bearded.[114] An inscribed stela, dedicated to Milqart, depicts the god as bearded, holding an axe, and wearing a conical cap, a motif which is repeated on a seal stone, a Carthaginian razor, and a decorated bowl [figs. 25-27].[115] On several of the seals, the axe wielding figure also carries a shield. Therefore I would interpret the figure on the prow of the Kef el-Blida war ship as representing the vessel's guardian deity, Milqart, much as the war ship, mentioned by Arrian, was dedicated to the Tyrian Herakles.[116]

Phoenician merchants are also recorded making sacrifices to their country's god, Tyrian Herakles, before setting sail from Greece on their way to Carthage.[117] In addition to thanking Milqart for giving one of the merchants victory in a competition with the Greeks, the sacrifice is made to the god to ensure a safe voyage to Carthage. Similarly, Strabo reports that Tyrian sailors offered sacrifices to Herakles on their voyages to found the city of Gader, in order to check the safety of future travel.[118] On two different expeditions the sacrifices were not favorable, so the ships turned back. The third attempt reached the island of Gader, and a temple was founded in honor of Milqart, the protector of the seafaring explorers.

Like the classical listing of headlands dedicated to the Tyrian Herakles, mentioned above, Phoenician inscriptions from Sicily and Carthage verify a cape dedicated to Milqart. These include coins from Sicily and two sacrificial stelae from Carthage, which refer to *Rōš Milqart*, "Promontory of Milqart".[119]

---

[114]J. Ferron, "La peinture funeraire de Kef-el-Blida," *Archéologia* 20 (1968), 54; and A. M. Bisi, "Le influenze puniche sulla religione libica: la gorfa di Kef el-Blida," *Studi e materiali di storia delle religioni* 37/1 (1966), 88.

[115]The seals are discussed in W. Culican's "Melqart Representations on Phoenician Seals," *Abr-Nahrain* 2 (1960-61), 41-54. For a representation of the bowl and the interpretation of the axe wielding figure as Milqart see Barnett, "Ezekiel and Tyre," 11-12, fig. 1.

[116]Barnett also interprets symbols shown below a scene with Milqart, depicted on a stone bowl, as possibly representing an anchor and a ship, *ibid.*, 10. Judging from the photographs provided, the lower symbol is too fragmentary to interpret as anything at all, let alone a ship, and the upper motif has somewhat of an anchor shape, with possible flukes and a rope-hole, but lacks an anchor stock. I would hesitate to call this an anchor, as Barnett does himself by placing a question mark after its identification, *ibid.*

[117]Heliodorus of Emesa, *Aethiopica*, IV.16.8.

[118]*Geography*, III.5.5.

[119]Z. S. Harris, *A Grammar of the Phoenician Language* (New Haven, CT:

What were Milqart's attributes which made him a guardian of seafarers? Scholars have often mistakenly given Milqart qualities of a storm god, based on the fact that he is called *Baʿl Ṣur*, and on his misidentification with the "marine" god riding the winged seahorse on Tyrian coins.[120] The appellation *Baʿl Ṣur* is more accurately translated as "the lord of Tyre" than "Baʿl (the storm god) of Tyre". This is proven in the Esarhaddon/Baʿl of Tyre treaty which lists the three aspects of the Tyrian storm god separately from Milqart (Akk. $^d mi\text{-}il\text{-}qar\text{-}tu$).[121] While *Baʿl Šamêm*, *Baʿl Malagê*, and *Baʿl Ṣapōn* control the marine storm, Milqart and *Išmun* are described as having effects on the land and its fecundity.[122] I have already discussed the problems of the identification of the god on the seahorse, above. It should be stressed, though, that there is no primary evidence which equates the god on the seahorse with Milqart.[123]

If Milqart was not a storm god and did not possess any attributes believed to affect the weather, as have all of the nautical patron deities described so far, why was he important to sailors? The answer seems to lie in a comparison with his Greek, Hurrian, and Mesopotamian counterparts, Herakles, *Iršappa*, and Nergal.

Herakles, through the tales of his adventurous twelve tasks, became the paradigm of the intrepid traveller.[124] Thus he was considered a guardian of voyagers. Though we are not left any textual details of his sea travels, Herakles is represented on gems sailing across the waters on a raft [fig. 28]. Pausanias records the story of an "Egyptian" statue of Herakles found in the god's temple in Erythrae, which he claims came over from Tyre on a wooden raft.[125] Pausanias

American Oriental Society, 1936), p. 145. Note Harris's corrected reading of *rš mlqrt* for *bt mlqrt*, CIS I.264, which is not emended in KAI 86 (=CIS I.264). The evidence is most recently reviewed in C. Bonnet's *Melqart*, vol. VIII, StudPhoen (Leuven: Uitgeverij Peeters, 1988), pp. 267-69.

[120]This notion is especially tenacious among French scholars, beginning with R. Dussaud's concept that Milqart was a fusion of the storm god, Baʿl-Haddu, and the deified sea, Yamm, represented on Tyrian coins by the god riding over the sea on the winged seahorse: "Astarté, Pontos et Baʿal," 215, and "Melqart," 205-30. Milqart is called *Baʿl Ṣur* in a Phoenician inscription from Malta, KAI 47.1.

[121]Rev. IV.10' names the storm gods, Rev. IV.14' names Milqart.

[122]Rev. IV.11'-13' and Rev. IV.14'-17'.

[123]This point was already made by Betlyon, *The Coinage and Mints of Phoenicia*, p. 46.

[124]L. Lacroix, "Héraclès, héros voyageur et civilisateur," *Bulletin de la Classe des Lettres et des Sciences morales et politiques de l'Academie royale de Belgique* 60 (1974), 34-59. Bonnet, *Melqart*, pp. 284-86.

[125]*Description of Greece*, VII.5.5.

most likely mistakes the Egyptianizing elements of Phoenician art for a truly Egyptian image, since he says the statue was Tyrian. Therefore, I believe that the story reflects a tradition of Tyrian Herakles-Milqart voyaging by raft.

The adventures of Greek Herakles also portray the hero-god as the vanquisher of monsters and beasts. One of these tales, lost to us textually but depicted on Greek black- and red-figure pottery, pits Herakles in a wrestling match against a creature who is human from the waist up, and fish from the waist down [figs. 30 and 32].[126] This fish-tailed monster has several different names, inscribed on a few of the vessels: Halios *Gerōn*, Triton, or Nereus. It is possible that Herakles's defeat of these sea monsters made him the hero and guardian of sailors, who feared mysterious sea creatures.

No such images of Milqart wrestling a fish-tailed monster are preserved in Phoenician iconography, though the motif of the fish-tailed creature is considered to have originated in the Near East.[127] The composite, marine creature is portrayed on Phoenician coins from Aradus, and on a Phoenician sealstone, but he is always depicted alone [figs. 29 and 31].[128] It is intriguing, however, to consider the possibility that Milqart, like his Greek counterpart, was revered for his protection of travellers on sea voyages, as well for vanquishing sea monsters.[129]

---

[126] S. B. Luce, "Heracles and the Old Man of the Sea," *AJA* 26 (1922), 174-92; K. Shepard, *The Fish-Tailed Monster in Greek and Etruscan Art* (New York: Privately printed, 1940); R. Glynn, "Herakles, Nereus and Triton: A Study of Iconography in Sixth Century Athens," *AJA* 85 (1981), 121-32; and G. Ahlberg-Cornell, *Herakles and the Sea-Monster in Attic Black-Figure Vase-Painting* (Uppsala: Almqvist & Wiksell, 1984).
[127] Shepard, *The Fish-Tailed Monster*, pp. 4-9.
[128] Betlyon, *The Coinage and Mints of Phoenicia*, pp. 79-80. Betlyon reviews past misidentifications of this deity as Dagnu or Milqart and concludes that the name of the god is unknown. It should be noted that "Triton" is one of the gods mentioned in the pantheon of Hannibal's treaty, Polybius, VII.9.2. Clearly "Triton" is the Carthaginian version of the fish-tailed god from Aradus, showing his presence in the Phoenician expansion to the western Mediterranean.
[129] I have already mentioned the myth of Baʿl-Haddu's defeat of Yamm from Ugarit and its parallel tale of Demarous's (Baʿl-Haddu's) defeat of Pontos (Greek deified sea=Yamm) preserved by Philo of Byblos, *Praep. Evang.*, 1.10.28, 35; see Dussaud, "Astarté, Pontos et Baʿal," 206-7, and Clapham, "Sanchuniathon: The First Two Cycles," 147-49. Milqart, who was not among the pantheon at Ugarit, is mentioned by Philo, *Praep. Evang.*, 1.10. 27. It must be noted that Milqart plays no role in Philo's description of the struggle with Sea (Pontos). Thus we posses West Semitic stories of mythic battles between the storm god and the god of the sea and Sea's divine helpers, but no similar myths or representations survive which involve Milqart that would parallel Herakles's struggles against sea gods or monsters.

Another clue which may help explain why Milqart was a patron of sailors comes from another neighboring group. The Hurrian god *Iršappa*, who is equivalent to Canaanite *Rašp* or Mesopotamian Nergal, and therefore also to be equated with *Rašp*'s later Phoenician form, Milqart, is a deity of commerce (Hurrian ^{d}*ir-ša-ap-pa dam-ki-ra-a-ši* and *ir-šap-pi-ni-iš DAM.GAR-ra-a-ši*).[130] This is also true of Nergal, who is referred to at Emar as the "lord of commerce, or the marketplace," (EN KI.LAM, *bēl maḫīri*).[131] So perhaps Milqart was important to Phoenician seafarers as a protector of commerce, much of which was conducted over the waters of the Mediterranean from the eastern littoral through the straits of Gibraltar, or as a guardian of travellers across the seas.

Summary

Levantine sailors prepared themselves for the tribulations of travel on the water, in part, by enlisting the guardianship of deities from their diverse pantheon of gods. Baʿl-Haddu, the storm god, was a tutelary deity of mariners in several of his aspects: there is evidence that *Baʿl Šamêm, Baʿl Malagê, Baʿl Ṣapōn*, Libyan Ammon, and *Baʿl Rōʾš* controlled the beneficial winds crucial to merchant ships dependant on sail power, winds which could be equally devastating in a tempest. Thus seafarers' appeasement and patronage of the storm god, in his many forms, was crucial for successful sailing.

Several marine deities protected sailors from the hazards of the water and its malevolent spirits. In the later periods, the Phoenician "Poseidon" was honored by mariners; and the hippokamp, the totem animal of a deity depicted riding on the creature's back over the waves of the sea, is portrayed as a guardian spirit of ships. The lack of data pertaining to either of these gods clouds their specific functions in the Phoenician pantheon, and therefore the attributes which made them important to mariners are uncertain. I would suggest that these two deities were in fact hypostases of the Phoenician storm god, with special

---

[130]*KUB* XXXIV 102 ii 13 and XXVII I rev. ii 23. The idea of these Bronze Age pestilence gods as patrons of commerce is put forth by W. L. Moran in *The Amarna Letters* (Baltimore: The Johns Hopkins University Press, 1992), p. 102, n. 4. For *Iršappa*'s Semitic equivalences see E. Laroche, "Glossaire de la langue hourrite," *Revue hittite et asianique* 34 (1976), 124-25. *Rašp* has been linked with Nergal and Milqart by Albright, *Yahweh and the Gods of Canaan*, pp. 128 n. 43, 139,145 n. 95, 243.

[131]D. Arnaud, *Recherches au pays d'Astata*, vol. 6/3, *Emar* (Paris: ERC, 1986), 373:74'; 378:10. See Moran, *Amarna Letters*, p. 102, n. 4.

control over marine winds, based on a comparison with the Greek Poseidon and on the iconography of the "marine" god. This would help explain their special importance to sailors.

Goddesses were nautical patrons as well. ʾAšerah appears to have been linked with the crescent, or new moon, which was an important astral guide to navigators. The crescentic new moon is known from other seafaring cultures to portend upcoming weather at sea, which is crucial for the safety of a ship and its crew . This lunar symbol was mounted at the stern of Phoenician vessels, the area where the pilot steered the ship, presumably to ensure the deity's divine aid in navigation and protection of those on board.

Similarly, the sign of the goddess Tinnit, the Carthaginian goddess equated with ʾAšerah, is found on ships' standards. Maritime symbols on sacrificial stelae dedicated to Tinnit are further evidence of her role as a guardian of seafarers.

Milqart, the Phoenician chthonic deity, is the final tutelary god of mariners. This is evident in the naming of promontories, islands, and harbors after the god. Ships and harbor temples are dedicated to Milqart, and sacrifices are made to him before venturing out to sea. Milqart possessed no attributes related to the weather or celestial connections critical for sailing. However, comparative evidence shows that Greek Herakles, who is directly equated with Milqart, was a guardian of travellers and vanquisher of sea monsters. Hurrian *Iršappa* and Mesopotamian Nergal, both of whom are comparable to Milqart, as well, were patrons of commerce. Phoenician seafarers' veneration of Milqart is possibly due to the god's role as a patron of voyagers and a heroic slayer of monsters, like his Hellenic counterpart, or his role as a guardian of commerce.

The importance of this array of different gods to Canaanite and Phoenician sailors is attested in coastal sanctuaries. Temples in port cities and shrines on isolated promontories dedicated to these guardian deities were sacral focal points which helped ensure the mariner's link to his divine protectors, both in harbor and while on a voyage.

Chapter 2
SEASIDE TEMPLES AND SHRINES

I have demonstrated that several different deities were important to Canaanite and Phoenician seafarers because of the divine protection which they provided during a voyage. The question then arises as to where sailors worshipped these deities, in order to appease the gods and ensure that their sacred patrons continued to guard their journeys at sea.

As the earthly residence of maritime gods, temples and shrines located in harbors and along the coast were sacred locations for classical and modern, traditional mariners:

> And a shrill wind sprang up to blow, and the ships ran swiftly over the teeming ways, and at night put in to Geraestus. There on the altar of Poseidon we laid many thighs of bulls, thankful to have traversed the great sea.[1]

> Yet of a surety do I deem that never in my benched ship did I pass by fair altar of thine (Zeus's) on my ill-starred way hither, but upon all I burned the fat and the thighs of bulls.[2]

Temples in harbors were important for they provided seafarers with places which linked them to their sacred benefactors. Port sanctuaries were a place for both ancient and modern mariners to pray to their gods

---
[1]Homer, *The Odyssey*, III.176-79. Trans. A. T. Murray, vol. 1, *The Loeb Classical Library* (Cambridge: Harvard University Press, 1984), p. 81.
[2]Homer, *The Iliad*, VIII.238-40. Trans. A. T. Murray, vol. 1, *The Loeb Classical Library* (Cambridge: Harvard University Press, 1924), p. 355. For further references see Homer, *The Odyssey*, XII.345-49; Livy, XL.52.5-7; Pausanias, *Description of Greece*, I.1.3, II.32.2; Rougé, *La marine dans l'Antiquité*, pp. 208-9; Semple, "Templed Promontories," 370-74; and Wachsmuth, ΠΟΜΠΙΜΟΣ Ο ΔΑΙΜΩΝ, p. 137, n. 237.

for safety on the waters before travel, and a location where thanks could be expressed to these deities after safely landing following a difficult voyage.³

Thank-offerings were presented to guardian deities which were representative of the sailors' environment. Sacred anchors, called sheet-anchors in English maritime vocabulary, were kept in reserve on board ship and were thrown overboard in emergencies during storms in hope of securing or slowing a vessel battered about by the elements.⁴ These special anchors were commonly placed in temples in honor of guardian gods for getting ships safely through tempests:

> There they cast away their small anchor-stone by the advice of Tiphys and left it beneath a fountain, the fountain of Artacie; and they took another meet for their purpose, a heavy one; but the first, according to the oracle of the Far-Darter, the Ionians, sons of Neleus, in after days laid to be a sacred stone, as was right, in the temple of Jasonian Athena.⁵

Models of ships were dedicated in thanks to patron deities, too, as were actual parts of ships, such as rudders, oars, or the prows of captured enemy vessels.⁶ The presence of a sacred building in a harbor site does not prove its importance to sailors. It is through the evidence of material remains of maritime votives, such as dedicatory anchors or model ships, that one may posit the significance of an ancient temple to the sacral needs of seafarers.

Similarly, shrines dedicated to classical and modern sailors' patron deities were built on seaside promontories, isolated from settlements along the coast:

---

³Herodotus, *The Persian Wars*, VIII.121-22; Pausanias, *Description of Greece*, I.40.5. Bassett, *Legends and Superstitions of the Sea*, pp. 379-98; Wachsmuth, ΠΟΜΠΙΜΟΣ Ο ΔΑΙΜΩΝ, pp. 133-42.

⁴Davaras provides a summary of the archaeological and textual evidence for sacred anchors in the classical world in "Une ancre minoenne sacrée?" 47-71. See also F. Carrazé, "L'ancre de miséricorde dans la marine antique," *Archéologia* 61 (1973), 13-19. For the usage of "sheet-anchor" in English see *The Oxford English Dictionary*, XV, pp. 225-26.

⁵Apollonius Rhodius, *Argonautica*, I.955-60. Trans. R. C. Seaton, *The Loeb Classical Library* (Cambridge: Harvard University Press, 1988), p. 69. See also Davaras, "Une ancre minoenne sacrée?" 47-71.

⁶For model ships see Canney, "Boats and Ships in Temples and Tombs," 50-57; A. Göttlicher, *Materialien für ein Corpus der Schiffsmodelle im Altertum* (Mainz: Philipp von Zabern, 1978), pp. 8-10; Johnston, *Ship and Boat Models in Ancient Greece*, pp. 127-28. For other types of maritime votives see W. H. D. Rouse, *Greek Votive Offerings* (Cambridge: Cambridge University Press, 1902), pp. 228-31; and Wachsmuth, ΠΟΜΠΙΜΟΣ Ο ΔΑΙΜΩΝ, pp. 133-42.

> They sailed along the coast of Italy . . . until they came to Rhegium, a promontory of Italy. There . . . they pitched a camp . . . in the precinct of Artemis.[7]

These shrines not only continued the sailors' link to their tutelary deities away from port, they also marked particularly dangerous areas, provided a land-bearing to aid navigation from the water, or commemorated a wrecked vessel.[8] Evidence for this type of shrine is scarce in the archaeological record, perhaps because the isolated locations make them difficult to discover. Fortunately they are also mentioned in texts, such as geographic accounts or periploi, which detail routes of navigation.

I shall review the nautical votives discovered in Levantine harbor temples in order to show that Canaanite and Phoenician mariners, like their classical and modern counterparts, were making distinct offerings to their patron deities in port. Votive anchors and model ships are present in several Canaanite and Phoenician port temples, but are completely absent from sacred structures excavated at inland sites. This evidence demonstrates that maritime offerings were limited to the coast and were not part of a cultural practice common in the hinterland, and suggests that these nautical votives are not part of common land based cult but are unique to seafarers' sacral practices.

Several Canaanite and Phoenician seaside shrines are identifiable at locations around the Mediterranean. Like parallel Greek and Roman promontory shrines, these Canaanite and Phoenician isolated sanctuaries presumably continued the sailors' link to their divine protectors while away from home port, as well as serving as landmarks which aided navigation and marked freshwater sources.

This evidence from harbor temples and seaside shrines demonstrates that Canaanite and Phoenician seafarers had special locations on land for their worship. These temples and shrines linked the sailors to their sacred patrons and were focal points for maritime cult.[9] The finds suggest that ceremonies were performed on land

---

[7]Thucydides, *History of The Peloponnesian War*, VI.44.2-3. Trans. C. F. Smith, vol. 3, *The Loeb Classical Library* (Cambridge: Harvard University Press, 1992), p. 263. For further references see Apollonius Rhodius, *The Argonautica*, IV.1693; Livy, XXIV.3.3-7; Thucydides, *History of The Peloponnesian War*, III.94.2, VI.3.1-2, VII.26.2; Rougé, *La marine dans l'Antiquité*, pp. 208-9; and Semple, "Templed Promontories," 374-83.

[8]Silius Italicus, *Punica*, II.580-83. Semple, "Templed Promontories," 360-65.

[9]For general observations on the role the temple played in Phoenician settlement and expansion throughout the Mediterranean see G. Bunnens, *L'expansion phénicienne en Mediterranée*, vol. 17, Études de philologie d'archéologie et d'histoire anciennes (Brussels: Intitut historique belge de Rome,

before sailing, to ensure safety while voyaging, or after a successful journey, in fulfillment of vows made at sea, as will be discussed in detail below in chapter 4.

Harbor temples

Before presenting the evidence for nautical votives in Canaanite and Phoenician temples, a *caveat* must be introduced regarding the identification of stone anchors in temple contexts. Stone anchors, in their most basic form, are dressed, flat stones with a rope-hole drilled toward their top. Typologically, these simple stone anchors could possibly be confused with perforated stone weights used to hold down a levered beam in an olive oil press. Some of these press weights have been found in sacred contexts.[10] However, press weights are typically rounded and squat, and their surfaces are only roughly finished, while anchors are flat and nicely finished.[11]

One may also compare the relative weights to try to distinguish between anchors and press weights. The data from Tel Miqne and Tel Batash indicate that press weights from clear olive oil producing contexts weigh between 70-120 kg.[12] Pierced stones known to be anchors because of additional rope or fluke holes weigh between 64-600 kg.[13] Anchors found on the Uluburun shipwreck weigh from 20-210 kg,

---

1979), pp. 282-85; and "Aspects religieux de l'expansion phénicienne," in *StudPhoen*, vol. IV, *Religio Phoenicia*, eds. C. Bonnet et al. (Namur: Société des études classiques, 1986), pp. 119-25.

[10]L. E. Stager and S. R. Wolff, "Production and Commerce in Temple Courtyards: An Olive Press in the Sacred Precinct at Tel Dan," *BASOR* 243 (1981), 95-102.

[11]Frost, "The Stone-Anchors of Byblos," 437. This distinction is not true at Ugarit, however, see below n. 39.

[12]At Miqne the weights varied from 90 to 120 kg, D. Eitam and A. Shomroni, "Research of the Oil Industry During the Iron Age at Tel Miqne: A Preliminary Report," in *Olive Oil in Antiquity*, eds. M. Heltzer and D. Eitam (Haifa: University of Haifa, 1987), p. 41; at Batash the weight was 70 kg, E. Ayalon, "Reconstructing a Traditional Olive Oil Plant at the Eretz Israel Museum, Tel Aviv," in *History and Technology of Olive Oil in the Holy Land*, ed. E. Ayalon (Arlington, VA: Oléarius Editions, 1994), p. 180.

[13]These data are derived from six three-holed anchors, and one with an L-shaped piercing from Ugarit weighing between 101-600 kg; Frost, "The Stone-Anchors of Ugarit," 244; four three-holed anchors from Kition weighing from 64-192 kg; H. Frost, "The Kition Anchors," in *Excavations at Kition*, vol. V, *The Pre-Phoenician Levels*, eds. V. Karageorghis and M. Demas (Nicosia: Cyprus Department of Antiquities, 1985), pp. 306-16; and two three-holed anchors from Kommos weighing 74-75 kg; J. W. Shaw, "Two Three-holed Stone Anchors from Kommos, Crete: Their Context, Type, and Origin," *The International Journal of Nautical Archaeology* 24/4 (1995), 283.

with the majority falling in the 121-210 kg range.[14] These data suggest that if a pierced stone weighs greater than 120 kg it is likely an anchor, but those weighing between 70-120 kg can be either an anchor or a press weight judging strictly by weight.

More complex stone anchors include typological features never found on press weights, such as extra holes to hold wooden flukes which helped the anchor grip the sea floor, and L-shaped piercings at the bottom of the anchor which held a second rope used to dislodge the anchor from the bottom and ease its retrieval.[15] Anchors with additional features besides the rope-hole should never be confused with press weights. Thus, I shall consider the interpretation of each pierced stone discovered in a sacred precinct based on weight and typological features, and so independent of its published identification.

Byblos

The earliest evidence we have of Canaanite maritime offerings in sacral contexts comes from the port site of Byblos, on the Lebanese coast. Byblos lies at one of the junctures of trade routes leading overland from Mesopotamia, and by sea or coastal roads from the Egyptian Delta. Thus the site flourished as an entrepot as both Mesopotamian and Egyptian states first developed and sought trade with one another and with territories in between, beginning in the Early Bronze Age.

The Tower Temple at Byblos, which dates to the end of the Early Bronze Age, had a flight of steps leading up to the building, the lowest course of which was constructed entirely from pierced stones [figs. 33 and 34].[16] Frost believes these stones are anchors, and represent a type of foundation offering. She strengthens her argument with the observation that all six anchors are actually replicas since their back sides are unfinished while their tops are carefully dressed.[17] Thus she

---

[14]The Uluburun wreck off of the Turkish coast has at least twenty-four stone anchors, six of which have been weighed and range between 121-208 kg, but there are also two small anchors each weighing only around 20 kg; see Shaw, "Stone Anchors from Kommos, " 288; and S. Wachsmann, *Seagoing Ships and Seamanship in the Bronze Age Levant* (College Station, TX: Texas A & M University Press, 1998), pp. 281-82.

[15]Frost, "The Stone-Anchors of Ugarit," 237-38.

[16]Frost, "The Stone-Anchors of Byblos," 429-30. Frost quotes the excavator, M. Dunand, as dating the building to the twenty-third c. B. C. E. M. Saghieh dates the Tower Temple to her JI/JII period, which is contemporary with ᶜAmuq J, Hama J4, Megiddo XV, or the Early Bronze IV-Middle Bronze I, *Byblos in the Third Millennium B.C.* (England: Aris & Phillips, 1983), p. 75, tab. 6, and p. 117, tab. 12.

calls these stones "dummy" anchors: none was ever used at sea; instead they were carved to resemble anchors and were placed together as a step to the Tower Temple, with their rope holes covered by the next course of steps. It is difficult to judge this evidence independent of the interpretations of Frost, since the temple and its associated finds have never been published by the excavator.[18] The stones are thin, and well dressed on the one side, clearly mimicking anchors and not press weights.[19] The practice of placing votive anchors in or around temples is not uncommon, though, for it is well attested from the following period at Byblos, as well.

The Temple of Obelisks at Byblos has four pierced stone votives from its Middle Bronze [MB] IIA phase which are ships' anchors [figs. 33 and 35].[20] Two of these anchors were placed on a type of stone bench, standing upright, and can be compared to the commemorative stone stelae, or obelisks, which also stood upright in the temple area.[21] A third anchor was found built into a bench, not set on top like the other two.[22] The fourth anchor was discovered built into the wall of the courtyard surrounding the cella of the temple. An offering deposit placed very near to this anchor contained hundreds of bronze objects, including ten model ships [fig. 39].[23] Another votive deposit from the temple included a single model ship, made out of bronze as well.[24] Thus the Temple of Obelisks was the repository for maritime offerings which included both anchors and models of ships.

Votive caches from Temple of Obelisks contained hundreds of figurines representing a male deity, and only a handful of female figurines.[25] The presence of anchor and ship model ex-votos in a

---

[17] "The Stone-Anchors of Byblos," 430.

[18] Frost, "The Stone-Anchors of Byblos," 427; Saghieh, *Byblos in the Third Millennium*, p. 74.

[19] Frost's drawings include profiles, demonstrating that these stones are neither rounded nor squat like press weights, their weights are not provided, "The Stone-Anchors of Byblos," 427, [fig. 34].

[20] Frost, "The Stone-Anchors of Byblos," 428-29. These four pierced stones [fig. 35] are all of the simple, one-hole, type, but they are thin and nicely dressed unlike press weights. Their weights are not provided.

[21] *Ibid.*

[22] *Ibid.*

[23] This was judged using photographs of the Temple of Obelisks, pls. XXII & XXIII, which show the anchor in situ and comparing its location with a plan, fig. 767, which shows the find spot of the cache containing the ten model ships (nos. 15068-77), M. Dunand, *Fouilles de Byblos*, vol. II text and vol. II plates (Paris: Librairie d'Amérique et d'Orient Adrien Maisonneuve, 1950-58).

[24] *Ibid.*, no. 17265.

[25] O. Negbi, *Canaanite Gods in Metal* (Tel Aviv: Tel Aviv University Institute of Archaeology, 1976), p. 123.

temple dedicated to a male deity would suggest that either a storm god or an earlier form of Milqart resided in the Temple of Obelisks.[26] The contemporary Syrian Temple at Byblos, dedicated to Baʻlat Gebal, has a fairly even representation of both male and female figurines.[27] The gods represented by these figurines seem to have been of less importance to Byblian sailors, though, for the Syrian Temple contains no maritime votives of any type.[28]

The "Sacred Enclosure" and the "Field of Offerings" at Byblos also had nautical offerings in the Middle Bronze IIA levels [fig. 33]. Though the function of each area is disputed, with Dunand stressing the sacral quality of the "Sacred Enclosure" and the "Field of Offerings" and Albright calling them both burial grounds, the number of votive caches in each area and a lack of interments seem to weigh on the side of Dunand's interpretation.[29] Four stone anchors are present in the "Sacred Enclosure": one was placed between two columns next to an entrance, and the other three most likely stood upright, like the obelisks and other anchors from the Temple of Obelisks [fig. 36].[30] Three jar deposits from the "Field of Offerings" contained bronze models of ships similar to those from the Temple of Obelisks; one had six ships, the second had two, and the last had one model ship [figs. 37 and 38].[31]

---

[26]Dunand believes the temple was dedicated to *Rašp*, the god of pestilence, based on an inscribed stela from the temple, *Fouilles de Byblos*, vol. II, p. 646. *Rašp* has been linked with Milqart; see Albright, *Yahweh and the Gods of Canaan*, pp. 128 n. 43, 139,145 n. 95, 243. Therefore, it is possible that the maritime offerings in the Temple of Obelisks were being dedicated to *Rašp* as a patron of sailors, just as much later on seafarers turned to Milqart for protection, see above ch. 1.

[27]For the connection of the temple to the goddess *Baʻlat Gebal* see N. Jidejian, *Byblos Through the Ages* (Beirut: Dar el-Machreq Publishers, 1971), pp. 17-20; and *KAI* 10. The figurines are reviewed in Negbi, *Canaanite Gods in Metal*, pp. 122-23.

[28]The lack of maritime votives in the temple dedicated to *Baʻlat Gebal* is curious given the more or less contemporary Egyptian coffin text, from the Middle Kingdom, which identifies Ḥathor with the Lady of Byblos, who is said to "hold the steering oars of . . . (funerary) barks," see Barguet, *Les textes des sarcophages égyptiens*, p. 200; and Faulkner, *Ancient Egyptian Coffin Texts*, p. 56.

[29]Dunand, *Fouilles de Byblos*, vol. II, pp. 394, 481, 653; W. F. Albright, "Remarks on the Chronology of Early Bronze IV-Middle Bronze IIA in Phoenicia and Syria-Palestine," *BASOR* 184 (1966), 26.

[30]Frost, "The Stone-Anchors of Byblos," 430-31. One of these pierced stones has an L-shaped piercing at its bottom [fig. 36, no. 21], identifying it as an anchor, while the remaining three have just the rope hole [fig. 36, nos. 17, 18, 22], but are thin and well-dressed. None of the weights of these pierced stones is provided.

[31]Dunand, *Fouilles de Byblos*, vol. II, nos. 10086-87, 10089-92; 10642-43; and 8816. It should be noted that S. Wachsmann has recently interpreted the ships from the "Field of Offerings" as either Egyptian models imported to Byblos or locally

Inland sites with temples contemporary to the sacred structures from the end of the Early Bronze Age and MBIIA at Byblos include Ebla, Alalakh, and Megiddo.[32] None of the temples at these sites show any evidence of maritime votives.[33]

Ugarit

The site of Ugarit, much like Byblos, lies at the confluence of a network of international trade routes which made it a hub of long-range commerce in the Bronze Age.[34] Though the city itself is set three km. inland from the coast, with an accompanying port settlement at Minet el-Beida, much of the economy of Ugarit was dependent on the sea and the avenues of communication and trade opened up by its proximity to the Mediterranean.[35]

Excavations at the mound of Ras Shamra, ancient Ugarit, have revealed two temples on the acropolis of the site, which the excavator has dated to the Middle Bronze through the Late Bronze Age [fig. 45].[36]

---

manufactured copies based on Egyptian models, *Seagoing Ships and Seamanship*, p. 54. His arguments are based on stylistic comparisons with Egyptian ship depictions and models, yet the Byblian model ships lack the high curved stern depicted in all of the Egyptian examples chosen by Wachsmann, and generally lack enough detail for specific comparisons. Therefore I disagree, and include these examples and the models from the Temple of Obelisks, overlooked by Wachsmann, as some of the few representations of Canaanite ships we have from the Middle Bronze Age.

[32]P. Matthiae, "Unité et développement du temple dans la Syrie du Bronze Moyen," in *Uitgaven van Het Nederlands Historisch-Archaeologisch Instituut te Istanbul*, vol. 37, *Le Temple et le Culte* (Istanbul: Nederlands Historisch-Archaeologisch Instituut, 1975), pp. 45-53; A. Mazar, "Temples of the Middle and Late Bronze Ages and the Iron Age," in *The Architecture of Ancient Israel*, eds. A. Kempinski and R. Reich (Jerusalem: Israel Exploration Society, 1992), pp. 161-62.

[33]P. Matthiae, *Ebla: An Empire Rediscovered*, trans. C. Holme (London: Hodder and Stoughton, 1977), pp. 125-32; L. Woolley, *Alalakh* (Oxford: The Society of Antiquaries, 1955), pp. 47-53; H. G. May and R. Engberg, eds., *Material Remains of the Megiddo Cult* (Chicago: University of Chicago Press, 1935).

[34]M. Heltzer, *Goods, Prices and the Organization of Trade in Ugarit* (Wiesbaden: Dr. Ludwig Reichert, 1978).

[35]E. Linder, "The Maritime Texts of Ugarit: A Study in Late Bronze Age Shipping," Diss. Brandeis University, 1970; and "Ugarit: a Canaanite Thalassocracy," in *Ugarit in Retrospect*, ed. G. D. Young (Winona Lake, IN: Eisenbrauns, 1981), pp. 31-42; J. M. Sasson, "Canaanite Maritime Involvement in the Second Millennium B.C.," *JAOS* 86 (1966), 126-38.

[36]The volume of the final publication of these temples and their contents was never completed. See C. Schaeffer's comments on the planned contents of this volume in the introduction to C. Virolleaud's *La légende phénicienne de Danel*, vol. I, *Mission de Ras-Shamra* (Paris: Librairie orientaliste Paul Geuthner, 1936),

Seaside Temples and Shrines 47

It is hard to judge this dating because items uncovered in the temples have not been published in detail, especially pottery finds which could narrow the time range for the buildings. It is more likely that the excavation represents the Late Bronze phases of the temples, considering that the two monumental structures were just under the surface of the mound. Broad horizontal exposure of the uppermost strata at Ugarit has revealed almost a quarter of the Late Bronze Age city, while the Middle Bronze Age has only been uncovered in a few deep soundings limited in their area, below the later levels.[37]

The two temples, called the Temple of Baʿl and the Temple of Dagnu because inscribed stelae dedicated to the deities were found in each respective sanctuary, are virtually identical in plan and layout [fig. 45].[38] One interesting difference between the two buildings is the presence of twelve votive stone anchors in the Temple of Baʿl and their complete absence from the Temple of Dagnu [figs. 41 and 43].[39] No

---

p. v. Interim reports published by the excavator, C. Schaeffer, leave out many specifics, but provide the only access to details of the architecture and small finds from the temples; see *Syria* 12 (1931), 8-14; 14 (1933), 119-26; 15 (1934), 124-31; 16 (1935), 154-56, 177-80. For a recent work providing an overview of the temples and the difficulty of working with the archaeological material, see M. Yon, "Sanctuaires d'Ougarit," *Travaux de la Maison de l'Orient*, vol. 7, *Temples et sanctuaires*, ed. G. Roux (Lyon: GIS-Maison de l'Orient, 1984), pp. 43-50.

[37]J. -C. Courtois, "Ras Shamra: Archéologie," *Supplément au Dictionnaire de la Bible*, vol. 9, ed. L. Pirot *et al.* (Paris: Letouzey & Ané, 1979), cols. 1150-1280. Curtois, however, follows Schaeffer and dates the buildings from the Middle through the Late Bronze Age, while I would consider the exposed phase as only Late Bronze, *ibid.*, cols. 1195-97.

[38]C. Schaeffer, *Syria* 16 (1935), 155-56.

[39]There are actually fifteen pierced stones from the precinct of the Temple of Baʿl. One of these pierced stones has an L-shaped hole at its bottom [fig. 44, no. 9], and five have additional piercings for flukes [fig. 42, nos. 4, 5; fig. 44, nos. 8, 15, 16]. Nine of these stones [fig. 42, nos. 1-3, 6; fig. 44, nos. 7, 11-14] are examples of the basic shape, with just the rope hole, but all are thin and well-dressed. However, thin, well-dressed olive oil press weights have also been identified at Ugarit; see O. Callot, "Les huileries du Bronze Récent a Ougarit," in *Ras Shamra-Ougarit*, vol. III, *Le centre de la ville*, ed. M. Yon (Paris: Édition recherche sur les civilizations, 1987), pp. 197-212, figs. 6 and 11. Because of this typological similarity one may turn to a comparison of weight to distinguish between possible press weights and anchors. Unfortunately Callot does not publish the weight of the two pierced stones found in obvious oil press contexts, in Ugarit's lower city. Other pierced stones from the lower city are identified by Frost as anchors, but weigh considerably less than the pierced stones which are clearly anchors [nos. 4, 5, 8, 15, 16] from the Temple of Baʿl: 40-60 kg vs. 101-600 kg; see Frost, "Anchors Sacred and Profane," 375-83. Thus if we consider this difference in weight, nos. 1-3, 6, and 7 should be taken as anchors, weighing between 125-400 kg each, whereas 11-13 could be either anchors or press weights, weighing 26.5-78 kg. The weight of no. 14 is not given, but is taken by Frost to be

other category of maritime votive, such as model ships, was present in either one of these acropolis temples.[40] A third sacred building, the Sanctuary of the Rhytons, located just west of the acropolis, also lacked any material remains of maritime offerings.[41]

The anchors dedicated at the Temple of Ba'l, which I have already mentioned briefly in chapter 1 in connection with *Ba'l Ṣapōn*, are most likely thank-offerings to the Canaanite storm god.[42] Five anchors were placed next to the entranceway to the cella of the temple; another five anchors were discovered built into the walls of the temple precinct; the last two were not recorded in situ, but appear to have been freestanding, set upright in the temple courtyard [fig. 43].[43]

Like the anchors in the earlier Temple of Obelisks at Byblos, some of the votive anchors at Ugarit were built into the walls of the Temple of Ba'l, or the temple precinct, while others were left free standing. This difference in offerings may represent a fulfillment of two different kinds of vows. The first type may be the outcome of a "foundation" vow since these offerings were made during the construction of the building. In other words, while in distress at sea, a sailor makes a pledge to found a building, or to add on to a sacred precinct, in order to honor a patron god. This practice is attested in the myth of Cadmus, the legendary Phoenician prince, who is reported to have founded a temple in honor of the Semitic "Poseidon" in return for the god's divine protection through several storms at sea.[44] Greek mariners are also recorded as founding new temples and shrines to guardian deities after being saved from peril at sea.[45]

The Temple of Ba'l at Ugarit, as one of the three principal sacred structures at the site, served as more than merely a sailors' chapel, however. The temple was most likely founded to serve the community as a whole in honor of one of the city's main deities. This does not negate the possibility that the Temple of Ba'l's foundation anchors were laid in order to consecrate the building to the storm god in honor of his protection of the seafarers of Ugarit. I would suggest that these

---

a miniature of an unfinished composite anchor, with suggestions of holes for flukes, *ibid.*, p. 380.

[40]A description of some of the small finds from the temples is presented in G. Saadé, *Ougarit: Métropole cananéenne* (Beirut: Imprimerie Catholique, 1979), pp. 133-43. The preliminary reports, detailed above in n. 39, describe a few of the objects.

[41]Yon, "Sanctuaires d'Ougarit," 48-50.

[42]Frost, "The Stone-Anchors of Ugarit," 242-43.

[43]Frost, "Anchors Sacred and Profane," 375-82.

[44]Diodorus, V.58.2.

[45]Pausanias, *Description of Greece*, II.32.2, III.24.7. Further classical references are found in Rouse, *Greek Votive Offerings*, p. 228.

anchors were built into walls in fulfillment of "foundation" vows made to *Ba˒l Ṣapōn* for his help at sea. Tribute to the storm god's favor continued to be offered by sailors after the completion of the temple, as is evident in the free standing votive anchors in the precinct of the Temple of Ba˒l.

Sacred structures from inland Syria-Palestine, contemporary with the Temple of Ba˒l, are numerous.[46] Major sites with temples in their Late Bronze Age levels include Emar, Alalakh, Kamid el-Loz, Hazor, Beth Shan, Megiddo, Shechem, and Lachish.[47] None of these temples, located in sites away from the Mediterranean coast, contain any type of maritime votive.

Kition

The harbor site of Kition, on the southeastern coast of Cyprus, has a long occupational history stretching from the Late Cypriot [LC] IIC period (Thirteenth century B. C. E.) through the early Hellenistic period (fourth century B. C. E.).[48] The ancient city, which lies directly below the modern town of Larnaca, has been excavated in several different areas, revealing a series of sacred buildings. These temples date to several different occupations at Kition, both in the northern part of the site and the area called the bamboula, or acropolis.[49]

---

[46]Mazar, "Temples," pp. 169-83; J. Margueron, "A propos des temples de Syrie du nord," in *Sanctuaires et clergés*, eds. M. Philonenko and M. Simon (Paris: Paul Geuthner, 1985), pp. 11-38.

[47]J. Margueron, "Rapport preliminaire sur les 3e, 4e, 5e et 6e campagnes de fouilles a Meskene-Emar," *Les annales archéologique arabes syriennes* 32 (1982), 233-49; J. Margueron, "Emar," *Les annales archéologique arabes syriennes* 33/2 (1983), 175-85; Woolley, *Alalakh*, 65-90; M. Metzger reviews the temple at Kamid el-Loz in "Über die spätbronzezeitlichen Tempel," in *Frühe Phöniker im Libanon*, ed. R. Hachmann (Mainz am Rhein: Philipp von Zabern, 1983), pp. 66-78; Y. Yadin, *Hazor* (London: Oxford University Press, 1972), pp. 67-105; A. Rowe, *The Four Canaanite Temples of Beth-Shan* (Philadelphia: University of Pennsylvania, 1940); G. M. Fitzgerald, *The Four Canaanite Temples of Beth-Shan*, vol. 2, *The Pottery* (Philadelphia: University of Pennsylvania, 1930); May, *Material Remains of the Megiddo Cult*; G. E. Wright, *Shechem* (New York: McGraw-Hill, 1964), 95-101, 122; O. Tuffnell, C. H. Inge, and L. Harding, *Lachish*, vol. II, *The Fosse Temple* (London: Oxford University Press, 1940), pp. 59-91; for the Lachish acropolis temple see D. Ussishkin, "Excavations at Tel Lachish--1973-1977, Preliminary Report," *Tel Aviv* 5 (1978), 10-25.

[48]V. Karageorghis, *A View from the Bronze Age* (New York: E.P. Dutton, 1976), p. 173. The absolute dates for the levels at Kition follow Karageorghis's presentation.

[49]V. Karageorghis and M. Demas, eds. *Excavations at Kition*, vol. V, *The Pre-Phoenician Levels* (Nicosia: Cyprus Department of Antiquities, 1985);

The sacred precinct of Area II, located next to the northern wall of the ancient city, was founded in the LCIIC with the initial phases of Temples 2 and 3.[50] Temple 2 contains numerous votive stone anchors, while Temple 3 has none.[51] The sacred area is rebuilt in the LCIIIA (1230-1190 B. C. E.) with some similarities in architectural layout, but other differences in tradition, such as the use of nicely dressed, ashlar masonry, and unprecedented cultic paraphernalia, such as oxen skulls and terra-cotta masks, presumably used in rituals.[52] Three new sanctuaries, Temples 1, 4, and 5 are founded in the LCIIIA phase.[53] Stone anchors are a prominent feature in Temples 1, 4 and 5, and the rebuilt Temple 2, while graffiti of ships, a sacred expression with a long life in the Aegean, are found carved on an altar in Temple 4 and on the outside of the ashlar masonry, southern closing wall of Temple 1.[54]

None of this evidence for maritime cult, however, can be called Canaanite. Despite the proximity and contemporaneity of the LCIIC Temple 2 at Kition with the Temple of Baʿl at Ugarit, and the similarity of votive anchors, the differences in architectural traditions and the assemblage of material culture at the sites point to distinct groups occupying each settlement. In the later LCIII phases at Kition, the assemblage has no similarity to contemporary Canaanite material culture, but rather reflects a blend of local Cypriot traditions, carried over from the earlier LCII, with new materials associated with the settlement of the Sea Peoples.[55] Thus the evidence from the LC temples at Kition nicely illustrates the Cypriot and Sea Peoples' use of votive anchors in maritime cultic practices, similar to Canaanite traditions. The presence of nautical graffiti, however, is the mark of an Aegean practice not paralleled in Canaanite or later Phoenician cult.[56]

Following the LCIII levels (1230-1050 B. C. E.), there is a continuation of the same settlement pattern in the Cypro-Geometric [CG] I in Area II (1050-1000 B. C. E.).[57] Kition is then abandoned;

Karageorghis, *A View from the Bronze Age*, pp. 95-141; A. Caubet, "Le sanctuaire Chypro-archaïque de Kition-Bamboula," in *Travaux de la Maison de l'Orient*, vol. 7, *Temples et sanctuaires*, ed. G. Roux (Lyon: GIS-Maison de l'Orient, 1984), pp. 107-18.
[50]Karageorghis and Demas, *Excavations at Kition*, vol. V, pp. 263-65.
[51]Frost, "The Kition Anchors," 286, 295-98.
[52]Karageorghis and Demas, *Excavations at Kition*, vol. V, pp. 265-66, 278.
[53]Karageorghis, *View from the Bronze Age*, pp. 62-72, 76-81; Karageorghis and Demas, *Excavations at Kition*, vol. V, pp. 243-45.
[54]Frost, "The Kition Anchors," 295-306; L. Basch and M. Artzy, "Ship Graffiti at Kition," in *Excavations at Kition*, vol. V, eds. Karageorghis and Demas, pp. 322-36.
[55]Karageorghis and Demas, *Excavations at Kition*, vol. V, pp. 269-78.
[56]Basch and Artzy, "Ship Graffiti at Kition," 322.

however the sanctity of the spot is renewed during a Phoenician inhabitation of the city, with the construction of the CGIII-Hellenistic I phases of Temples 1 and 4 (850-312 B. C. E.).[58] The other temples are not rebuilt during the Phoenician occupation of the site. Temple 1 in its Phoenician phases has stone anchors worked into its architecture.[59] It is not clear, however, that these anchors were placed as offerings. They may merely be reused stones robbed from earlier buildings.[60]

In the Cypro-Archaic [CA] period (750/725-500 B. C. E.), a second sacred area is established at Kition on the bamboula of the site.[61] The CA sanctuary has four different phases, all attributed to continued Phoenician occupation of Kition.[62] The second and third phases of the sanctuary both have anchors within their confines [figs. 48 and 49].[63] A weight anchor, similar to earlier Bronze Age stone anchors, was uncovered in the courtyard of the second phase of the sanctuary, dating to the beginning of CA II, ca. 650-550 B. C. E. [fig. 50].[64] The anchor

---

[57]Karageorghis, *View from the Bronze Age*, p. 173.
[58]*Ibid.*, pp. 94-141.
[59]Frost, "The Kition Anchors," 305-306.
[60]*Ibid.*, 286.
[61]Early excavations of the sacred structures of the bamboula are found in E. Gjerstad *et al.*, *The Swedish Cyprus Expedition*, vol. III (Stockholm: The Swedish Cyprus Expedition, 1937), pp. 1-75; later excavations are reported by Caubet, "Le sanctuaire Chypro-archaïque de Kition-Bamboula," 107-118. Gjerstad identified the sacred area as dedicated to Herakles-Milqart, based on a number of statues of the god wearing his lion skin cloak and brandishing a club, p. 75. This iconography was adopted by the Phoenicians, under Greek influence, and was used to represent Milqart in addition to the more traditionally Phoenician depiction of the god as bearded, holding an axe, and wearing a kilt and conical cap, C. Bonnet, "Le culte de Melqart à Carthage: un cas de conservatisme religieux," in *StudPhoen*, vol. IV, *Religio Phoenicia*, eds. C. Bonnet *et al.* (Namur: Société des études classiques, 1986), pp. 209-22. The votive statues, however, are not limited to only Herakles-Milqart types: There is a striding figure of a weather god, Zeus or Ba‘l; see Gjerstad, *The Swedish Cyprus Expedition*, vol. III, pl. XIV; and the later excavations uncovered numerous miniature stone stelae with carved Ḥathor masks, representing the goddess ʾAšerah (she is shown with a Ḥathor wig in earlier Qudšu depictions from Egypt); see Caubet, "Le sanctuaire Chypro-archaïque de Kition-Bamboula," 115. This mixture of cult statues and stelae shows that the bamboula sanctuaries were dedicated to several deities, all of which were patrons of mariners.
[62]*Ibid.*, 117.
[63]*Ibid.*, 112, 115; H. Frost, "The Birth of the Stocked Anchor and the Maximum Size of Early Ships.," *Mariner's Mirror* 68 (1982), 263-73.
[64]Caubet, "Le sanctuaire Chypro-archaïque de Kition-Bamboula," 112 ; Frost, "Stocked Anchor," 265-66. The identification of this pierced stone as an anchor is questionable because it is not particularly flat nor well-dressed, and no weight or drawing of the object is provided. Despite this, Honor Frost, the leading authority on stone anchors calls the find a "weight-anchor", an identification

was found placed against the southern wall of the chapel, locus 527. In phase 3 of the building, CAII, ca. 550-500 B. C. E., the chapel fell out of use and an altar and hearth were set up in its place [fig. 49]. Just north of these sacred features a stone stock from an anchor was placed standing upright like a stela [fig. 50].[65]

This votive anchor stock represents a continuation in the practice of dedicating anchors in port temples, despite the morphological changes taking place in the shapes of anchors. The older stone anchors, shaped from stone blocks with circular rope-holes carved at the top, were being replaced by wooden anchors shaped like the anchors we still use today.[66] Initially the weighted cross-piece, or stock, on these wooden anchors was made of stone. However, the stone stock was quickly replaced by one made of cast lead.[67] This may help to explain why the stone stock in the sanctuary at Kition-Bamboula is the latest evidence we have of an anchor placed in a Phoenician temple: it is likely that wooden anchors with lead stocks, or just the lead stocks, continued to be offered in thanks to protective deities by Phoenician seafarers. Wood is not long preserved, however, and metals are generally recycled; thus one would not expect to find any traces of votive anchors after stone fittings are no longer commonly in use.

No inland temples exist which are considered both Phoenician and contemporary with the sanctuary at Kition-Bamboula.[68] This may be due to a paucity of excavated Phoenician sites from this period, but it may also reflect the fact that Phoenician settlements from the Iron Age were largely coastal or in the immediate hinterland.[69]

Tell Sūkās

The mound of Tell Sūkās, located south of Ras Shamra on the eastern Mediterranean coast, has a series of superimposed temples in

---

which I favor over a press weight, especially in consideration of the slightly later offering of an anchor stock.
[65]Caubet, "Le sanctuaire Chypro-archaïque de Kition-Bamboula," 114-6; Frost, "Stocked Anchor," 267-8. For stone anchor stocks in sacred contexts in the classical world see P. A. Gianfrotta, "First Elements for the Dating of Stone Anchor Stocks," *The International Journal of Nautical Archaeology and Underwater Exploration* 6/4 (1977), 285-92.
[66]F. Moll, "The History of the Anchor," *Mariner's Mirror* 13 (1927), 293-332; G. Kapitän, "Ancient Anchors--Technology and Classification," *The International Journal of Nautical Archaeology and Underwater Exploration* 13/1 (1984), 33-44.
[67]Kapitän, "Ancient Anchors," 33-40.
[68]Harden, *The Phoenicians*, pp. 82-91; Moscati, *The World of the Phoenicians*, pp. 44-48.
[69]Harden, *The Phoenicians*, pp. 23-39.

its Period G.[70] These levels, dated from the first quarter of the seventh century B. C. E. to the beginning of the fifth century, have been called Greek by the excavator P. J. Riis.[71] While the preceding Period H and following Period F are termed Phoenician and Neo-Phoenician, Riis believes that Period G represents a large Greek presence at Sūkās because of the large quantity of Greek pottery excavated at the site.[72] However, this misleading picture is corrected by J. Boardman's publication of estimated percentages of imported pottery at Sūkās, which were only around 5-11%.[73] Indeed, even Riis admitted that the assemblage of remains viewed as a whole is not that of a pure Greek colony, but seems to represent Greeks settling among Phoenicians.[74] However, he does not publish any of the non-Greek pottery from Sūkās, and devotes the majority of the volume to the Greek pottery and "Greek" levels of the site.[75] This is balanced in a later publication which details the non-Greek pottery and small finds from Sūkās, showing that the assemblage of material culture from Period G is definitely not purely Greek.[76]

Riis also sees Hellenic parallels to the architecture of the three phases of temples in Period G.[77] I disagree with this interpretation, since the plan of the Period G^3 temple is close to that of the Tinnit/ ʿAštart temple excavated at the Phoenician site of Sarepta.[78] The

---

[70]P. J. Riis, *Sūkās*, vol. I, *The North-East Sanctuary and the First Settling of Greeks in Syria and Palestine* (Copenhagen: Munksgaard, 1970), pp. 40-91.

[71]*Ibid.*, p. 127.

[72]*Ibid.*, p. 126-75.

[73]The figure was provided to Boardman in a personal letter from Riis, see "Al Mina and History," *Oxford Journal of Archaeology* 9/2 (1990), 173.

[74]*Sūkās*, vol. I, p. 129.

[75]For a note of warning on a similar bias in the publication of the nearby site of Al Mina, and the resulting skewed view of the site's inhabitants, see P. M. Bikai, "Black Athena and the Phoenicians," *Journal of Mediterranean Archaeology* 3/1 (1990), 68-69.

[76]M. -L. Buhl, *Sūkās*, vol. VII, *The Near Eastern Pottery and Objects of Other Materials from the Upper Strata* (Copenhagen: Munksgaard, 1983). Although calling Period G Greek, Riis admits that "the general impression which we get from the finds at Sūkās taken as a whole is that of a Phoenician town with a strong, at times very strong Greek element," *Sūkās*, vol. I, p. 129. Riis, however, only describes the Greek elements and leaves us guessing what the Phoenician evidence is like. For further arguments against the "Greekness" of Period G see H. I. MacAdams, review of *Sūkās VIII: The Habitation Quarters*, by J. Lund, *JNES* 50/2 (1991), 153-55.

[77]*Sūkās*, vol. I, p. 52-54.

[78]Compare Riis, *Sūkās*, vol. I, fig. 18, with J. B. Pritchard *et al.*, *Sarepta: A Preliminary Report on the Iron Age* (Philadelphia: University of Pennsylvania, 1975), fig. 2.

Period G² building, a tripartite sanctuary with a pillared entrance, is paralleled by the north Syrian temples at Tell Taʿyinat and ʿAin Dara, and is similar to the descriptions of the Solomonic temple, built for the Israelites by Phoenician craftsmen [figs. 51-53].[79]

This Period G² tripartite temple has a broken stone anchor covering a stone lined pit in the chamber furthest from its pillared entrance [fig. 51].[80] This pit in the "holy of holies" contained ox and pig bones, a clay lamp, pottery sherds, and white ashes.[81] Riis, not recognizing the perforated stone as an anchor, believed the ash to be the burnt remains of a wooden post which would have stood upright in the hole bored through the stone. It is more likely, however, that this ash was the burnt remains of offerings, of which some were animal, such as ox and pig. The presence of a perforated weight anchor in a level which Riis dates to 588-552 B. C. E. is unusual, since stocked wooden anchors were commonly in use at this time.[82] With the introduction of the stocked anchor, however, the use of perforated stone anchors did not completely stop; they are even in use today.[83] It is also possible that an heirloom anchor from an earlier time period was dedicated in the Period G² temple at Sūkās.[84]

Like our previous example of Kition-Bamboula, there are no Phoenician temples inland which are contemporary with the Period G² temple at Sūkās. Again, the fact that Phoenician settlements were largely coastal during the end of the Iron Age, along with a dearth of contemporary excavated sites, limits the realm of comparison.

---

[79]For descriptions of the temple of Solomon see I Kings 5-8.

[80]The anchor was originally published as a "perforated stone", Riis, Sūkās, vol. I, p. 64. Buhl, however, identifies the stone as part of an anchor, Sūkās, vol. VII, p. 105. Unfortunately, Buhl but does not provide a drawing of the stone to aid independent identification, nor is its weight published.

[81] Riis, Sūkās, vol. I, p. 64.

[82]For the date of Period G, Phase II, see Riis, Sūkās, vol. I, p. 127. For the change in anchor morphology see Frost, "Stocked Anchor," 263-73; Gianfrotta, "Dating of Stone Anchor Stocks," 285-92; and Kapitän, "Ancient Anchors," 33-40.

[83]Frost, "Stocked Anchor," 268; J. W. van Nouhuys, "The Anchor," Mariner's Mirror 37 (1951), 20-22.

[84]Recently an heirloom stone anchor identical with ones excavated in Early Bronze Age contexts from sites around the Sea of Galilee was found buried beneath the altar of a Byzantine church, Y. Hirschfeld, "The Anchor Church at the Summit of Mt. Berenice, Tiberias," BA 57/3 (1994), 122-33.

Isolated Seaside Shrines

Seaside shrines, the second category of sanctuaries important to sailors, are more difficult to identify than temples in harbor sites. They are generally located away from settlements, which makes them harder to detect archaeologically because their ruins are relatively small and difficult to discover. It is not clear that maritime votives were left at these shrines. Instead, this nautical tribute was made in port at either end of a journey.[85] Promontory shrines, rather, marked points along the journey which were particularly hazardous; commemorated an event, such as a battle or shipwreck; or were erected as a sighting or landmark to aid navigation from the water:

> Next she sought the mound which Amphitryon's son (Hercules) had built on the topmost peak of the mountain, as a sea-mark for sailors and a welcome tribute of honor to the dead.[86]

Seafarers would have stopped to pay homage at these shrines, or prayed to the resident god from the sea.[87] Some of the shrines were also constructed near freshwater sources, which may indicate that ships landed at these spots to re-supply their stores of drinking water.

Syro-Palestinian Coastal Shrines

Isolated shrines along the Syro-Palestinian coast vary in date of use and location. The earliest example was founded at the beginning of the Middle Bronze Age, at the site of Nahariyah [fig. 54].[88] The Nahariyah shrine, contemporary with the sacred buildings at Byblos which contained votive anchors and model ships, was constructed one hundred m. from the sea and eight hundred m. away from the settlement site of Nahariyah [fig. 54].[89] The sanctuary was devoted to

---

[85] Apollonius Rhodius, *Argonautica*, I.955-60; Bassett, *Legends and Superstitions of the Sea*, pp. 59, 383.

[86] Silius Italicus, *Punica*, II.580-83. Trans. J. D. Duff, vol. 1, *The Loeb Classical Library* (Cambridge: Harvard University Press, 1983), p. 103. For further examples see Semple, "Templed Promontories," 362-69, 382-86.

[87] Homer, *The Iliad*, VIII.238-40; Homer, *The Odyssey*, III.176-79; see quotations above. Bassett, *Legends and Superstitions of the Sea*, p. 416; Wachsmuth, ΠΟΜΠΙΜΟΣ Ο ΔΑΙΜΩΝ, pp. 394-423.

[88] I. Ben-Dor, "A Middle Bronze-Age Temple at Nahariya," *QDAP* 14 (1950), 1-41; M. Dothan, "Sanctuaries Along the Coast of Canaan in the MB Period: Nahariyah," in *Temples and High Places in Biblical Times* (Jerusalem: The Nelson Glueck School of Biblical Archaeology of Hebrew Union College - Jewish Institute of Religion, 1981), pp. 74-81.

a goddess, judging by the discovery of female figurines and a mold used to manufacture the likeness of a goddess, although we cannot be sure which one.[90] A freshwater spring is present just below the surface of the sea, directly opposite the shrine at Nahariyah [fig. 54].[91] Presuming a slightly lower sea level in the Middle Bronze Age, the shrine would have been a landmark visible from the Mediterranean, which signaled a source of drinking water for passing sailors.

Farther south from Nahariyah, on the Syro-Palestinian coast, is the harbor site of Ashkelon. In the Middle Bronze IIC (ca. 1600-1550 B. C. E.) a shrine was founded on the outside of the settlement's ramparts, towards the sea from the northern city gate [fig. 55].[92] The road from the sea to the city's main entrance passed by the shrine, and the building may have served as a place of offering for merchants and sailors as they approached or exited the site.[93] A cultic figurine of a bull calf was discovered in a storeroom of the sanctuary building, housed in a pottery model shrine.[94] The bull calf is the companion animal of the storm god, Baʿl-Haddu, which suggests that the sanctuary was dedicated to a patron deity of seafarers and may have been a focal point of maritime cult practices.[95]

---

[89]Ben-Dor, "Temple at Nahariya," 1; Dothan, "Sanctuaries," 74.

[90]Ben-Dor was the first to propose that this goddess was ʾAšerah of the Sea (ʾAṯiratu yammi) presumably based on the locality of the shrine, "Temple at Nahariya," 41. This identification is logical, given ʾAšerah's links to the sea and importance to mariners detailed above in ch. 1, yet it cannot be proved and should remain in the realm of conjecture.

[91]Ibid.

[92]L. E. Stager, Ashkelon Discovered (Washington, DC: Biblical Archaeological Society, 1991), pp. 3-6; "Ashkelon," in The New Encyclopedia of Archaeological Excavations in the Holy Land, vol. 1, ed. E. Stern (New York: Simon and Schuster, 1993), p. 106.

[93]Stager, Ashkelon Discovered, 4.

[94]Ibid., 3-6.

[95]Ibid., 6. For the link between the bull calf and the storm god see W. F. Albright, From the Stone Age to Christianity (New York: Doubleday, 1957), pp. 299-301, especially n. 33. This symbolism continues in Israel as the bull calf, Heb. ʿegel, was one of Yahweh's companion animals which was preferred in the iconography of the Northern Kingdom (ibid.); see also Exod 32, I Kings 12:28, 32. In the pantheon from Ugarit, we know that the chief god, ʾĒl, was represented by the mature bull for he is referred to as ṯōr, "bull", in the texts; see KTU 1.3.V.10, 13, 35 for a few of numerous examples. In one instance, Baʿl is compared to a bull calf, Ug. ʿigl= Heb. ʿegel, while ʿAnat is the mother cow, Ug. ʾarḫ, KTU 1.6.II.7-9, 28-30; and a cylinder seal from Ugarit's port, Minet el-Beida, depicts Baʿl sitting on the back of a young bull [fig. 8]. In another Ugaritic text, a minor figure in the pantheon, ʿAtik, is called "ʾĒl's calf (progeny)", ʿigl ʾIlu, KTU 1.3.III.44; this same epithet, ʿigl ʾIlu, is repeated in KTU 1.108.12 without the name of the deity. One of the forms of Baʿl at Palmyra is ʿAglibōl, which is possibly a

During the Late Bronze Age an isolated temple was built at the site of Tel Mevorakh.[96] The sanctuary encompasses the entire mound in this period, and has been interpreted by its excavator as a shrine built for travellers using the coastal highway [fig. 56].[97] The building stands alone, over twelve km. from the nearest contemporary cities at Tel Dor and Zeror.[98] It is possible that the temple was used by travellers coming from the sea, as well. Mevorakh is around two km. from the shore, and could have been reached by boats travelling the short distance up the Tanninim river from the Mediterranean [fig. 56].

The Persian period temple at Makmish, near the settlement site of Tel Michal four hundred m. to its south-west, is another example of a seaside sanctuary [fig. 57].[99] The building is around three hundred fifty m. from the shore, and was built next to a rivulet which may have provided safe anchorage in antiquity [fig. 57].[100] Not much is known about this shrine at Makmish because its architectural plans were never published; however, from descriptions and photographs Stern has determined that it belongs to the category of "Broad Temples" known

---

derivation from ^{c}egel + Ba^{c}l; see J. G. Février, *La religion des palmyréniens* (Paris: Librairie philosophique J. Vrin, 1931), p. 85. Similar bovine imagery is known from the Hurrian and Mesopotamian pantheons. The Hurrian storm god *Tešub* is represented by a mature bull and his son *Šarruma* was called "*Tešub*'s calf" (hieroglyphic Hurrian ^{d}*Šarruma ti-su-pi x-pi-ti*, and cuneiform Hurrian ^{d}*Šarruma Teššuppi ḫupiti*), although the companion animal on which *Šarruma* rides in the inscribed relief is a panther, see E. Laroche, "Le dieu anatolien Sarrumma," *Syria* 40 (1963), 285-287. In Mesopotamia the storm god Adad is accompanied by a bull, and rain clouds were referred to as Adad's bull calves, (Akk. *bu-ru ekdu ša* ^{d}*IM*, "fierce bull calf of Adad"), J. Black and A. Green, *Gods, Demons and Symbols of Ancient Mesopotamia* (London: British Museum Press, 1992), pp. 110-11; for the Akkadian see I. J. Gelb, *et al.*, eds., *The Assyrian Dictionary*, B vol. 2 (Chicago: Oriental Institute, 1965), p. 342a.

[96]E. Stern, *Qedem*, vol. 18, *Excavations at Tel Mevorakh, Part Two: The Bronze Age* (Jerusalem: The Institute of Archaeology, the Hebrew University of Jerusalem, 1984), pp. 3-44. There is also a Late Bronze IIB seaside temple at Tel Nami, but the cult objects from the building and nearby ship graffiti on the cliffs of Nahal Me^{c}arot seem to have Aegean affinities, rather than Canaanite; see M. Artzy, "Conical Cups and Pumice, Aegean Cult at Tel Nami, Israel," in *Thalassa: L'Égée péhistorique et la mer*, eds. R. Laffineur & L. Basch (Liège: Université de Liège, 1991), pp. 203-6.

[97]Stern, *Tel Mevorakh*, p. 36.

[98]E. Stern, "A Late Bronze Temple at Tell Mevorakh," *BA* 40 (1977), 91.

[99]N. Avigad, "Excavations at Makmish, 1958," *IEJ* 10 (1960), 90-96; N. Avigad, "Makmish," in *Encyclopedia of Archaeological Excavations in the Holy Land*, vol. III, eds. M. Avi-Yonah and E. Stern (Englewood Cliffs, NJ: Prentice-Hall, 1977), p. 768.

[100]Avigad, "Excavations at Makmish, 1958," 96.

from similar Persian period buildings in Syria and Cyprus.[101] Votive clay figurines of several types attest to the presence of different deities worshiped at the shrine.[102] An inscribed jar fragment dedicated to *Ba'l Šamêm*, most likely coming from the temple, suggests that a patron deity of sailors also resided at the site of Makmish.[103]

Contemporary with the temple at Makmish is a Persian period sanctuary near the site of Tell Sūkās, which continued to be used through the Late Hellenistic period [fig. 58].[104] The temple was founded across the southern harbor from the city in Period G^1, in an area isolated from the settlement which was otherwise used as a cemetery.[105] It is likely that Milqart was worshiped at this temple, perhaps in his role of protector of travellers or mariners, given the discovery of the fragmentary remains of a statue with the typical lion skin and club of Herakles-Milqart.[106] Votives of several other unidentifiable deities were also deposited in the sanctuary, as well.[107]

Coastal Shrines Beyond the Phoenician Homeland

Classical authors detail numerous seaside sanctuaries dedicated to the god Milqart, established by the Phoenicians during their expansion westward throughout the Mediterranean.[108] Perhaps the best detailed is the temple of Milqart built on the island of Gader.[109] Voyagers arriving safely on the island would give their thanks to Milqart at the temple, located at the southernmost end of the island, isolated from the settlement site in the north of Gader.[110] The Milqart temple precinct also contained a freshwater spring within its boundaries, located next to the edge of the sea.[111]

[101] *Material Culture of the Land of the Bible in the Persian Period 538-332 B.C.* (Warminster: Aris & Phillips, 1982), p. 64.
[102] Avigad, "Excavations at Makmish, 1958," 93-95. The types included both seated, bearded male and pregnant or suckling female figurines.
[103] A. F. Rainey, "The 'Lord of Heaven' at Tel Michal," in *Excavations at Tel Michal, Israel*, eds. Z. Herzog, G. Rapp, and O. Negbi (Minneapolis: The University of Minnesota Press, 1989), pp. 381-82.
[104] P. J. Riis, *Sūkās*, vol. VI, *The Graeco-Phoenician Cemetery and Sanctuary at the Southern Harbour* (Copenhagen: Munksgaard, 1979), pp. 33-68.
[105] For the location see the map in Riis, *Sūkās*, vol. I, fig. 3.
[106] Riis, *Sūkās*, vol. VI, pp. 67-68.
[107] *Ibid.*, Riis believes some of the votives represent 'Aštart, but his evidence is not specific enough to differentiate between the three main West Semitic goddesses.
[108] See the above section on Milqart in ch. 1.
[109] Strabo, *Geography*, III.5.5
[110] *Ibid.*

A Phoenician seaside temple was also dedicated to the Semitic "Poseidon."[112] The temple was founded on a wooded promontory by the Carthaginian captain, Hanno, during a colonizing voyage by sea along the Atlantic coast of Africa.[113] This example is a nice illustration of the Phoenician practice of commemorating newly found headlands, discovered in nautical explorations, to sailors' patron deities.

Four temples have been excavated which can be classified as Phoenician seaside sanctuaries. The earliest is at Kommos, on the southern coast of Crete.[114] Temple B at Kommos is an isolated shrine overlooking the water [fig. 59].[115] The building, dated to ca. 800-600 B. C. E., has been interpreted as Phoenician based on its shrine, made up of three standing pillars, and the Phoenician pottery excavated both inside the building and in dumps surrounding the temple.[116] I would also add that the votive, Egyptianized faience figurines and small bronze bull found around the tripillar shrine are also typically Phoenician, and that the architecture of Temple B is paralleled by the two Period G^1 temples at Sūkās, one on the mound and one just across the southern harbor, both of which I consider Phoenician structures.[117] The temple site at Kommos also marked a source of freshwater, and the excavator elaborates on the shrine's function as a landmark, calling the building a "watering and trading point" for passing ships.[118]

Much farther west, in Sardinia, is the promontory temple at Capo San Marco, which dates to the fifth century B. C. E. [fig. 60].[119] This temple is situated over a thousand m. south of the Phoenician-Punic settlement of Tharros, in a location visible to ships sailing towards the city from the west [fig. 61, the building is labeled "Archaic Temple"].

---

[111]*Ibid.*, III.5.7

[112]*GGM*, vol. I, p. 13.

[113]Moscati, *The World of the Phoenicians*, pp. 181-84.

[114]J. W. Shaw, "Phoenicians in Southern Crete," *AJA* 93/2 (1989), 165-83. I would like to thank Prof. I. Winter for pointing this out to me.

[115]*Ibid.*

[116]*Ibid.*

[117]For the small finds associated with Kommos Temple B see J. W. Shaw, "Excavations at Kommos (Crete) During 1979," *Hesperia* 49/3 (1980), 229-37. Similar Egyptianized faiences are found in the temple from the Phoenician site of Sarepta, Pritchard, *Sarepta: A Preliminary Report*, pp. 29-33. For the plan of Kommos Temple B see Shaw, "Phoenicians in Southern Crete," fig. 3; for the Sūkās Period G^1 temples see Riis, *Sūkās*, vol. I, fig. 33; and Riis, *Sūkās*, vol. VI, fig. 220. It should be noted that these Sūkās temples post-date the one at Kommos by at least a century.

[118]Shaw, "Phoenicians in Southern Crete," 182.

[119]F. Barreca, "Tharros (S. Giovanni di Sinis, Cagliari)-Scoperte a Capo S. Marco," *Notizie degli scavi di antichità* 12 (1958), 409-12.

None of the small finds was published from the excavation of the building, which consisted of an open main room, with pillars to support a roof, and a small side chamber.[120] The focus of the main room, and presumably of the worship, was a stone baetyl.[121]

South of the site of Kition, on Cyprus, is an isolated temple dedicated to Milqart, or Išmun-Milqart [fig. 77].[122] The temple stood on top of a small hill around three hundred m. from the settlement site, with vantages over the nearby Salt Lake and the sea. Not many details are known about the structure of this temple. It can be dated to the fifth-fourth century B. C. E. based on finds of Attic Black-Glazed wares, one sherd of which had a graffito naming the god Milqart.[123] Further Phoenician graffiti incised on Attic wares and fragments of white marble bowls with Phoenician inscriptions were unearthed in the temple, and date paleographically to the fourth century.[124] Similar graffiti were discovered on Attic wares from the contemporary levels of Temples 1 and 4, inside of Kition's city walls.[125]

The fourth seaside temple is from the Tunisian promontory of Ras ed-Drek, which is an important landmark on the main sailing route between Sicily and Carthage, and dates to between the fourth and second century B. C. E. [fig. 62].[126] Unfortunately, the building contained no votives to give clues to the nature of ceremonies performed there, or to hint at the temple's deities.[127] The sanctuary, however, did have a cistern, which follows the tradition that these isolated sacred buildings often marked sources of freshwater.[128]

---

[120]Barreca, "Capo S. Marco," 409-11.
[121]*Ibid.*, 411. The placement of the baetyl is shown in fig. 60.
[122]K. Nicolaou, *The Historical Topography of Kition*, vol. 43, *Studies in Mediterranean Archaeology* (Göteborg: Paul Åström, 1976), pp. 111-13.
[123]*Ibid.*, 113.
[124]*Ibid.*, 112-13; and A. Caubet, "Les sanctuaires de Kition à l'époque de la dynastie phénicienne," in *StudPhoen*, vol. IV, *Religio Phoenicia*, ed. C. Bonnet et al. (Namur: Société des études classiques, 1986), p. 166.
[125]A. W. Johnston, "Graffiti on Attic Vases," in *Excavations at Kition*, vol. IV, *The Non-Cypriote Pottery*, V. Karageorghis, et al. (Nicosia: Cyprus Department of Antiquities, 1981), pp. 45-49; Karageorghis, *A View from the Bronze Age*, p. 173.
[126]M. Fantar, "Le temple de Ras ed-Drek," in *Prospezione archeologica al Capo Bon*, vol. II, eds. F. Barreca and M. Fantar (Rome: Consiglio nazionale delle ricerche, 1983), pp. 43-63.
[127]*Ibid.*, 57.
[128]*Ibid.*, 53-55.

Summary

Harbor temples dedicated to nautical guardian deities provided space for the mariner to propitiate his gods. Material records of these offerings have come down in the form of maritime votives, such as stone anchors, anchor stocks, and model ships, dedicated in port sanctuaries. Contemporary sacred structures from inland Canaanite and Phoenician sites show no evidence of nautical votives, demonstrating that these offerings were not part of the cultures' general religious practices but were limited to use along the coast. Shrines dedicated to patron deities were erected on seaside promontories, isolated from settlement sites. These sanctuaries renewed the seafarers' link to their sacred protectors while away from port, and had the more profane function of serving as landmarks for taking bearings from sea, marked dangerous straits, commemorated wrecks, and often signaled sources of freshwater, a staple which needed to be constantly renewed aboard ship.

Having established the importance of specific temples and shrines on land to the sacral welfare of Canaanite and Phoenician sailors, we need to see how mariners' religious needs were met while at sea. I shall demonstrate that ships were considered to be the residence of a god or goddess, like temples or shrines on land. Thus, the hull of the vessel provided a physical barrier against the sea and its threats, while the deity imbued in the ship created a spiritual block against the deep. Sacred spaces aboard ship also provided seafarers with areas for worship and cultic activities while on the water, which perpetuated the links to their divine protectors.

Chapter 3
SACRED SPACE ABOARD SHIP

I have demonstrated that harbor temples and seaside shrines served to link Canaanite and Phoenician seafarers with their guardian deities. The question then arises as to how these Levantine mariners maintained the divine contact they needed for protection against the constant threat of the sea while they were away from port or out of sight of a shrine on shore.

Sailors in both classical and modern societies regard their ships as imbued with a divine spirit.[1] Perhaps the most overt indication of this phenomenon is the prow figure, usually a representation of a god or totem, which protects the ship:

> He sails in the huge (ship) Triton, . . . its shaggy front, as it floats, shows a man down to the waist, its belly ends in a fish; beneath the monster's breast the wave gurgles in foam.[2]

Apotropaic eyes, painted on the sides of the ship to ward off danger, also represent a very literal expression of the deity within the vessel.[3] Ships' appellations may also indicate a spiritual link since vessels are generally named after a tutelary god or goddess:

---

[1] Göttlicher, *Kultschiffe und Schiffskulte im Altertum*; Hornell, "The Prow of the Ship," 121-28, and "The Cult of the Oculus," 285-89; Rivers, "Ships and Boats," 473-74; Rougé, *La marine dans l'Antiquité*, pp. 206-7; Svoronos, "Stylides," 81-152.

[2] Virgil, *Aeneid*, X.209-12. Trans. H. R. Fairclough, vol. 2, *The Loeb Classical Library* (Cambridge: Harvard University Press, 1986), p. 185. It should be noted, too, that the image of the prow figure, which is half-man, half-fish, is that of the god Triton, whom the ship is named after. For further examples see Bassett, *Legends and Superstitions of the Sea*, pp. 463-65; Hornell, "The Prow of the Ship," 121-28; Svoronos, "Stylides," 130-43; and Wachsmuth, ΠΟΜΠΙΜΟΣ Ο ΔΑΙΜΩΝ, pp. 237-51.

[3] Hornell, "The Cult of the Oculus," 285-89; Rougé, *La marine dans l'Antiquité*, p. 207; Torr, *Ancient Ships*, p. 69; and Wachsmuth, ΠΟΜΠΙΜΟΣ Ο ΔΑΙΜΩΝ, pp. 256-57.

The chief priest consecrated a ship . . . he took a lighted torch, an egg, and sulphur, uttered prayers of great solemnity with reverent lips, and purified the ship thoroughly, naming it and dedicating it to the goddess.[4]

Worship of protective deities and cultic ceremonies took place at specific areas of the ship. Generally the prow, the guiding point of the moving vessel, is considered sacred space, but sometimes the stern is a holy area, as well.[5]

I shall argue that similar concepts of the deified ship and sacred areas aboard vessels existed in Canaanite-Phoenician tradition, based on evidence which is found in diverse sources.[6] There are very few texts with nautical subjects which were written by the Canaanites or Phoenicians themselves.[7] Fortunately, foreign, classical observers have left some records which detail sacred aspects of Phoenician vessels. Archaeology also provides evidence, but this is quite limited because of the few number of Canaanite, Phoenician, or Punic shipwrecks which have been discovered and excavated.[8] The majority

---

[4] Apuleius, *The Golden Ass*, XI.16. Trans. J. A. Hanson, vol. 2, *The Loeb Classical Library* (Cambridge: Harvard University Press, 1989), p. 323. For further evidence see L. Casson, *Ships and Seamanship in the Ancient World* (Princeton: Princeton University Press, 1971), pp. 348-60; Rougé, *La marine dans l'Antiquité*, pp. 206-7; and D. Jones, *A Glossary of Ancient Egyptian Nautical Titles and Terms* (London: Kegan Paul International, 1988), pp. 231-45.

[5] Apollonius Rhodius, *The Argonautica*, IV.1592-1602; Herodotus, *The Persian Wars*, VII.180, VIII.121; Silius Italicus, *Punica*, XV.158-62; Virgil, *Aeneid*, III.527-32, V.775-78. Rivers, "Ships and Boats," 474; Wachsmuth, ΠΟΜΠΙΜΟΣ Ο ΔΑΙΜΩΝ, pp. 342-93.

[6] For general works on Canaanite or Phoenician ships see P. Bartoloni, "Navires et navigation," in *La civilisation phénicienne et punique*, ed. V. Krings, *Handbuch der Orientalistik*, abt. 1, *Der Nahe und Mittlere Osten*, bd. 20 (Leiden: E. J. Brill, 1995), pp. 282-89; Bartoloni, "Ships and Navigation," 72-77; J.-G. Février, "L'ancienne marine phénicienne et les découvertes récentes," *La nouvelle Clio* 1-2 (1949-50), 128-43; G. de Thierry, "Schiffahrt der Phöniker," *Technik Geschichte* 27 (1938), 123-28; Wachsmann, *Seagoing Ships and Seamanship*, pp. 39-60.

[7] For the Canaanite evidence see Linder, "The Maritime Texts of Ugarit;" Sasson, "Canaanite Maritime Involvement," 126-38; and J. Hoftijzer and W. H. van Soldt, "Texts from Ugarit Pertaining to Seafaring," appendix to *Seagoing Ships and Seamanship in the Bronze Age Levant*, by S. Wachsmann (College Station, TX: Texas A & M University Press, 1998), pp. 333-44. There is no equivalent corpus of Phoenician maritime texts. Nautical words or themes are found scattered through the wide range of Phoenician inscriptions, see Tomback, *Lexicon of the Phoenician and Punic Languages*.

[8] The country of origin of the two Bronze Age ships excavated off the Turkish coast by G. F. Bass is not absolutely certain because of the wide range of products each ship carried, "Cape Gelidonya: A Bronze Age Shipwreck," *Transactions of*

of data come from pictorial representations of Canaanite and Phoenician ships which appear in a variety of media.

This textual, archaeological, and pictorial evidence shows that Canaanite and Phoenician ships, like numerous counterparts in other ancient and modern seafaring communities, housed divine spirits just as temples did on land. These deities protected the sailors from the dangerous waters. Contact with the ship's god could be made in the sacred space aboard the vessel, generally located in the prow or stern, a practice which also parallels the use of a temple on land. While at sea, these sacred areas also provided sailors with a link to other deities, not present in the ship's hull, who were important to the safety of the crew and the well being of each voyage.

Textual evidence

The Bronze Age textual evidence which suggests the concept of the divinity of ships comes from the Ugaritic corpus and from an Egyptian papyrus. I have already detailed references from the Kirta Epic and Papyrus Sallier IV, which equate the deified Mt. Ṣapōn and Baʿl Ṣapōn with the Ugaritic or Canaanite term *any*, which means "ship."[9] These demonstrate that the storm god and his sacred mountain were represented, and were likely worshipped, in the form of a ship. It is not surprising that the Canaanite storm god was symbolized as a boat, given the importance of the deity who controlled the winds to the good fortune and survival of those on board a vessel. This practice is paralleled by Greek seafarers who dedicated ships to Zeus Kasios, Baʿl Ṣapōn's direct Hellenic equivalent, or to the more general Zeus Soter, Zeus the savior.[10]

The personification of the spirit in ships from Ugarit is also demonstrated in a Ugaritic prose text describing a shipwreck.[11] This

---

the *American Philosophical Society* 57/8 (1967); "A Bronze Age Shipwreck at Ulu Burun (Kaş): 1984 Campaign," *AJA* 90 (1986), 269-96; G. F. Bass *et al.*, "The Bronze Age Shipwreck at Ulu Burun: 1986 Campaign," *AJA* 93 (1989), 1-29. To my knowledge, only one Iron Age or Persian period ship has been excavated which may be Phoenician. This is the Maʿagan Mikhael wreck, uncovered recently off of the Israeli coast near Haifa, E. Linder, "The Maʿagan Mikhael Shipwreck Excavations," *Qadmoniot* 24/1-2 (1991), 39-46 (Hebrew). Punic wrecks are few, as well; see H. Frost, ed., "Lilybaeum (Marsala)-The Punic Ship: Final Excavation Report," *Notizie degli scavi di antichità*, Supplement, 30 (1976); and A. Arribas *et al.*, *El Barco de El Sec* (Mallorca: Universitat de les Illes Balears,1987).

[9]See above, ch. 1, pp. 14-18.
[10]Albright, "Baal-Zephon," 11-12; Svoronos, "Stylides," 92.
[11]*KTU* 2.38.

tablet was sent by the king of Tyre to the king of Ugarit, reporting on the wreck of a vessel sailing south from Ugarit. The ship (Ug. *any*) is said to have "died in a terrible rain" (Ug. *mītat bi gašmi ʾaduri*).[12] The ship was not lost or sunk; it literally died as its spirit perished in the wake of the storm.[13]

The tutelary, or guardian, spirit of a Punic warship was another form of the Phoenician storm god. Libyan Ammon, the Latinized name for the Phoenician storm god, was worshipped at the stern of the galley, where a statue or figurine of the deity was in place.[14] Ammon's presence was not limited to the stern, however, for the ship was named after the deity, which indicates that his essence was embodied throughout the vessel.[15]

From the same source, Silius Italicus's *Punica*, we learn of other names of Punic warships: the *Io*, the *Elissae*, and the *Sidon*.[16] Other ships are mentioned, but the text does not clarify whether they are Roman or Carthaginian. Io is the name of a mythological priestess, who is identified with Isis or Ḥathor in Egypt, and may have had links to the moon.[17] Given *ʾAšerah*'s and *Tinnit*'s connection with the crescent moon and crescent-and-disk symbol, and the images of ships dedicated to Tinnit on Punic sacrificial stelae, it is possible that the name of the *Io* was *ʾAšerah* or *Tinnit* in the original Phoenician.[18] Elissae is the name of the mythical Tyrian princess, who sailed from her homeland to found the Phoenician colony at Carthage, where she was called Dido.[19] Thus the vessel *Elissae* was dedicated to a heroine, who may have protected mariners in her role as a mythic adventurer. The final ship appears to have been embodied with the spirit of the

---

[12]*KTU* 2.38.13-14; the form *mtt* is the 3fs perfect of the root *mwt* "to die". For the vocalization of Ugaritic *adr* see Huehnergard, *Ugaritic Vocabulary in Syllabic Transcriptions*, p. 104.

[13]This has been noted by J. M. Sasson, who attributes the personification to the common practice of anthropomorphizing ships, *Jonah* (New York: Doubleday, 1990), pp. 96-97. However, Sasson fails to realize that this anthropomorphization takes place because ships possess spirits.

[14]Silius Italicus, *Punica*, XIV.436-40, 458-61. For details of prayers and sacrifices given to this ship's god see below, ch. 4.

[15]*Ibid.*, XIV.572.

[16]XIV.517-18, 573, 580.

[17]K. Dowden, "Io," in *The Oxford Classical Dictionary*, 3rd ed., eds. S. Hornblower and A. Spawforth (Oxford: Oxford University Press, 1996), pp. 762-63.

[18]For *ʾAšerah*-Tinnit's link to the crescent and crescent-and-disk symbol see above ch. 1, pp. 26-32.

[19]C. Bailey and P. R. Hardie, "Dido," in *The Oxford Classical Dictionary*, 3rd ed., eds. S. Hornblower and A. Spawforth (Oxford: Oxford University Press, 1996), p. 467.

eponymous ancestor of one of the important cities of the Phoenician homeland, Sidon. We know from Philo of Byblos that Sidon was the daughter of the deified sea Pontos/Yamm.[20] It is possible, given her ancestry, that Sidon was a marine deity important to the welfare of sailors, but Philo details the goddess's discovery of singing only.[21]

Herodotus mentions that the prows of Phoenician warships were ornamented with a pigmy-like figure.[22] It is not absolutely clear what Herodotus was referring to in these figures since possible parallels from the rendering of ships on Phoenician coins are too small to show details of the sculpted prows [figs. 65 and 66].

Arrian, writing of Alexander the Great's capture of the city of Tyre, mentions a Phoenician ship taken by the Macedonian victor.[23] This ship was especially important because it was dedicated to Tyrian Herakles, the god Milqart, who was a guardian of seafarers.[24] Alexander pays tribute to Herakles, in thanks for his victory, by inscribing the ship with his own dedication to the god.[25] This act further demonstrates the hallowed nature of the vessel and shows that the ship was a symbol of the deity Herakles as important to Alexander as any anthropomorphic image of the god.

Strabo mentions the *hippoi*, or horse-headed boats, of the Phoenicians from Gader.[26] He relates a story of a horse figurehead which washed ashore in Egypt, from a vessel which wrecked after it had strayed from the coast of Spain. Local shipmasters identified the figurehead as coming from small fishing boats, called "horses" (Gk. *hippoi*) after the carving on their prow.[27] I interpret the horse-headed prow as representative of the spirit of the Phoenician winged seahorse and its companion deity, which was imparted in these *hippoi*.[28]

Archaeological evidence

The exploration of Canaanite and Phoenician shipwrecks is still in its infancy. Two Late Bronze Age ships, one Persian period wreck, and

---

[20]*Praep. Evang.*, 1.10.26. Dussaud, "Astarté, Pontos et Baʿal," 206-207; Clapham, "Sanchuniathon: The First Two Cycles," 147-49.
[21]*Praep. Evang.*, 1.10.26-27. A. I. Baumgarten, *The Phoenician History of Philo of Byblos* (Leiden: E. J. Brill, 1981), p. 209.
[22]*The Persian Wars*, III.37.
[23]*Anabasis of Alexander*, II.24.6.
[24]"kai tēn naun tēn Tyrian tēn hieran tou Herakleous," ibid.
[25]*Ibid.*
[26]*Geography*, II.3.4.
[27]*Ibid.*
[28]See above, ch. 1.

three Punic vessels have been excavated which may, with some caution, be considered Canaanite or Phoenician.²⁹ One must be careful when interpreting the ethnicity of a vessel because of the mixed nature of goods on board ships, collected at every possible stop, make it difficult to determine the home port of a wreck.³⁰

The Bronze Age shipwreck excavated off of the Turkish coast at Uluburun has finished products and raw materials originating from at least five distinct cultural areas.³¹ Recently, a female figurine, made of cast bronze and partially sheeted in gold foil, was uncovered in a section believed to have been the prow of the ship.³² This figurine, holding out her left hand in a sign of benediction, is clearly a goddess [fig. 68]. Though the type is unique, the style and craftsmanship are definitely Canaanite and can be compared to other goddess figurines found on land in the Levant.³³

This goddess figurine, protectress of the Uluburun vessel, is material evidence of the tradition of ships housing representations of their guardian deities, which has already been demonstrated by the literary reference to the image of Libyan Ammon placed at the stern of a Punic war galley.³⁴ Thus the practice of keeping figurines of tutelary gods on board Canaanite and Phoenician ships spans at least the Late Bronze Age through the Roman period. It is possible that the figurine is a representation of ʾAšerah, since she is the only goddess in the Late Bronze Age pantheon who was a protectress of Canaanite sailors.³⁵

Pictorial evidence

The largest group of data which attest to the notion of divine spirits in Phoenician ships comes from pictorial representations. These nautical depictions appear in royal Assyrian reliefs, a tomb painting, coins, and sacrificial stelae.³⁶

---

²⁹Bass, "Cape Gelidonya: A Bronze Age Shipwreck," and "Ulu Burun (Kaş): 1984 Campaign," 269-96; Bass *et al.*, "Ulu Burun: 1986 Campaign," 1-29; Linder, "The Maʿagan Mikhael Shipwreck Excavations," 39-46 (Hebrew); Frost excavated two Punic ships off of the Italian coast; see "Lilybaeum (Marsala)-The Punic Ship,"; and Arribas *et al., El Barco de El Sec.*
³⁰Wachsmann, *Seagoing Ships and Seamanship*, pp. 211-12.
³¹Bass, "Ulu Burun (Kaş): 1984 Campaign," 269-96; Bass *et al.*, "Ulu Burun: 1986 Campaign," 1-29.
³²Wachsmann, *Seagoing Ships and Seamanship*, pp. 206-208.
³³Especially Negbi's " 'Syro-Egyptian' Group," *Canaanite Gods in Metal*, p. 88.
³⁴Silius Italicus, *Punica*, XIV.436-40, 458-61.
³⁵See above, ch. 1.
³⁶Curiously the Canaanite ships from the tomb of Kenamun show no evidence

A scene of Tyrians bearing tribute to the Assyrian ruler is shown on bronze bands from the gate of Shalmaneser III's palace at Balawat. From the island of Tyre, portrayed at the left of the register, goods are loaded onto small boats with horse-headed prow and stern ornaments, which ferry the tribute across to waiting attendants on the mainland [fig. 64]. Similar boats, but with only a horse-head at their prows, are carved on a relief from Khorsabad from the reign of Sargon II [fig. 63]. This scene details Phoenician sailors towing logs at sea, in boats similar to the *hippoi* used for fishing ventures out of Gader.

A different prow figure is shown on a warship painted on the wall of a Phoenician tomb at Kef el-Blida in Tunisia [fig. 24]. This figure is identical to certain versions of the Canaanite or Phoenician iconographic type called the "smiting god", and is depicted as bearded, wearing a conical cap, with an axe held in his raised hand and a shield in the lowered one.[37] These same attributes are known from a figure found on an earlier engraved stela discovered near Aleppo, whose inscription identifies the god as Milqart [fig. 27]. The motif of the axe-bearing Milqart is also preserved on Phoenician seals, a Phoenician bowl, and a Carthaginian razor [figs. 25 and 26]. However, Phoenician artists more commonly portrayed Milqart in hellenized attire, with lion skin cloak and club, because of the god's close identification with Greek Herakles. Thus I view the war galley from Kef el-Blida as under the divine protection of Milqart, whose figure adorns and guides the prow of the ship, much like the Tyrian ship described by Arrian.

Anthropomorphic figures, both male and female, are also shown on the prows of warships on Phoenician coins [fig. 65 and 66]. Because of their size, however, the representations are not very detailed, which makes the identification of the prow figure impossible.

Some coins from Byblos, however, show clear representations of war galleys guided by either horse- or lion-headed prows [figs. 21 and

---

of prow figures, stylides, apotropaic eyes, or sacred areas [figs. 76a and 76b]. It is possible that these ships carried figurines of deities, like that found on the roughly contemporary Uluburun wreck, which escaped the view of the Egyptian artist who rendered the foreign vessels. Other depictions of Phoenician vessels, such as those on the Assyrian relief which shows ships leaving the island of Tyre, reveal no evidence of sacred objects or areas on board ship; see Barnett, "Ezekiel and Tyre," 6, pl. 1, fig. 1. Two representations of ships generally considered Phoenician, one on the reliefs from Karatepe and the second on a sarcophagus from Sidon, shall not be detailed since their stern figures are a bird and goose head, which are typical Aegean and Roman symbols; see Casson, *Ships and Seamanship*, pp. 57-58, 347-48; and C. Picard, "Le dauphin au trident sur le sarcophage sidonien 'au navire'," *Syria* 14 (1933), 318-21. Birdlike iconography was not carved on Phoenician ships.

[37]Ferron, "La peinture funeraire," 54; Bisi, "La gorfa di Kef el-Blida," 88.

22].³⁸ The symbolism of the horse is familiar from other sources which I have already detailed, but the lion is unique. I have argued above that this feline was the companion animal of the goddess ʾAšerah, since she is often depicted riding on the back of a lion [figs. 2-6, and 8], and is called Labiʾt, "lioness", in Ugaritic.³⁹ Given her marine attribute (Ug. ʾAṯiratu yammi), it is not surprising that sailors placed "ʾAšerah of the Sea's" totem animal on the prows of their ships, imbuing the vessels with her spirit in order to protect themselves from the dangers of the waters and its spirits.⁴⁰

Another symbol of ʾAšerah and her later form Tinnit, the crescent or crescent-and-disk, is shown mounted on a staff placed near the stern of many galleys rendered on Phoenician coins [fig. 66].⁴¹ The placement of this symbol at the rear of the ship, near where the pilot guided the vessel, indicates the goddess's importance in navigation. Often the crescent-and-disk *stylis*, or standard, is placed on ships whose prow depicts the figure or totem of a different deity, which demonstrates that more than one Phoenician god was guarding the vessel at the same time [fig. 66]. This is not surprising given the specialized powers and attributes of deities in the Phoenician pantheon, and hints at a possible variety of spirits residing in each ship, which we are unable to detail because of a dearth of evidence.

The eyes depicted on the prows of warships on Phoenician coins are a very literal expression of the divine spirit in these vessels [figs. 21, 65, and 66].⁴² The deity who looks through these oculi guides the front of the ship and helps to avoid danger. The eye is also known as a symbol which wards off trouble or harm.⁴³

---

³⁸Basch, "Phoenician Oared Ships," 230; Betlyon, *The Coinage and Mints of Phoenicia*, pl. 8.8, 9.2.

³⁹See above, ch. 1, n. 95; and Cross, *Canaanite Myth and Hebrew Epic*, pp. 33-35. For the Ugaritic allusion to ʾAšerah as the "lioness" see CTA 5.1.14 (the corresponding text in KTU 1.5.I.14 reads *lbim* instead of *lbit*).

⁴⁰For a listing of all the occurrences of the goddess's watery epithet see Whitaker, *A Concordance of the Ugaritic Literature*, p. 43. It is also possible that the lion headed prow represents the god Milqart, see above ch. 1, n. 96.

⁴¹Betlyon, *The Coinage and Mints of Phoenicia*, p. 10, n. 37.

⁴²Hornell, "The Cult of the Oculus," 285-89; Hornell, "The Prow of the Ship," 122; Torr, *Ancient Ships*, p. 69; F. T. Elworthy, *The Evil Eye* (1895; reprinted, New York: Julian, 1958), pp. 133-34; C. Maloney, "Don't Say 'Pretty Baby' Lest you Zap it with Your Eye--The Evil Eye in South Asia," in *The Evil Eye*, ed. C. Maloney (New York: Columbia University Press, 1976), p. 129; L. W. Moss and S. C. Cappannari, "Mal'occhio, Ayin ha ra, Oculus fascinus, Judenblick: The Evil Eye Hovers Above," in *The Evil Eye*, ed. C. Maloney (New York: Columbia University Press, 1976), pp. 11-12.

⁴³Hornell, "The Cult of the Oculus," 285-89; Elworthy, *The Evil Eye*; Maloney, ed., *The Evil Eye*. Oculi are also found depicted on the horse blinkers from Iron

Sacred Space Aboard Ship 71

The symbolism of the horse-head prows, described above, becomes clearer through iconography unique to Phoenician coinage. A winged seahorse, or hippokamp, is depicted swimming beneath ships on coins from Byblos and Aradus, or conversely the ships ride on top of this composite creature who guards the vessel from the dangers of the sea [figs. 21 and 22]. I interpret the horse's head on Phoenician ships as the head of this hippokamp, whose sea-serpent body and bird's wings were represented metaphorically by the hull and oars, or steering rudders of the vessel.[44] Just as the lion prow symbolized ʾAšerah's presence in a ship, the horse prow symbolized the essence of the "marine" deity, who is shown riding across the waves on the back of his totem, the hippokamp [fig. 23].

The concept of the sacral nature of different areas of Phoenician ships is best demonstrated on sacrificial grave markers from Carthage.[45] Nautical representations on these stelae include parts of ships, such as the prow, stern, rudder, or anchor, which signify the sanctity of these maritime symbols [figs. 16-19, 67a, and 67b].[46] This is not surprising, since we have already discussed how figurines of deities were housed either fore or aft in a ship, in areas which were clearly delineated as sacred space. One of these figurines is actually depicted on a stela, housed in a small shrine placed behind the steering rudders at the stern of a ship [figs. 19 and 69]. Depictions of the sacred anchor continued the tradition, manifested in a slightly different form, of dedicating actual anchors or anchor parts in temples. The rudder, most common of all the nautical figures on these burial markers, represents the desire for divine guidance in navigating a vessel.[47] Votive rudders

---

Age Cyprus, showing that ships are not the only mode of transport protected by the eyes of deities, see M. A. Littauer and J. H. Crouwel, *Wheeled Vehicles and Ridden Animals in the Ancient Near East* (Leiden: E. J. Brill, 1979), p. 125, fig. 73. I would like to thank Prof. I. Winter for pointing this out to me.

[44] Classical parallels for the metaphor of the ship as a horse or winged horse are collected together in Torr, *Ancient Ships*, p. 114. See also above ch. 1, n. 36.

[45] Apollonius Rhodius, *The Argonautica*, IV.15925-1602; Herodotus, *The Persian Wars*, VII.180, VIII.121; Silius Italicus, *Punica*, XV.158-62; Virgil, *Aeneid*, III.527-32, V.775-78. Hornell, "The Prow of the Ship," 121-28; Rivers, "Ships and Boats," 474; Wachsmuth, ΠΟΜΠΙΜΟΣ Ο ΔΑΙΜΩΝ, pp. 342-93.

[46] C. Picard, "Les représentations de sacrifice molk sur les stèles de Carthage," *Karthago*, 18 (1978), 17, 28, 53-54; Hours-Miedan, "Les stèles de Carthage," pls. XXXVIII, XXXIX.

[47] In the sample studied by Picard there were five anchors, twenty-two ships or ships' parts, and forty-seven rudders, "Sacrifice molk sur les stèles," 17, 28, 53-54. Greek seafarers held the belief of the "holy steering rudder" (Gk. *hagnoteros pēdaliou*); see Diogenianus, I.10.11; Wachsmuth, ΠΟΜΠΙΜΟΣ Ο ΔΑΙΜΩΝ, pp. 218-220.

must have been important symbols to Carthaginian pilots who were responsible for the safe and accurate guiding of a ship.

In general the depictions of ships or parts of ships on Punic sacrificial stelae are not detailed enough to determine which Phoenician gods were present in the vessel, except for symbols of Tinnit. Most of the boats display the apotropaic oculus [figs. 16, 18, 67a, and 67b], and one example has a prow figure which is undistinguishable [fig. 70].[48]

The one goddess who is clearly represented as the patron of a ship on these sacrificial stelae is Tinnit. The sign of Tinnit is shown on poles placed both fore and aft on a vessel, flanking what may be a standard with a caduceus [fig. 16]. Another stela depicts the prow of a war galley, with a caduceus mounted on a *stylis* [fig. 18]. Morphological changes in the motif found on sacrificial stelae demonstrate that the Carthaginian caduceus developed from the stylization of the palm tree, which is a symbol of the goddess *ʾAšerah*-Tinnit.[49]

Summary

While away from shore, the ship itself provided sacred space for Canaanite and Phoenician sailors. Levantine ships were considered to be imbued with a spirit that protected crews from the dangers of the waters and its divine creatures. This is best attested in the portrayal of deities, totems, and apotropaic eyes at the prow of vessels. Ships were often named after gods, demonstrating both the animate and sacred nature ascribed to these vessels. Sacred areas aboard ships allowed mariners to maintain contact with deities whose presence was not imparted in the vessel itself. The prow, the guiding point of a ship, was an especially sacred location on the vessel. The stern had holy qualities, too, as is shown in the placement of sacred standards, figurines of deities, and portable altars at the rear of Phoenician ships.

I have established the importance of harbor temples, seaside shrines, and ships in linking Canaanite and Phoenician mariners to the gods who watched over their voyages. The question then arises as to what ceremonies were being performed by sailors, both on land and at sea, in order to ensure the continued favor of their divine patrons.

---

[48] Also see A. Moore, "A Ship at Carthage," *Mariner's Mirror* 1 (1911), 281.
[49] R. A. Oden, *Studies in Lucian's 'De Syria Dea'* (Missoula: Scholars Press, 1977), pp. 141-44, 151-55. For a review of the various interpretations of the symbolism connected with the Punic caduceus see Brown, *Late Carthaginian Child Sacrifice*, pp. 131-34.

Chapter 4
RELIGIOUS CEREMONIES PERFORMED BY LEVANTINE SAILORS

Port temples, promontory shrines, and holy places aboard ship were all sacred spaces important to Canaanite and Phoenician sailors. These spaces provided mariners with links to their tutelary gods while on land and at sea. The question remains, however, as to what rituals Levantine sailors were practicing at these locations to maintain contact with their divine patrons, in order to ensure sacred favor and guidance during a voyage or to give thanks after a successful journey.

The performance of religious ceremonies in port and on board ship is common practice among sailors from other seafaring cultures, both ancient and modern:

> When the ships had been manned and everything had at last been put aboard which they were to take with them on the voyage, the trumpeter proclaimed silence, and they offered the prayers that were customary before putting out to sea, not ship by ship but all together, led by a herald, the mariners as well as the officers throughout the whole army making libations with golden and silver cups from wine they mixed.[1]

> Then father Anchises wreathed a great bowl, filled it with wine, and standing on the lofty stern called on the gods: 'Ye gods, lords of the sea and earth and storms, waft us onward with easy wind, and blow with favoring breath!'[2]

---

[1] Thucydides, *History of the Peloponnesian War*, VI.32.1-2. Trans. C. F. Smith, vol. 3, *The Loeb Classical Library* (Cambridge: Harvard University Press, 1992), p. 241.
[2] Virgil, *Aeneid*, III.527-32. Trans. H. R. Fairclough, vol. 1, *The Loeb Classical Library* (Cambridge: Harvard University Press, 1986), p. 383.

> Then he bids slay three steers to Eryx and a lamb to the Tempests, and duly loose the moorings. He himself, with temples bound in leaves of trimmed olive, standing apart on the prow, holds the cup, flings the entrails into the salt flood, and pours the liquid wine.[3]

Specific cultic practice varies among different seafaring societies, but usually involves some sort of sacrifice, offering, prayer, libation, or vow at stages in the voyage which require sacred protection.[4] This type of cultic activity when traversing a cultural or geographic threshold, or liminal zone, is common on land as well, as a type of rite of passage.[5] Thus one may view setting out on the sea as entering a doubly liminal zone, since sailors are both away from their home and away from the familiarity of the land.

I shall argue that Canaanite and Phoenician nautical rituals follow a similar pattern. The sacrifices of Phoenician sailors, both on land before setting sail and after safe landing, are mentioned by classical authors. Maritime votives found in Canaanite and Phoenician temples, and nautical imagery displayed on Phoenician stelae that commemorated child burials are evidence which suggests specialized cult practiced by seafarers while in harbor.

Depictions of Canaanite and Phoenician rituals conducted on board ship while leaving and entering port are found in Egyptian sources. Ceremonies performed at sea while passing a promontory shrine are suggested by the presence of several isolated Canaanite and Phoenician sacred structures. Other vows, prayers, and sacrifices offered at sea in times of danger are found in diverse sources.

These cultic data demonstrate that Canaanite and Phoenician sailors had specialized religious practices which took place at points of transition in a voyage. Rituals were conducted on land, both before

---

[3] Virgil, *Aeneid*, V.775-78. Trans. H. R. Fairclough, vol. 1, *The Loeb Classical Library* (Cambridge: Harvard University Press, 1986), p. 497. For further classical and modern examples see Apollonius Rhodius, *The Argonautica*, IV.1595-1602; Apuleius, *The Golden Ass*, XI.16; Arrian, *Anabasis of Alexander*, VI.3.1; Diodorus, XVII.104.1; Herodotus, *The Persian Wars*, VII. 180; Homer, *The Odyssey*, II.430-34; Silius Italicus, *Punica*, I.617-23; Bassett, *Legends and Superstitions of the Sea*, pp. 379-425; Rougé, *La marine dans l'Antiquité*, pp. 209-10; Sébillot, *Le folk-lore des pêcheurs*, pp. 88-132; Semple, "Templed Promontories," 383-86; and Wachsmuth, ΠΟΜΠΙΜΟΣ Ο ΔΑΙΜΩΝ, pp. 113-77, 319-483.

[4] For artifactual evidence of these practices on Greek vessels see Kapitän, "Rituals on Ancient Ships," 147-62.

[5] See the pioneering work of A. Van Gennep, *The Rites of Passage*, trans. M. B. Vizedom and G. L. Caffee (Chicago: The University of Chicago Press, 1960); and V. W. Turner, *The Ritual Process* (Chicago: Aldine Publishing, 1969).

sailing and after safe arrival; on board ship, while leaving and entering port; and at sea, when passing a promontory shrine, and in times of distress, in order to ensure a safe journey and the appeasement and protection of patron gods.

Maritime cult in port

Evidence of the specialized cultic practices of Canaanite and Phoenician sailors while in port is scarce. On several voyages to Gader reported by Strabo, Phoenician mariners are recorded making sacrifices to Herakles-Milqart.[6] These sacrifices take place while on shore, both before setting sail and after having reached the destination of Gader safely. The author, however, does not detail what type of sacrifices were made, but he does add that after an inauspicious offering was given before setting sail for Gader, the voyagers turned their vessels homeward rather than continue on with a bad omen.[7]

Similarly, Heliodorus reports that Tyrian merchants prepared sacrifices in port, to honor and ask for the guidance of Herakles-Milqart before setting sail to Carthage.[8] What was actually sacrificed to Herakles-Milqart and the contents of the prayers, though, are not mentioned by the author.

Material cultural evidence of mariners' ceremonies on land is found in the nautical offerings placed in Canaanite and Phoenician harbor temples.[9] These objects uncovered in sacred contexts include stone anchors from Byblos, Ugarit, Kition-Bamboula, and Tell Sūkās; an anchor stock, from Kition-Bamboula; and model ships from Byblos [figs. 34-39, 42, 44, 50, and 51].[10] What were the rites conducted at port temples in connection with these maritime votives, and why were these ceremonies performed? Unfortunately, no Canaanite or Phoenician cultic texts have been preserved which shed light on the religious practices which included the dedication of anchors or model ships.[11] Comparative evidence, however, suggests an interpretation.

[6]*Geography*, III.5.5.
[7]*Ibid*.
[8]*Aethiopica*, IV.16.8.
[9]See above, ch. 2.
[10]Frost, "The Stone-Anchors of Byblos," 425-42; "The Stone-Anchors of Ugarit," 235-45; "Anchors Sacred and Profane," 355-410; "Stocked Anchor," 265-8; Buhl, *Sūkās*, vol. VII, p. 105. For the model ships see Dunand, *Fouilles de Byblos*, vol. II, nos. 8816, 10086-87, 10089-92, 10642-43, 15068-77, and 17265.
[11]In his comprehensive study of the cult at Ugarit, Tarragon cannot find an explanation in the Ugaritic texts for the anchors placed in and around the Temple of Baʿl, *La culte à Ugarit*, p. 182.

Ancient Greek votives include a wide variety of nautical objects. Offerings of anchors, anchor stocks and miniature anchors have been discovered in excavations of sacred structures; anchor stocks are found inscribed with the names of protective deities; and texts and cultic lists refer to the placement of anchors in temples.[12] These anchors and anchor parts were dedicated to various gods, as is attested by inscriptions on their stocks and the different temples in which they were placed as votives.

Apollonius's account demonstrates that it was Greek sailors who were offering up anchors, both at a freshwater well and in a temple dedicated to Athena.[13] The question remains as to why anchors were chosen as votives. Several anchors were stored on board Greek ships, including the sacred anchor (Gk. *hiera agkura*), which was used only in emergencies, to stabilize the ship in a storm.[14] It is likely these sacred anchors which were placed in temples after successfully bringing a ship through a tempest, much as other offerings were vowed by Greek sailors in times of peril at sea and dedicated back in port.[15]

Model ships were also placed as offerings in sacred buildings in ancient and modern seafaring communities.[16] These models represented the ships whose hull and divine spirit guarded sailors from the dangers of the water, and were dedicated as offerings of thanks to patron deities.[17]

Given this comparative evidence, it is not surprising that Canaanite and Phoenician mariners offered up maritime votives in port temples. The motives behind ancient and modern seafarers' offerings of sacred anchors and model ships suggest that the parallel Canaanite and Phoenician votives were dedicated to guardian gods who saw sailors through perils at sea.

Another group of Phoenician nautical votives is found in representations on Punic sacrificial stelae. Maritime motifs on these stelae include depictions of ships [figs. 16, 67a, and 67b]; sacred parts of

---

[12]Apollonius Rhodius, *The Argonautica*, I.955-960; Arrian, *Periplus Maris Euxini*, XI; Pausanias, *Description of Greece*, I.4.5. Davaras summarizes the classical textual and archaeological evidence, "Une ancre minoenne sacrée?" 47-71. See also Gianfrotta, "Dating of Stone Anchor Stocks," 285-92.
[13]*The Argonautica*, I.955-960.
[14]Davaras, "Une ancre minoenne sacrée?" 57; Svoronos, "Stylides," 105-110.
[15]Pausanias, *Description of Greece*, II.32.2, III.24.7, IX.11.4. Further classical references are summarized in Rouse, *Greek Votive Offerings*, p. 228.
[16]Bassett, *Legends and Superstitions of the Sea*, p. 394; Canney, "Boats and Ships in Temples and Tombs," 50-57; Göttlicher, *Corpus der Schiffsmodelle*, pp. 8-10, *Kultschiffe und Schiffskulte im Altertum*; Johnston, *Ship and Boat Models*, pp. 127-28.
[17]See above ch. 3, and Rouse, *Greek Votive Offerings*, p. 230.

ships, including both the prow and the stern [figs. 18, 19, and 70]; and equipment from ships, such as anchors and rudders [figs. 17, 20, 67a, and 67b].[18] Why were these maritime symbols dedicated on children's sacrificial stelae?

These stelae have been excavated from tophets, sacrificial burial grounds, and were used to mark the places of offering urns which contained the remains of sacrificed children or substitute sacrifices of animals.[19] In her comprehensive study on child sacrifice, S. Brown has concluded that such offerings were often made by Phoenicians in response to situations of great crisis, based on classical textual sources.[20] It is possible that nautical imagery was carved on sacrificial stelae as a fulfillment of seafarers' vows, made in response to the dangers or stresses occurring at sea. In other words, when sailors or navigators were faced with certain dire situations out on the water they could make a vow to offer their child in order to placate the angry deity causing the trouble.[21]

Mariners may have commemorated these vows taken at sea by placing sacred images of their profession on their dedicatory monuments:[22] ships, whose seaworthiness and guardian spirit shielded their crew from the harmful waters; sacred areas of ships, demonstrated by the representation of only the prow or stern of a vessel; sacred anchors, which were a sailor's last hope for safety during a storm; and the rudder, the instrument responsible for safe guidance of a vessel and successful navigation.[23] In a unique example from a

---

[18]Picard "Sacrifice molk sur les stèles," 17, 28, 53-54.

[19]Brown summarizes the most recent studies of the human and faunal remains from the burial urns associated with the sacrificial stelae, based on the unpublished works of J. Schwartz, *Late Carthaginian Child Sacrifice*, pp. 52-53. See also L. Stager, "The Rite of Child Sacrifice at Carthage," in *New Light on Ancient Carthage*, ed. J. Pedley (Ann Arbor: University of Michigan Press, 1980), pp. 1-11, and "Carthage: A View from the Tophet," in *Phoenizier im Westen*, ed. H. G. Niemeyer (Mainz am Rhein: Philipp von Zabern, 1982), pp. 155-66.

[20]*Late Carthaginian Child Sacrifice* , p. 33.

[21]This would be the nautical rendition of one of the three main reasons offered by Brown for child sacrifice: "to appease the gods who had shown anger by inflicting disasters such as war or plagues," Brown, *Late Carthaginian Child Sacrifice*, p. 22.

[22]For symbols of other professions depicted on Carthaginian sacrificial stelae, including craftsmen's and carpenters' tools, farmers' plows, and a chariot, see Hours-Miedan, "Les stèles de Carthage," 65-66, pl. XXXVIIa-h.

[23]These interpretations differ from those presented by Hours-Miedan and Picard, who recognize the sacredness of ships but do not give the same attribution to anchors or rudders; see Hours-Miedan, "Les stèles de Carthage," 66-68; and C. Picard, "Les représentations de sacrifice molk sur les ex-voto de Carthage," *Karthago* 17 (1976), 77, 84-85, 112. For sacred anchors see Carrazé,

possible tophet discovered near Tyre, an actual stone anchor may have been used to mark the sacrificial urn instead of a stela with carved symbols or a dedication [fig. 71].[24] These maritime symbols may represent a specific event at sea which demanded a vow of the sacrifice of a sailor's or pilot's child, or a substitute animal, once safe haven had been found back in harbor.

Rituals performed while leaving or entering port

Early representations from Old Kingdom Egypt depict Syrians aboard Egyptian ships, pulling into port near Memphis.[25] The nautical reliefs from the mortuary complex of Sahu-Re, the second pharaoh of the Fifth Dynasty, show several boats with clearly Egyptian characteristics transporting both Egyptian and Syrian passengers [fig. 73].[26] All of the people on board have their arms raised up, with their forearms bent back and the palms of their hands facing forwards.[27]

A very similar scene is depicted on a funerary causeway of the Pharaoh Ounas, the last ruler of Egypt's Fifth Dynasty [fig. 74].[28] Like the scene from Sahu-Re's monument, the ships shown docking are Egyptian, but the people on board are both Syrian and Egyptian. All have their arms raised with the palms of their hands open and facing forwards, as the ships pull into port, like the passengers depicted in the Sahu-Re relief. This posture can be identified as a typical Egyptian gesture of prayer or praise.[29] Therefore I suggest that the Egyptians

"L'ancre de misericorde," 13-19; Davaras, "Une ancre minoenne sacrée?" 57; Svoronos, "Stylides," 105-110. For the idea of the "holy steering rudder" (Gk. *hagnoteros pēdaliou*) among the Greeks see Diogenianus, I.10.11; Wachsmuth, ΠΟΜΠΙΜΟΣ Ο ΔΑΙΜΩΝ, pp. 218-220.

[24]This tophet was not excavated in situ, but discovered from the sale of objects removed illicitly from the ground. The stone anchor was found among a clandestine cache of sixty stelae, and was also presumed to have been a sacrificial stela, see H. Seeden, "A *Tophet* in Tyre?" *Berytus* 39 (1991), 43 and H. Sader, "Phoenician Stelae from Tyre," *Berytus* 39 (1991), 101.

[25]It is not clear if we can call the inhabitants of the Levant in the Early Bronze Age, the period of the Egyptian Old Kingdom, Canaanites. I have included this material, however, because it clearly depicts the religious actions of Levantine peoples aboard ship.

[26]*ANEP*, fig. 42. For discussions on the ship design see L. Basch, "Anchors in Egypt," *Mariner's Mirror* 71 (1985), 454-55; Casson, *Ships and Seamanship*, pp. 20-21.

[27]I would like to thank Prof. E. Marcus for pointing this out to me.

[28]S. Hassan, "The Causeway of *Wnis* at Sakkara," *Zeitschrift für Ägyptische Sprache und Altertumskunde* 80 (1955), 138-39.

[29]H. Brunner, " Gebet," *Lexikon der Ägyptologie*, vol. II, col. 453; *ANEP*, figs. 4, 46, 47, 52, 339, 542.

and Syrians in both the Sahu-Re and Ounas reliefs are offering prayers of thanks as they approach a safe landing at their port of destination in Lower Egypt.

As for the Late Bronze Age, our finest representations of Canaanite ships are found in paintings from the Eighteenth Dynasty tomb of Kenamun in Thebes [figs. 76a and 76b].[30] A flotilla, whose crew members are all depicted with Canaanite traditional garb and hairstyles, is shown docking in Egypt at the end of its voyage. As the vessels are landing, different crew members are engaged in various activities, which include giving prayers of thanks and making offerings at the conclusion of a successful journey. Several of the mariners, both a finely dressed captain and ordinary members of the crew, are depicted with their hands raised in prayer, much like the earlier, Old Kingdom reliefs [figs. 76a and 76b]. This captain leans out over the prow of his docked ship with his arms raised before him, while crew members, positioned in the crow's nest and rigging of another ship, hold their hands aloft in an identical gesture. While the crew prays from the rigging, the captain of the vessel stands on the deck or hull of the ship making an offering of thanks, with a cup raised in one hand, and a brazier of smoking incense in the other [figs. 76a and 76b].[31] Another high ranking crew member kneels before this captain, steadying a storage jar, which may have held the necessary incense or the liquid which fills the offering cup. Similarly, on one of the docked vessels, two high ranking crew members make offerings: one holds a carinated bowl and a cup aloft in either hand, while the second has also raised up an incense stand with its smoldering contents [figs. 76a and 76b].

Small fragments from a bronze incense stand were uncovered from the Cape Gelidonya shipwreck, which dates slightly later than this Theban tomb.[32] It is not clear whether this is an indication of similar practices of making incense offerings aboard the ship, or merely represents bits of scrap metal brought on the vessel to trade as a commodity rather than utilizing the object in its primary function.

Several musical instruments were discovered among the material cultural remains from the Uluburun shipwreck, which may have been used in ceremonies performed while leaving or entering port, or while the ship was out at sea.[33] These include a horn made from a

[30]G. Daressy, "Une flotille phénicienne," *Revue archéologique* 27 (1895), 286-92; N. de G. Davies and R. O. Faulkner, "A Syrian Trading Venture to Egypt," *Journal of Egyptian Archaeology* 33 (1947), 40-46.
[31]Daressy, "Une flotille phénicienne," 287; Davies and Faulkner, "Syrian Trading Venture," 44.
[32]Bass, "Cape Gelidonya: A Bronze Age Shipwreck," 107-109.
[33]The ritual interpretation of these musical instruments on the Uluburun

hippopotamus tooth, a matching pair of bronze finger cymbals, a possible whistle made from tin, and five tortoise shells which were used as sound boxes for stringed instruments such as lutes or lyres. Some of these instruments may have also been used to make more profane music, which would have served to entertain the crew while the ship was away from port.

Several of the crew members shown in the Canaanite flotilla from the Theban tomb wear circular medallions around their necks [figs. 76a and 76b].[34] The representation is not detailed enough to tell which specific pendants the sailors are wearing, although several Canaanite types are known from excavations.[35] Presumably these amulets, representative of guardian deities, had apotropaic qualities which helped protect their owners at sea.[36]

From the Persian period comes a scene of a ship leaving port, inscribed on a scapula, unearthed at the harbor site of Tel Dor on the eastern Mediterranean littoral [fig. 75].[37] During this time, Dor was a Phoenician settlement; however, it is not clear whether the nautical depiction can be properly termed "Phoenician." The ship represented is of an Aegean type and there is an inscription on one side in Cypro-Syllabic script.[38] It is more likely a Cypriot votive offering meant to be placed in a Phoenician shrine at Dor, like parallel examples of Cypriot dedicatory inscriptions discovered in the Phoenician mainland sites of Sidon and Sarepta.[39] The scapula's context does not add any information to its origin or function since it was discovered thrown in a pit, cut into a street.[40] The scene shows a priestess with an offering bowl raised up in one hand, blessing the ship as it pulls out to sea, and is evidence for Cypriot or Aegean maritime religion [fig. 75].[41]

---

shipwreck is posed by G. F. Bass in his "Prolegomena to a Study of Maritime Traffic in Raw Materials to the Aegean During the Fourteenth and Thirteenth Centuries B.C." in *TEXNH: Craftsmen, Craftswomen and Craftsmanship in the Aegean Bronze Age*, vol. 16, *Aegaeum*, eds. R. Laffineur and P. P. Betancourt (Liège: Université de Liège, 1997) 168. I would like to thank Prof. E. Marcus for bringing this to my attention. The instruments are also described in Wachsmann, *Seagoing Ships and Seamanship*, p. 306.

[34]Davies and Faulkner, "Syrian Trading Venture," 44.

[35]P. McGovern, *Late Bronze Palestinian Pendants* (Sheffield, England: JSOT, 1985).

[36]K. R. Maxwell-Hyslop, *Western Asiatic Jewellery* (London: Methuen, 1971), pp. 138-57.

[37]E. Stern, "A Phoenician-Cypriote Votive Scapula from Tel Dor: A Maritime Scene," *IEJ* 44 (1994), 1-11.

[38]*Ibid.*, 7-10.

[39]*Ibid.*, 7.

[40]*Ibid.*, 2-3.

Rituals at Sea

After the ceremonies performed while leaving port, Canaanite and Phoenician sailors faced the trepidations of the open water. While at sea, it is probable that cultic activities took place aboard ship when passing promontories.

The sacredness of headlands to Canaanites and Phoenicians is demonstrated, as we have discussed, by West Semitic references to *Baʿl Rōʾš*, "Lord of the promontory"; *Rōʾšu Qudši*, "sacred promontory"; and *Rōš Milqart*, "Promontory of Milqart".[42] Classical references detail headlands dedicated by the Phoenicians to Herakles-Milqart and "Poseidon", and archaeological evidence demonstrates the existence of Canaanite and Phoenician isolated seaside shrines and temples.[43] No direct evidence remains, however, of the religious practices conducted by Canaanite and Phoenician seafarers while passing these sacred spaces and templed promontories.

While between landings it was not uncommon for classical seafarers to give prayers or sacrifices to various promontory gods.[44] Shrines on headlands served as a focal point for offerings, which were conducted on land at the sacred precinct, or while at sea within sight of the coastal sanctuary.[45] These rituals continued the crew's connection to their divine patrons, carried over from rites conducted in port and while setting sail, while en route to their final destination. One may posit that ceremonies were performed from on board Canaanite and Phoenician ships while passing sacred headlands, based on this comparative classical data and the textual and archaeological evidence for Canaanite-Phoenician sea side shrines.[46]

---

[41]*Ibid.*, 10-11, fig. 8.

[42]Lipinski, "*Baʿli-Raʾši* et *Raʾšu Qudšu*," 84-92; Février, "Les inscriptions puniques de Sousse," 561; Simons, *Egyptian Topographical Lists*, list I.48, XXIII.1, and XXVII.108; Harris, *Grammar of Phoenician*, p. 145. Note Harris's corrected reading of *rš mlqrt* for *bt mlqrt*, CIS I.264, which is not amended in KAI 86 (=CIS I.264); see Bonnet, *Melqart*, pp. 267-69.

[43]Geographical features dedicated to Herakles-Milqart are summarized in Gsell, *Histoire*, vol. IV, p. 307, n. 2; the founding of a promontory temple dedicated to "Poseidon" is described in the periplus of Hanno, GGM, vol.I, p. 13; Canaanite and Phoenician seaside shrines have been discovered throughout the Mediterranean, see above ch. 2.

[44]Homer, *The Iliad*, VIII.238-40. Semple, "Templed Promontories," 383-86.

[45]Homer, *The Odyssey*, III.176-79. Bassett, *Legends and Superstitions of the Sea*, p. 416; Rougé, *La marine dans l'Antiquité*, pp. 208-9; Wachsmuth, ΠΟΜΠΙΜΟΣ Ο ΔΑΙΜΩΝ, pp. 394-423.

[46]See above ch. 2.

During times of distress at sea, both ancient and modern sailors call upon their guardian deities for help either in reaction to storms or during battle.[47] A Greek legend tells how the Phoenician prince Cadmus called upon "Poseidon" to protect him during several storms on his voyage from Phoenicia to Greece.[48] Cadmus vowed to establish a temple in honor of the god if he survived the tempests, and fulfills his promise by erecting the building upon his safe arrival on the island of Rhodes. He even leaves several Phoenicians from his ship to oversee the new temple.

In the book of Jonah, the prophet tries to escape from Yahweh by boarding a ship in the port of Jaffa.[49] The nationality of the ship and its crew is not detailed in the account, but the vessel leaves port for the Phoenician city of Tarshish and is clearly crewed by non-Israelites.[50] The sailors were likely of mixed nationalities, because when threatened by a tempest at sea each sailor "cried out to his god(s)" (Heb. *wayyizʿăqû ʾîš ʾel-ʾĕlōhāyw*) for help in this time of danger.[51] When the sea calmed, the seafarers made sacrifices and offered vows to Yahweh (Heb. *wayyizbaḥû-zebaḥ la YHWH wayyiddarû nədārîm*), presumably to thank him for ending the storm without harm to the vessel or its crew.[52] This passage is an example of seafarers, possibly Phoenicians, calling out to patron deities for protection during a storm, and the offering of sacrifices and vows to their divine guardian while at sea, in thanks after danger is past and the storm is calmed.[53]

During a naval battle against the Romans, Sabratha, a Carthaginian warrior, prays to the guardian deity of his war galley.[54]

---

[47] Apollonius Rhodius, *The Argonautica*, IV.1701-4; Livy, XXIX.27.1-4; Lucretius, *De Rerum Natura*, V.1226-32. Bassett, *Legends and Superstitions of the Sea*, pp. 393-95; Wachsmuth, ΠΟΜΠΙΜΟΣ Ο ΔΑΙΜΩΝ, pp. 424-50.
[48] Diodorus, V.58.2.
[49] Jonah 1:3.
[50] M. Elat, "Tarshish and the Problem of Phoenician Colonization in the Western Mediterranean," *Orientalia lovaniensia periodica* 13 (1982), 55-69; and E. Lipinski, "Carthage et Tarshish," *Biblioteca Orientalis* 45 (1988), 59-81. The sailors are clearly non-Israelite since they have to ask what land Jonah comes from and with which nation he is affiliated (Jonah 1:8).
[51] Jonah 1:5.
[52] Jonah 1:16.
[53] The motif of Yahweh as storm god, taken over from Baʿl-Haddu's attributes, is well known from other biblical passages, Deut 33:26-29, Ps 18:8-16, Ps 65:8, Ps 77:17-20, Ps 89:10, Ps 148:7-8. See Cross, *Canaanite Myth and Hebrew Epic*, pp. 147-63. Yahweh's raising and calming of a storm at sea and his patronage of sailors during a tempest as described in Ps 107:23-30 is a particularly striking parallel to Jonah 1.
[54] Silius Italicus, *Punica*, XIV.436-41.

He asks the vessel's protector, Libyan Ammon, for help in the heat of the battle and to aid the aim of his spear, which kills an enemy. Later on, when it is clear that the ship is sinking, its navigator sacrifices himself to the same deity.[55] He offers his own blood to Ammon, and, in a very literal gesture, stabs himself and lets his blood flow onto the figurine of the god set up at the stern of the warship.

Another instance of Carthaginian human sacrifice is related by Valerius Maximus with regard to ships.[56] Roman prisoners of war captured in naval combat were tied to the keels of Carthaginian vessels, and crushed to death beneath the weight of the ship. Though no details are preserved in Valerius's account, it is possible that the victims were not merely executed, but were sacrificed to the gods of each vessel. These ships were consecrated with the blood of the prisoners, which covered their hulls.[57]

A possible depiction of a maritime human sacrifice is painted on the walls of the Punic tomb at Kef el-Blida [fig. 24]. I have already discussed the tomb's warship with regard to the representation of Milqart on its prow.[58] A figure is shown stretched out in midair in front of the prow, as if he has just leapt from the front of the ship.[59] I would interpret this figure as a sacrificial victim who is being thrown from the galley as a propitiatory offering.

Predictions

One practice I have not detailed with regard to the safety of travel at sea is divination, or the prediction of the future, used in order to anticipate the fortune of a voyage.[60] I have mentioned the Carthaginian expedition which turned homeward rather than continue on towards Gader, because of a bad omen discovered in a sacrifice offered to Herakles-Milqart before setting sail.[61] Bato, the Carthaginian pilot who sacrifices himself to his ship's god, is praised by Silius

---

[55] *Ibid.*, XIV.458-61.
[56] IX.2, ext.1. For comments on this passage, and an interpretation of the sacrifice as a launching ceremony, see H. Gaidoz, "Un sacrifice humain à Carthage," *Revue archéologique* 7 (1886), 192-93.
[57] For comparative evidence for human sacrifice among other seafaring groups see Bassett, *Legends and Superstitions of the Sea*, pp. 379-82; and Rivers, "Ships and Boats," 471-74.
[58] See above chs. 1 and 3.
[59] Ferron, "La peinture funeraire," 54.
[60] For comparative evidence see Bassett, *Legends and Superstitions of the Sea*, pp. 452-55.
[61] Strabo, *Geography*, III.5.5.

Italicus for his ability to foretell what the winds would be like on the following day.⁶²

In Hanno's colonizing venture from Carthage along the Atlantic coast of Africa, "soothsayers" (Gk. *manteis*) were brought on the voyage.⁶³ Details of these diviners' actions, however, are not given, and the original Phoenician term from which *manteis* was translated is not known.⁶⁴

One method of foretelling the future or determining divine will was through cleromancy, the reading of omens from lot casting. The sailors aboard ship with Jonah cast lots (Heb. *wənappîlâ gôrālôt*) in order to determine who brought wrath upon the voyage.⁶⁵ What was used for lots, however, is not specified in the story.

Often astragali, or sheep's knucklebones, were rolled like dice to determine omens.⁶⁶ Depictions of astragali are found on numerous classical lead anchor stocks, put there as symbols of good fortune.⁶⁷ One actual astragal was uncovered from the Cape Gelidonya shipwreck, and hints at attempts of the crew to determine the future fortunes of the vessel, which was eventually lost beneath the waves.⁶⁸

Summary

Special religious ceremonies were performed by Canaanite and Phoenician sailors on land and at sea, in order to appease protective gods and ensure the crew's safety during a voyage. This cult typically took place during transition points of a journey: in port, before leaving or upon safe arrival; and on board ship while leaving or entering harbor, passing a headland or landmark, or in times of peril.

---

⁶²*Punica*, XIV.455-56.

⁶³Periplus of Hanno § XIV, *GGM*, vol. 1, pp. 1-14.

⁶⁴The closest parallel in biblical Hebrew is *ḥōzeh*, "seer", but this is not translated as *mantis* in Septuagint Greek, see E. Hatch and H. Redpath, *A Concordance to the Septuagint*, vol. II (Oxford: Clarendon, 1897), pp. 1232b, 1316a. The Phoenician equivalent to Hebrew *ḥōzeh* is not attested in any inscriptions.

⁶⁵Jonah 1:7. For an overview of cleromancy in the Hebrew Bible see Sasson, *Jonah*, pp. 108-11.

⁶⁶T. Hopfer, "Astragalomanteia," in *Real-Encyclopädie der classischen Altertumswissenschaft*, Supplement vol. 4, eds. A. Pauly et al. (Stuttgart: J. B. Metzler, 1924), cols. 51-56.

⁶⁷Kapitän, "Rituals on Ancient Ships," 152-53. For a link between depictions of astragali and the goddess Aphrodite-Venus, protectress of mariners, on lead anchor stocks see Queyrel, "Aphrodite et les marins," 284.

⁶⁸Bass, "Cape Gelidonya: A Bronze Age Shipwreck," 133. I would like to thank Prof. E. Marcus for bringing this to my attention.

Sacrifices made to divine guardians by Phoenician sailors are attested before setting sail and after safe arrival on land. Harbor temples with special maritime votives show material evidence of the offerings seafarers left related to their trade, presumably in hope for a safe and prosperous voyage or in thanks to divinities for surviving dangers on the water. Similarly, it is possible that nautical symbols on dedicatory stelae mark the sacrifice of young victims vowed by sailors while at sea in order to placate angry gods.

Several nautical scenes depict sailors praying and making sacrifices on board ship as they enter port. Sacred promontories were likely the focus of ritual activity on vessels, conducted from the water. While sailing, mariners often made vows to their sacred patrons in times of threat from tempest or battle, which were fulfilled once the safety of shore had been reached. There is also evidence which indicates that Canaanite and Phoenician seafarers practiced divination to try to foretell future sailing conditions and the will of the gods.

These indications of specialized ritual practices of Canaanite and Phoenician sailors hint at a much larger array of sacrifices, prayers, vows, and divination specific to the sacral needs and concerns of mariners. At liminal points in a voyage and in times of danger, Levantine seafarers performed ceremonies to ensure their safety and welfare; what, however, occurred when these precautions failed and a mariner died at sea or back in port?

Chapter 5
MARITIME MORTUARY RITUAL
AND BURIAL PRACTICES

Thus far, we have discussed Canaanite and Phoenician seafarers' adoption of patron deities and the worship of these gods in harbor temples, promontory shrines, and aboard Levantine ships. This specialized cult was maintained in order to appease the gods who controlled sailors' fate at sea and protected their lives, but what transpired when a mariner died?

Death, the treatment of the dead, and the elicited responses of the living are all occurrences charged with sacred significance which entail prescribed ritual behavior.[1] Despite the general dearth of maritime texts related to the Canaanites and Phoenicians, a glimpse of the mourning rites and laments of Tyrian seafarers caused by the wreck of a ship and the death of its crew is recorded in a metaphoric way in the book of Ezekiel.[2] This example is unique; further evidence of funereal practices with maritime connections is found only in burial contexts.

Mortuary remains preserve part of a culture's religious traditions and ritual activity connected with the interment and well-being of their

---

[1] For social anthropological studies on mortuary ritual see R. Hertz, "A Contribution to the Study of the Collective Representation of Death," in *Death and the Right Hand*, trans. R. and C. Needham (Glencoe, IL: The Free Press, 1960), pp. 27-86; R. Huntington and P. Metcalf, *Celebrations of Death: The Anthropology of Mortuary Ritual* (Cambridge: Cambridge University Press, 1979); L. -V. Thomas, "Funeral Rites," trans. K. Anderson, in *The Encyclopedia of Religion*, vol. 5, ed M. Eliade (New York: Macmillan, 1987), pp. 450-59; Van Gennep, "Funerals," *The Rites of Passage*, pp. 146-65. For classical studies see W. Burkert, "Funerary Ritual," in *Homo Necans: The Anthropology of Ancient Greek Sacrificial Ritual and Myth*, trans. P. Bing (Berkeley: University of California Press, 1983), pp. 48-58; and I. Morris, *Burial and Ancient Society* (Cambridge: Cambridge University Press, 1987), pp. 29-54.
[2] Ezek 27:26-36.

dead.³ Therefore, it is not surprising to find maritime symbols, so important for the protection and welfare of sailors during their lives, carried over to the grave.⁴ Like the material remains from maritime ritual in harbor temples, Canaanite and Phoenician nautical mortuary symbols are of two types: anchors and representations of ships.

The evidence of mortuary rituals and funeral dirges performed by Phoenician sailors, and of burials which include nautical grave goods, suggests that the funereal practices of Levantine seafarers had certain specialized aspects. The mortuary ceremonies conducted by mariners are paralleled by terrestrial practices, but nautical imagery found in interments of sailors is unique when compared to the typical items associated with burials in Canaanite and Phoenician societies.⁵

Nautical mortuary ritual

Mortuary ritual consists of the sacral rites and ceremonies performed by the living in honor of the dead. As noted, our only example of the mourning practices of Phoenician sailors, in tribute to the loss of fellow mariners at sea, is preserved in the book of Ezekiel. Ezekiel 27 is presented as a dirge by the Israelite prophet over the Phoenician city of Tyre, which compares the city metaphorically to a ship and contains a wealth of information regarding Phoenician ship construction and maritime trade.⁶ At the end of the chapter, the

---

³Despite renewed interest in societal information which can be deduced from burials, brought on with the processual archaeology movement, most interpreters have shied away from the ritual aspects associated with interments. For an overview and critique of these works see E. -J. Pader, "Death and Ritual: Anthropological and Archaeological Perspectives," in *Symbolism, Social Relations and the Interpretation of Mortuary Remains*, vol. 130, B. A. R. International Series (Oxford: B. A. R., 1982), 36-68.

⁴Canney, "Boats and Ships in Temples and Tombs," 50-57; Casson, *Ships and Seamanship*, pp. 355-56; Frost, "Anchors Sacred and Profane," 360-62, 383; Göttlicher, *Corpus der Schiffsmodelle*, pp. 5-7; Johnston, *Ship and Boat Models*, pp. 127-28; Rivers, "Ships and Boats," 472-73; R. C. Rudolph, "Boat-Models From Early Chinese Tombs," *AJA* 78 (1974), 65-68.

⁵For the most recent overviews of mortuary ritual and burial in Canaan and Phoenicia see R. S. Hallote, "Mortuary Archaeology and the Middle Bronze Age Southern Levant," *Journal of Mediterranean Archaeology* 8/1 (1995), 93-122; R. Gonen, *Burial Patterns and Cultural Diversity in Late Bronze Age Canaan* (Winona Lake, IN: Eisenbrauns, 1992); B. Margalit, "Death and Dying in the Ugaritic Epics," in *Death in Mesopotamia*, vol. 8, *Mesopotamia*, ed. B. Alster (Copenhagen: Akademish Forlag, 1980), pp. 243-54; M. Gras, P. Rouillard, and J. Teixidor, "The Phoenicians and Death," *Berytus* 39 (1991), 127-76.

⁶For specialized studies on Ezek 27 see S. Smith, "The Ship Tyre," *PEQ* (1953), 97-110; Van Dijk, *Ezekiel's Prophecy on Tyre*; Barnett, "Ezekiel and Tyre," 6-13; E. Lipinski, "Products and Brokers of Tyre According to Ezekiel 27," in

"ship" Tyre, sinks in a storm and all of her crew is lost beneath the waves; they literally "fall into the heart of the seas," (v. 27, *yiplû bəlēv yammîm*). Hearing the cries of the drowning sailors in the distance (v. 28, *ləqôl zaʿăqat ḥōbəlāyīk*), Tyrian seafarers from other ships leave their vessels and stand on shore (v. 29, *wəyārədû mēʾonîyôtêhem . . . ʾel-hāʾāreṣ yaʿămōdû*) in order to mourn their dying comrades. The fact that the sailors conduct their rites on land may indicate a possible taboo against celebrating the dead while aboard ship.

The mourning rites performed by the mariners do not exhibit any special nautical practices. The Tyrian seafarers wail and cry bitterly over the sunken ship, throw dust on their heads and roll in ashes (v. 30, *wəhišmîʿû ʿălayik bəqôlām, wəyizʿăqû mārāh, wəyaʿălû ʿāpār ʿal-rāʾšêhem, bāʾēper yitpallāšû*); they shave their heads and wear sackcloth, weeping and mourning bitterly (v. 31, *wəhiqrîḥû ʾēlayik qorḥāh, wəḥāgərû sakkîm, ûbākû ʾēlayīk bəmar-nepeš, mispēd mār*); and they end their rites with a lament (vv. 32-36). This lament is presented as a quotation from the mourning song of the sailors, but was most likely fabricated by the prophet to fit his polemic against the city of Tyre and should not be taken as an actual nautical dirge. The Phoenician sailors' actions are identical to Israelite rituals for the dead known from other texts in the Hebrew Bible, which attests to cultural similarities between the two neighboring groups.[7]

Although these rituals performed for drowned sailors are not unique, special nautical indicators have been discovered in burials. Two maritime symbols are found associated with graves: representations of anchors and ships.

Anchors in graves

Canaanite burials with associated anchors are rare, and are found only at Byblos, Akko, Ashkelon, and Ugarit. In Byblos's necropolis "K", a series of chamber tombs were excavated, revealing interments from the Early Bronze through the Iron Age, with some evidence of

---

StudPhoen, vol. III, *Phoenicia and its Neighbours* (Leuven: Uitgeverij Peeters, 1985), pp. 213-20; M. Liverani, "The Trade Network of Tyre According to Ezek. 27," in *Ah, Assyria*, vol. 33, *Scripta Hierosolymitana*, ed. M. Cogan and I. Ephʿal (Jerusalem: Magnes, 1991), pp. 65-79; I. M. Diakonoff, "The Naval Power and Trade of Tyre," *IEJ* 42 (1992), 168-93.

[7] I Sam 4:12; II Sam 3:31; Jer 16:6-7; Amos 8:10; Mic 1:8-10. R. de Vaux, "Death and Funeral Rites," in *Ancient Israel: Its Life and Institutions*, trans. J. McHugh (London: Darton, Longman, and Todd, 1961), pp. 56-61; B. B. Schmidt, *Israel's Beneficent Dead*, vol. 11, *Forschungen zum Alten Testament* (Tübingen: J. C. B. Mohr, 1994), pp. 132-273.

Hellenistic and Roman grave goods.[8] The majority of finds, however, come from the Middle and Late Bronze Age.[9] A stone anchor was discovered near the passageway between two of the interior burial chambers, and may have been used to block the entranceway at some point of the tomb's use [fig. 40].[10] The anchor was not found in a stratified context, and is thus datable only through typological means. It has been compared by J.-F. Salles, the excavator of necropolis "K", with a votive anchor discovered in the Middle Bronze Age levels of the Sacred Enclosure at Byblos [fig. 36, no. 17].[11] The original placement of the anchor in the tomb may thus be contemporary with the offerings of votive anchors and model ships in the temples of Byblos.

An unpublished, Middle Bronze IIB tomb from the port site of Akko contained a stone anchor [fig. 78].[12] The anchor was originally attributed by the excavators to an adult burial (area AB, locus 851). However, the anchor appears to have cut this burial, as the stone itself disturbed the skull of the adult skeleton, and is therefore later than the adult burial. I would associate the anchor with a burial of a child that also dates to Middle Bronze IIB (area AB, locus 848), which is superimposed above the adult burial. The child's feet are positioned adjacent to the anchor, as if they were rested against the anchor stone before decomposition. Given the young age of the interred it is unlikely that this child was a sailor, but it is possible that its father or other relations had connections to the sea as Akko was a major port city in the Middle Bronze Age. It is possible that the child was sacrificed to fulfill vows made at sea (see above ch. 4).[13]

---

[8] J. -F. Salles, *La nécropole "K" de Byblos* (Boulogne: Maison de l'Orient, 1980), pp. 98-99.
[9] *Ibid.*, p. 99, pl. 31.
[10] *Ibid.*, p. 12. The pierced stone is thin and well dressed, thus presumably an anchor. Its weight is not provided.
[11] *Ibid.*
[12] I am currently working on the publication of the Bronze and Iron Age finds from areas A, AB, and H at Tel Akko through a generous grant from the Shelby White-Leon Levy Program for Archaeological Publications. I would like to thank the patrons and members of the White-Levy committee for making this possible, and Prof. M. Artzy for allowing me access to the unpublished material at the University of Haifa, Israel. The pierced stone associate with the burial is thin and well dressed, no weight is provided with the excavation notes. The object itself has not been found in storage at the University of Haifa, so I have not been able to weigh the stone myself.
[13] Unfortunately no scientific report on the skeletal material from the child burial is available among the notes on locus 848. I have not been able to locate the bones to check for cut marks or other signs which might suggest that the child was sacrificed.

A tomb from the Middle Bronze IIB-IIC was recently excavated at the ancient harbor site of Ashkelon which utilized an anchor in its construction [fig. 79].[14] The feature was a structural tomb constructed of local kurkar stones, and was located just outside and west of the city's northern gate, near the road which lead to the sea. The anchor, which weighs 70 kg, was part of the top of the tomb's construction and may have acted as a capstone, as the tomb contained multiple burials spanning a range of time from the Middle Bronze IIB to IIC.[15] During its later use, the tomb would have been contemporaneous with Ashkelon's nearby extramural shrine, less than three meters to the west of the tomb, which contained the figurine of a bull-calf (see above ch. 2). The presence of a stone anchor in a burial close to this Middle Bronze IIC shrine adds credence to my interpretation that the shrine was a site of worship for sailors entering or leaving port at Ashkelon.

Tomb 36 at the site of Ugarit, located in the area of the lower city to the north-east of the acropolis, has a pair of identical stone anchors flanking its entranceway [fig. 46, no. 22].[16] The tomb contained burials from the Middle and Late Bronze Age, as is clear from the pottery sequence excavated from the chamber, and the anchors have been attributed to either period of the tomb's use.[17] The anchors show no sign of having been used at sea, and were most likely carved to be fit directly into the entrance to Tomb 36.[18] Thus they are more appropriately viewed as replicas or symbols of anchors.

From Ugarit's harbor, Minet el-Beida, there are five anchors associated with burials.[19] Details are not readily available for three of

---

[14]I would like to thank Prof. L. Stager, director of the Ashkelon Excavations, for allowing me to publish this tomb material. A fuller report on the tomb and its anchor is forthcoming.

[15]I would like to thank T. Barako, Ashkelon Lab Director, for providing me with photographs of the pierced stone and its weight, and L. Dawson, Ashkelon Excavation's physical anthropologist, for information on the scanty skeletal remains from this tomb. The pierced stone is thin and well finished, and its 70 kg weight is at the lower end of the 70-120 kg range of both stone anchors and olive oil press weights, as discussed above in ch. 2.

[16]C. F. A. Schaeffer, "Ras Shamra-Ugarit et le monde egéen," *Ugaritica* 1 (1939), 57, fig. 45. No information is provided on the sexing of the skeletal remains. For the tomb's location see Frost, "Anchors Sacred and Profane," 382, pl. Ia. Each pierced stone is thin and well finished, and weighs 100 kg each. This weight is in the 70-120 kg range of both stone anchors and olive oil press weights, as discussed above in ch. 2. There is no particular reason, however, to doubt that these pierced stones represent anchors.

[17]Frost, "Anchors Sacred and Profane," 382. For the pottery excavated from Tomb 36 see Schaeffer, "Ugarit et le monde egéen," figs. 43, 44, 46-48.

[18]Frost, "Anchors Sacred and Profane," 360, 382.

[19]*Ibid.*, 360.

these burials, however, and their anchors were removed without recording their exact provenance. Frost's anchor no. 36 was built into the dromos of a thirteenth century B. C. E. tomb, which contained one skeleton and imported Mycenaean and Cypriot grave goods [figs. 46, no. 36, and fig. 47].[20] Anchor 37, and another lost anchor, were found in Tomb 3, their positions in the tomb, however, are not clear [fig. 46, no. 37].[21]

Although the anchors from tombs at Ugarit and its port, Minet el-Beida, cannot be precisely dated, they belong to either Middle or Late Bronze interments. Thus these grave anchors are more or less contemporary with the anchors dedicated in the Temple of Ba‛l on the acropolis of the site.

Ships in graves

The site of Achziv, on the eastern Mediterranean coast, was a Phoenician city in the Iron Age and Persian period. Numerous Phoenician burials have been excavated from several different cemeteries which surrounded the area of settlement.[22] Two clay model ships have been reported from Achziv, but their provenance is unfortunately not described [fig. 72].[23] Given the intact condition of the ships, which would be rare from a stratified context, and the overwhelming number of graves which have been excavated at Achziv compared with the paucity of work done on the settlement itself, it is fair to assume that the two models came from burial contexts.[24]

Punic tombs excavated in North Africa have revealed further examples of ship imagery in burials. Two graves have been found with model ships, and a third burial contained a vase in the form of a ship's prow among its funerary offerings.[25] Representations of ships have

---

[20]*Ibid.*, 386-87, pl. X. The skeleton is assumed to be a male warrior because of the presence of weapons in the grave, not the sexing of the skeleton. The pierced stone weighs 70 kg and is thin and well dressed. I follow Frost in calling it an anchor.

[21]*Ibid.*, 387. No information is provided on the skeletal remains. The pierced stone weighs 85 kg and is thin and well dressed. I follow Frost in calling it an anchor.

[22]M. W. Prausnitz, "Achzib," in *The New Encyclopedia of Archaeological Excavations in the Holy Land*, vol. 1, ed. E. Stern (New York: Simon and Schuster, 1993), pp. 32-35.

[23]Göttlicher, *Corpus der Schiffsmodelle*, p. 30, nos. 102-103.

[24]Prausnitz, "Achzib," 32-35.

[25]For the model boats see P. Gauckler, *Nécroples Puniques*, vol. I (Paris: A. Picard, 1915), pp. 28-29, pl. CXXXV and *ibid.*, vol. II, pl. CCXLVI. The prow shaped vase is in C. Picard, *Catalogue du musée Alaoui*, vol. I (Tunis: 1957), p.

also been discovered painted on three Punic tombs.[26] The only detailed example of this group is the war galley depicted on the wall of the sixth-fifth century B. C. E. tomb at Kef el-Blida in Tunisia [fig. 24]. The ship has been discussed above, first with respect to the "smiting god" figure at its prow, and second with regard to a human figure shown suspended in the air, stretched out in front of the prow as if he has been thrown as a sacrifice from the ship.[27] Other details include the depiction of the vessel at full sail with twin rudders at its stern, the hull crowded with Punic marines holding spears and shields at the ready. It is significant that the motif of a warship was included in a Punic tomb, since representations of warships are known primarily from Phoenician coinage meant for use by the living [figs. 21, 22, 65, and 66].[28]

Interpretations

In his study of mortuary practices, L. R. Binford has defined six categories related to the dead which may affect their burial: cause and location of death, age and sex of the dead, social position, and affiliation of the deceased.[29] The appearance of maritime symbols in graves can be related to a few of these possibilities.

Following Binford's analysis, it is possible that maritime offerings reflect either the cause of death of the individual or his identity/ profession in Canaanite-Phoenician society. In the first case, if a mariner or traveler perished at sea perhaps the deceased was interred with a reminder of the voyage. This scenario seems unlikely, however, if one draws inferences from other seafaring cultures whose taboos prevent a corpse from remaining on board a ship, and practice burial at sea instead.[30]

The second possibility, the social affiliation of the deceased, seems a more likely explanation for the appearance of nautical symbols in mortuary contexts: sailors or marines formed a small subset of the Canaanite and Phoenician population, and in some instances may have brought representations of their profession with them to the grave.[31]

125, pl. LXXXIV.
[26]M. Fantar, *Eschatologie phénicienne-punique* (Tunis: Ministère des affaires culturelles, 1970), pp. 26-30.
[27]*Ibid.*, 54. See above, ch. 1, pp. 33-34; and ch. 4, p. 83.
[28]An exception is the depiction of the prow of war galleys on Carthaginian sacrificial stelae, marking rituals also related to death [figs. 18 and 70].
[29]"Mortuary Practices: Their Study and their Potential," *Memoirs of the Society for American Archaeology* 25 (1971), 16-25.
[30]Virgil, *Aeneid*, VI.149-51. Bassett, *Legends and Superstitions of the Sea*, pp. 135-37; Wachsmuth, ΠΟΜΠΙΜΟΣ Ο ΔΑΙΜΩΝ, pp. 277-79.

Thus, regardless of whether sailors died at sea or on land, the symbols of the anchor or ship which played such an important role in the sacral welfare of mariners during their lives also likely accompanied seafarers in death. It is possible that these maritime symbols of the anchor and ship may have had a continued cultic significance for sailors in the world of the dead, as well.

M. Fantar has interpreted the different representations of ships from Punic tombs as evidence of the Phoenician belief in the deceased's journey across an underworld ocean, presumably based on classical parallels.[32] If this were the case, I would expect many more representations of boats from Phoenician tombs, considering the thousands of burials which have been excavated; in fact, however, we only have a handful of examples from throughout the Mediterranean. Given this paucity of ship representations I disagree with the view that these vessels plied chthonic waters.

Summary

When religious precautions failed, and a ship went down at sea, fellow mariners performed religious rites for their lost comrades. These ceremonies included mourning rituals and the singing of lamentations for their dead. A number of Canaanite and Phoenician burials include nautical grave goods and symbols, such as offerings of anchors and model ships, and the depiction of ships in tomb paintings. The anchor and ship representations are the same symbols which were offered during a sailor's lifetime to patron deities, and may have perpetuated sacred connections after the death of a seafarer.

---

[31]Johnston, *Ship and Boat Models in Ancient Greece*, p. 11.
[32]*Eschatologie phénicienne-punique*, p. 31. For a similar interpretation based only on the painted tomb at Kef el-Blida see Ferron, "La peinture funeraire," 54.

CONCLUSIONS

Bronze Age Canaanites and their descendants, the Phoenicians, ventured out in ships from their home ports on the Levantine coast, to trade, settle, and explore throughout the waters of the Mediterranean. These mariners faced uncertainties and fears posed by the literal and psychological boundary of the sea. The dangers of navigating on the Mediterranean and the seeming whimsy of its winds and tides generated religious needs of seafarers which were not shared by members of Canaanite and Phoenician society who never left dry land.

The constant threats faced at sea led Canaanite and Phoenician sailors to adopt specific guardian deities. These tutelary gods generally had links to meteorological and celestial phenomena which made them crucial to mariners, because their powers over the elements could either benefit or devastate a voyage.

The storm god's importance to seafaring is vividly attested in the Esarhaddon/Baʿl of Tyre treaty. The treaty's section of curses calls on three epithets of the Phoenician storm god, *Baʿl Šamêm*, *Baʿl Malagê*, and *Baʿl Ṣapōn*, to raise an evil wind which will cause the waves of the sea to sink Tyrian ships. There is no further evidence which connects either *Baʿl Šamêm* or *Baʿl Malagê* to sailors, but other data show that *Baʿl Ṣapōn* was a patron of mariners.

Baʿl Ṣapōn's residence was on Mt. Ṣapōn, just north of the site of Ugarit. The height of the mountain, and its proximity to the sea made it both a landmark and a probable navigational aid for the maritime traffic leaving and entering port at Ugarit. Of Ugarit's three excavated temples, one contained an inscribed stela dedicated to *Baʿl Ṣapōn* along with numerous stone anchors; the other two lacked any maritime votives. These anchors in the temple with the dedication to Baʿl were either built into the sacred structure or left standing upright in the temple or its precinct, presumably as offerings from sailors who had made vows to the storm god. Mt. Ṣapōn is compared to a ship (*any*) in the Ugaritic Kirta epic, and the ship of Ba⁽l Ṣapōn (Eg. ⁾i-na-yat= Ug. *any*) is part of a triad of Canaanite gods worshipped in Egypt. A harbor between the Egyptian Delta and southern Canaan was named Ba⁽al Ṣəpôn (Heb.) in tribute to the god, and an early cylinder seal from the site of Tell el-Dabᶜa depicts Ba⁽l Ṣapōn and his companion bull protecting a ship at sail. The storm god, whose palace was constructed on Mt. Ṣapōn, is also known from the Ugaritic epics as the slayer of the deified sea, Yamm. Although it is not clear what role this myth played for Canaanite seafarers, it may be taken as a metaphor of Ba⁽l Ṣapōn as a guardian deity who protected mariners from the dangers of the sea through quelling the spirit of the waters.

Other forms of the Phoenician storm god were important to sailors. A figurine of Libyan Ammon was set up at the stern of a Carthaginian war galley, and was a focus of prayer and sacrifice during battle. Libyan Ammon is equated with the storm god Jove/Jupiter and should not be mistaken for the Carthaginian patriarchal deity, Ba⁽l Ḥamōn, who is called Saturn in Latin texts. Ba⁽l Rō⁾š, the "lord of the promontory", is known to have guarded his sacred headland, and presumably those who sailed within its sight, near the Phoenician city of Tyre.

Marine deities also had special links to seafarers. Carthaginian voyagers dedicated a promontory temple in honor of the Phoenician "Poseidon," and the commander of the Carthaginian navy prepared sacrifices to the god after the fleet's safe arrival in Sicily, before waging war on the Greeks. The Greek myth of Cadmus relates how the legendary Phoenician prince is said to have prayed to "Poseidon" for protection during several storms. After his safe arrival in port on the island of Rhodes, Cadmus founded a temple dedicated to "Poseidon" in accordance with his vows to the god, made in distress at sea. Another Phoenician marine deity is portrayed on Tyrian coins, riding over the waves of the Mediterranean on the back of his companion beast, which has a horse head, sea serpent body, and wings. This winged seahorse is depicted on other coins riding beneath ships, as a guardian spirit. Phoenician ships are often represented with horse-headed prows, which I interpret as an abbreviated form of the winged seahorse, symbol of the marine deity who rode on the hippokamp's back and watched over these particular vessels.

Goddesses played a role in the protection of sailors. ⁾Ašerah, known to have marine attributes from her description in the Ugaritic corpus as "⁾Ašerah of the sea" with her divine helper "Fisherman", was linked to the symbol of the crescent moon or crescent-and-disk. This lunar attribute is found on the headdress of the goddess *Qudšu* / *ʾAšerah* who is shown riding on the back of a lion, typically grasping snakes in her hands. The identical pose to the goddess on the *Qudšu* stelae is found in the iconography of Canaanite gold pendants, which show *ʾAšerah* riding a crescent, instead of the usual lion, or with crescents in her headdress. The crescent or crescent-and-disk symbol is important because it is shown on coins, placed on standards at the stern of Phoenician ships. I interpret this as representing the guardianship of the goddess *ʾAšerah* over these vessels, and her protection of navigation which was controlled by pilots who maneuvered steering oars at the stern of ships.

The placement of crescentic motifs in nautical contexts is sensible if one interprets them as representations of the new moon. Both ancient and modern, traditional sailors held the belief that impending weather patterns could be predicted from reading signs visible in the new moon. The light of the moon is also crucial for sailing at night.

Two pieces of evidence from the Middle Bronze Age also indicate *ʾAšerah* as a protectress of navigation. An Egyptian coffin text from the Middle Kingdom says that *Ḥathor*, who is equated in the text with the Canaanite Lady of Byblos, or *ʾAšerah*, holds the rudders to guide the voyage of funerary boats. Similarly, *ʾAšerah*'s head is depicted directly over the steering oars of opposed ships on a Canaanite cylinder seal.

Further evidence connecting *ʾAšerah* to mariners includes the dedication of a port, *ʾĒlat*, to the goddess under her original name. "*ʾĒlat* of Tyre" is inscribed on a coin which shows the goddess standing in a galley as its tutelary deity. *ʾAšerah*'s totem animals, the lion and snake, known from her depictions on the *Qudšu* stelae and Canaanite gold pendants, are represented on the seal from Tell el-Dabʿa which depicts *ʾAšerah*'s companions and symbols of *Baʿl Ṣapōn* watching over a ship at sail. Byblian galleys, portrayed on coins, have the head of a lion as their prow ornament, which I interpret as representative of the spirit of *ʾAšerah* imbued in these warships.

The goddess Tinnit has similar maritime and lunar aspects, which strengthens the argument equating her with *ʾAšerah*. Thus lunar symbols with maritime associations could represent either aspect of the goddess, *ʾAšerah*-Tinnit. The sign of the goddess Tinnit is represented with dolphins or fish, and is commonly associated with the crescent or crescent-and-disk. The sign of Tinnit is also shown on poles placed both fore and aft in a ship carved on a sacrificial stela, and other stelae dedicated to the goddess depict ships and sacred parts of ships, such as the prow or stern of the vessel, anchors, and rudders.

A final Phoenician god, Milqart, must be mentioned as a guardian of sailors. Classical sources demonstrate that numerous promontories, islands, and harbors were named after the Phoenician Herakles, who is Milqart. This is backed by the attestation of the "promontory of Milqart", *Rōš Milqart*, known from Phoenician inscriptions. From an account of Alexander the Great's conquest of Tyre comes the detail of a Tyrian ship dedicated to Herakles-Milqart, and a figure of Milqart in his "smiting" pose, with axe and shield, is shown on the prow of a war galley painted on a Carthaginian tomb. Classical texts further reveal that sacrifices were made to Herakles-Milqart by Tyrian traders, to ask the god for protection before setting sail for Carthage, and by Carthaginian voyagers seeking out the route to Gader. Once a colony was founded on the island of Gader, a temple was dedicated to Milqart, which was visited by travellers after their safe arrival by sea.

Milqart, however, did not have powers over the weather or celestial connections important to mariners like the other deities who were patrons of seafarers. No West Semitic evidence describes the qualities which made Milqart indispensable to sailors; however, attributes of his Greek, Hurrian, and Mesopotamian counterparts are revealing. The Greek Herakles was a guardian of travellers because of his legendary adventures, and is depicted sailing the Mediterranean on a raft. Similarly, Pausanias records a tradition that a Tyrian statue of Herakles-Milqart floated to Erythrae on a raft. One of Greek Herakles's tasks pitted him against a sea monster who was half-man, half-fish, a creature who is also known from Phoenician iconography. Given the weight of the evidence linking Milqart to the safety of seafarers, it is possible that Milqart was considered a patron of Phoenician travellers and may have been known as a vanquisher of sea monsters, like his Greek counterpart. It is also possible that Milqart was a divine protector of commerce, since comparative evidence shows that equivalent Bronze Age gods, Hurrian *Iršappa* and Mesopotamian Nergal, have this attribute.

The patron deities of sailors were members of a divine pantheon, and were worshipped for alternate reasons by people on land. For instance, the storm god brought the rains which were crucial for growing crops that brought sustenance to cities and villages; ʾAšerah and Tinnit were mother goddesses and protectresses of animals; and Milqart was an underworld deity, who had control over both health and pestilence.

Conclusions

This array of gods and goddesses was worshipped by sailors on shore in order to guarantee protection on the water or to give thanks after a safe landing. Harbor temples dedicated to nautical guardian deities provided space for the mariner to give propitiations to his gods. Evidence of Canaanite maritime votives is clear in the dedicatory anchors and model ships from the temples of Byblos. The practice of offering anchors is continued in later periods at the Temple of Baʿl in Ugarit, and at Phoenician temples from Kition-Bamboula and Tell Sūkās. No sacred structures from contemporary inland sites ever contain maritime votives. This demonstrates that nautical offerings were not commonplace throughout the society, but were specialized and limited to the zone directly affected by the sea.

At sea, isolated promontory shrines were visible to sailors in their voyages between harbors. These shrines served sacral and functional purposes: they continued the link between seafarer and holy patrons away from port, served as landmarks for navigation, and typically marked the location of freshwater sources. Phoenician isolated temples and shrines mentioned by classical authors are paralleled by excavated examples. Discoveries at Nahariyah, Ashkelon, Mevorakh, Makmish, Sūkās, Kommos, Capo San Marco, Kition, and Ras ed-Drek show physical remains of these shrines which marked Canaanite-Phoenician routes throughout the Mediterranean.

Temples in harbors and shrines on promontories were not for the sole use of seafarers. Temples were the houses of deities, and focal points for human contact with divinities whose multiple functions affected all members of Canaanite and Phoenician society. Thus sailors would have worshipped where farmers or craftspeople made vows, perhaps leaving different offerings, or similar offerings for varying concerns. Shrines outside of settlements may have served the needs of overland travelers, as well as mariners, if the sacred structures were within proximity of a road.

Ships in both ancient and modern traditional seafaring societies are considered to house divine spirits which guard mariners from the dangers of the sea. This belief is manifested in several literal forms: the representation of a god figure or totem placed at the prow, or sometimes the stern of a vessel; oculi, depicted at the prow to both guide the ship and ward off harm; and ships' names, which are often those of a deity known for traits which benefit sailors. These spirits and other divinities were worshipped at holy areas on board ship, typically found at the prow or stern of a vessel.

Evidence for divine ships among the Canaanites and Phoenicians is found in diverse sources. There are very few extant Canaanite or

Phoenician maritime texts, yet we know from the Ugaritic Kirta epic and a parallel reference from an Egyptian papyrus that *Baʿl Ṣapōn* was worshipped in the form of a ship. A letter from the king of Tyre to the king of Ugarit also suggests that Canaanite ships possessed spirits, since it mentions a ship wrecked in a storm as having literally died in the tempest. Classical texts also supply some details about Phoenician ships: the names of Punic warships, the presence of horse and pigmy figureheads, the worship of a figurine of the storm god at the stern of a galley, and the dedication of a ship to Tyrian Herakles-Milqart, are all mentioned by Greek and Latin authors.

Shipwrecks provide a source of material remains. The discovery of a Syro-Palestinian figurine of a goddess in the excavations of the Late Bronze age ship at Uluburun (Turkey) gives physical evidence of deities on board a vessel. The location of the figurine among the scatter of artifacts also indicates that it was housed at the prow of the ship.

Pictorial evidence comes from Assyrian reliefs, a tomb painting, coins, and sculpted sacrificial stelae. These representations show anthropomorphic prow ornaments, including a figure of Milqart, and animal totems, such as the horse and lion. The sign of Tinnit and the goddess's caduceus are displayed on vessels, and the crescent or crescent-and-disk symbol, representative of either Tinnit or ʾAšerah, commonly adorns the standard placed at the stern of warships. Oculi are very common. Representations of parts of ships, prows, sterns, rudders, and anchors on Punic sacrificial stelae show that specific areas of vessels or objects on board had sacral significance which was carried over in the use of their symbols on land.

Special religious ceremonies have been performed by ancient and modern sailors in order to ensure their safety during a voyage. These typically take place at points of transition: in port, before leaving or upon safe arrival; on board ship while leaving or entering harbor, passing a headland or landmark, or in times of peril or need.

Classical authors mention Phoenician seafarers making sacrifices to Herakles-Milqart before setting sail and after landing in harbor. Material remains of anchors and model ships placed as offerings in temples in Canaanite and Phoenician coastal sites suggest that celebrations were performed, presumably after mariners survived dangers at sea. Similarly, dedicatory stelae with nautical imagery are found in port. It is possible that these stelae commemorate the sacrifice of a seafarer's child, offered in a vow to placate angry gods at sea. In an example from a tophet near Tyre, a stone anchor was used to mark the placement of the urn rather than a carved, sacrificial stela.

While away from the safety of port, Canaanite and Phoenician sailors ensured continued contact with their protective deities through the dedication of promontories to their sacred patrons, and the construction of shrines on headlands. Presumably these sacred structures were a focus of seafarers' cultic activity from the water, and may have marked landing spots where ritual needs could be looked after, while more profane tasks like gathering freshwater could be attended to.

Evidence for prayers of thanks being given on board ships arriving in port is found in Egyptian representations. Old Kingdom reliefs show Syrian passengers on Egyptian vessels, with their hands held up in prayer as the ships dock in Memphis. A New Kingdom tomb painting represents a flotilla of Canaanite ships docking after their voyage to Egypt. Some crew members hold their hands up in prayer, while captains and high ranking crew members present libations and burn incense in celebration of their safe arrival. Musical instruments discovered on the Uluburun shipwreck may have been used in ceremonies performed aboard ship.

Mariners often made vows to their guardian deities in times of threat from tempest or battle. Cadmus, the legendary Phoenician prince, prayed to "Poseidon" for help when his ship was buffeted by storms. To fulfill the promises he made to the god, Cadmus built a temple dedicated to "Poseidon" once he had made a safe landing. The crew of Jonah's ship cry out to their storm gods, to try to enlist their aid in ending a storm. After the sea is calmed, the sailors offer sacrifices and make vows to Yahweh, to thank him as the god responsible for quelling the tempest.

During a naval battle with the Romans, a Carthaginian crew member prays to his ship's tutelary god for help and good aim before he lets loose his spear. When this same vessel is doomed to sink, its Carthaginian navigator sacrifices himself to the warship's protective spirit by stabbing himself and letting his blood flow on the figurine of the deity carried on board. Similarly, Roman soldiers captured in a naval battle were tied to the keels of Punic ships and crushed beneath the weight of the vessels, and a person is shown being thrown overboard from a Punic warship painted on a tomb at Kef el-Blida.

Because of the dangers at sea, predictions were important for the safety of a crew. One voyage, heading for Gader, turned back towards Carthage when a sacrifice to Herakles-Milqart produced a bad omen. A Carthaginian pilot is praised for his ability to sense what the winds will be like a day before they occur, and soothsayers were among the crew in a Carthaginian colonizing voyage along the Atlantic coast of

Africa. The crew on board ship with Jonah cast lots in order to determine who is responsible for triggering the storm that threatens their vessel. An astragal, a knucklebone rolled to read omens, discovered on the Cape Geledonya shipwreck gives a clue as to one method used by navigators or soothsayers to try to divine sailing conditions or the will of the gods.

Life on land was accompanied by prescribed religious ceremonies and practices, too. These included monthly or annual feasts and celebrations, and it is possible that there were daily routines, as well. Concerns on land and sea were mitigated by contact with the gods and through their appeasement with sacrifices, offerings, and prayers.

Maritime sacral beliefs and practices protected Canaanite and Phoenician sailors during their lifetime at sea, and are also reflected in the interment of their dead. Our only evidence of mourning rites performed by Phoenician seafarers is given in Ezekiel 27. The text notes specifically that the mariners did not conduct mortuary rituals aboard their vessels, but waited to disembark and grieve on shore. It is possible that mourning at sea was considered an act which would contaminate or bring ill fortune to a ship and was therefore taboo.

Further mortuary rituals and sacred beliefs can be inferred, in part, from the excavation and interpretation of burials. Stone anchors are found in a chamber tomb from Byblos, a burial at Akko, a structural tomb from Ashkelon, a shaft tomb from Ugarit, and several burials from Minet el-Beida. Model ships come from graves from Phoenician sites in the eastern Mediterranean and North Africa, and depictions of ships are painted in several Carthaginian tombs. These rare examples show that the maritime symbols so important to seafarers' lives were also brought, on occasion, to the grave.

It is possible that these anchors, model ships, and paintings of ships from mortuary contexts are markers of the deceased's profession. Mariners may have taken the same sacral symbols with them to the grave which they had offered in thanks to their patron deities during a lifetime of sailing. These familiar votives not only reflected the occupation of the interred, but were also offerings charged with sacred significance in the cultic practices of seafarers, and may have been placed in graves as tribute to a sailor's divine guardian.

Maritime religion, I have argued, was a discrete subset of the general religious beliefs and cultic practices of Canaanite and Phoenician society, generated by the unique uncertainties and dangers faced while living and voyaging at sea. This is what I consider a specialized religion; groups within a culture have different sacral needs and concerns based on their professions and their roles or ranking within their society or kinship structure. While certain religious beliefs and practices are shared throughout a group, others vary based on the individual's position within his or her culture. This concept has generally been overlooked in the study of Canaanite and Phoenician religion, which is typically presented in a monolithic form, reconstructed from data which derive from elite strata of each society.

I have combined archaeological, textual, and pictorial evidence to investigate the sacral beliefs and practices of seafarers, traditionally a non-elite group within their culture. I have used comparative material from other contemporary and modern seafaring societies to aid my interpretations of this evidence, in order to demonstrate that a specialized religion existed among Canaanite and Phoenician sailors. The picture developed permits us to connect this aspect of Canaanite and Phoenician life with what we have long known of the crucial importance of maritime technology and trade to the early Levantine cultures that pioneered seafaring and exploration throughout the Mediterranean.

BIBLIOGRAPHY

Abou-Assaf, A. *Der Tempel von ʿAin Dara*. Vol. 3, *Damaszener Forschungen*. Mainz am Rhein: Philipp von Zabern, 1990.
Ahlberg-Cornell, G. *Herakles and the Sea-Monster in Attic Black-Figure Vase-Painting*. Uppsala: Almqvist & Wiksell, 1984.
Aimé-Giron, N. "Adversaria Semitica III: Baʿal Ṣaphon et les dieux de Taḥpanḥès dans un nouveau papyrus phénicien." *Annales du Service des antiquités de l'Egypte* 40 (1941), 433-60.
Albright, W. F. "Zabûl Yam and Thâpiṭ Nahar in the Combat Between Baal and the Sea." *Journal of the Palestine Oriental Society* 16 (1936), 17-20.
—"Baal-Zephon." In *Festschrift Alfred Bertholet*, ed. W. Baumgartner et al. Tübingen: J. C. B. Mohr, 1950, pp. 1-14.
—*From the Stone Age to Christianity*. New York: Doubleday, 1957.
—"The Role of the Canaanites in the History of Civilization." In *The Bible and the Ancient Near East*, ed. G. E. Wright. Garden City, NY: Doubleday, 1961, pp. 328-62.
—"Remarks on the Chronology of Early Bronze IV-Middle Bronze IIA in Phoenicia and Syria-Palestine." *BASOR* 184 (1966), 26-35.
—*Yahweh and the Gods of Canaan*. New York: Doubleday, 1968.
Alexander, J. A. "The Archaeological Recognition of Religion: The Examples of Islam in Africa and 'Urnfields' in Europe." In *Space, Hierarchy and Society: Interdisciplinary Studies in Social Area Analysis*, vol. 59, B. A. R. International Series, eds. B. C. Burnham and J. Kingsbury. Great Britain: B. A. R., 1979, pp. 215-28.
Arribas, A. et al. *El Barco de El Sec*. Mallorca: Universitat de les Illes Balears, 1987.
Artzy, M. "Unusual Late Bronze Age Ship Representations From Tel Akko." *Mariner's Mirror* 70 (1984), 59-64.
—"Conical Cups and Pumice, Aegean Cult at Tel Nami, Israel." In *Thalassa: L'Égée péhistorique et la mer*, eds. R. Laffineur & L. Basch. Liège: Université de Liège, 1991, pp. 203-6.
Arnaud, D. *Recherches au pays d'Astata*. Vol. 6/3, *Emar*. Paris: ERC, 1986.
Astour, M. "Place Names." In *Ras Shamra Parallels*, vol. II, ed. L. R. Fisher. Rome: Pontificum Institutum Biblicum, 1975, pp. 249-369.
Attridge, H. W. and R. A. Oden. *The Syrian Goddess (De Dea Syria) Attributed to Lucian*. Missoula: Scholars Press, 1976.
—*Philo of Byblos: The Phoenician History*. Washington, DC: The Catholic Biblical Association of America, 1981.
Avigad, N. "Excavations at Makmish, 1958." *IEJ* 10 (1960), 90-96.
—"Makmish." In *Encyclopedia of Archaeological Excavations in the Holy Land*, vol. III, eds. M. Avi-Yonah and E. Stern. Englewood Cliffs, NJ: Prentice-Hall, 1977, pp. 768-70.
—"A Hebrew Seal Depicting a Sailing Ship." *BASOR* 246 (1982), 59-62.
Ayalon, E. "Reconstructing a Traditional Olive Oil Plant at the Eretz Israel Museum, Tel Aviv." In *History and Technology of Olive Oil in the Holy Land*, ed. E. Ayalon. Arlington, VA: Oléarius Editions, 1994, pp. 159-188.
Babelon, E. *Monnaies Grecques et Romaines*. Vol. II, part 2. Paris: E. Leroux, 1910.

Bailey, C. and P. R. Hardie "Dido." In *The Oxford Classical Dictionary*, 3rd ed., eds. S. Hornblower and A. Spawforth. Oxford: Oxford University Press, 1996, p. 467.
Baramki, D. *Phoenicia and the Phoenicians.* Beirut: Khayats, 1961.
Barguet, P. *Les textes des sarcophages égyptiens du Moyen Empire.* Paris: Les éditions du Cerf, 1986.
Barkai, R. "A Seafarer's Prayer." *Mediterranean Historical Review* 1 (1986), 117-20.
Barnett, R. D. "Early Shipping in the Near East." *Antiquity* 32 (1958), 220-31.
—"Ezekiel and Tyre." *EI* 9 (1969), 6-13.
Barr, J. "Philo of Byblos and His 'Phoenician History'." *Bulletin of the John Rylands University Library of Manchester* 57/1 (1974), 17-68.
Barré, M. L. *The God-List in the Treaty Between Hannibal and Philip V of Macedonia: A Study in Light of the Ancient Near Eastern Treaty Tradition.* Baltimore: The Johns Hopkins University Press, 1983.
Barreca, F. "Tharros (S. Giovanni di Sinis, Cagliari)-Scoperte a Capo S. Marco." *Notizie degli scavi di antichità* 12 (1958), 409-12.
—*La civiltà fenicio-punica in Sardegna.* Sassari, Italy: Carlo Delfino, 1988.
Barth, F. Introduction to *Ethnic Groups and Boundaries: The Social Organization of Culture Difference*, ed. F. Barth. Boston: Little, Brown, 1969, pp. 9-38.
Bartoloni, P. "Le figurazioni di carattere marino rappresentate sulle più tarde stele di Cartagine I. Le navi." *RSF* 5/2 (1977), 147-63.
—"Le figurazioni di carattere marino rappresentate sulle più tarde stele di Cartagine II. Le imbarcazioni minori." *RSF* 7/2 (1979), 181-91.
—"Ships and Navigation." In *The Phoenicians*, ed. S. Moscati. Milan: Bompiani, 1988, pp. 72-77.
—"Navires et navigation." In *La civilisation phénicienne et punique*, ed. V. Krings. *Handbuch der Orientalistik*, abt. 1, *Der Nahe und Mittlere Osten*, bd. 20. Leiden: E. J. Brill, 1995, pp. 282-89.
Basch, L. "Phoenician Oared Ships." *Mariner's Mirror* 55 (1969), 139-62, 227-45.
—"Anchors in Egypt." *Mariner's Mirror* 71 (1985), 453-67.
—*Le musée imaginaire de la marine antique.* Athens: Institut Hellénique pour la préservation de la tradition nautique, 1987.
Basch, L. and M. Artzy. "Ship Graffiti at Kition." In *Excavations at Kition*, Vol. V, *The Pre-Phoenician Levels*, eds. V. Karageorghis and M. Demas. Nicosia: Cyprus Department of Antiquities, 1981, pp. 322-36.
Baslez, M. -F. "Cultes et dévotions des Phéniciens en Grèce: les divinités marines." In *StudPhoen*, vol. IV, *Religio Phoenicia*, eds. C. Bonnet *et al.* Namur: Société des études classiques, 1986, pp. 289-305.
Bass, G. F., "Cape Gelidonya: A Bronze Age Shipwreck." *Transactions of the American Philosophical Society* 57/8 (1967).
—"A Bronze Age Shipwreck at Ulu Burun (Kaş): 1984 Campaign." *AJA* 90 (1986), 269-96.
—"Prolegomena to a Study of Maritime Traffic in Raw Materials to the Aegean During the Fourteenth and Thirteenth Centuries B.C." In *TEXNH: Craftsmen, Craftswomen and Craftsmanship in the Aegean Bronze Age*, vol. 16, *Aegaeum*, eds. R. Laffineur and P. P. Betancourt. Liège: Université de Liège, 1997, 153-70.

Bass, G. F., ed. *A History of Seafaring Based on Underwater Archaeology.* New York: Walker, 1972.
Bass, G. F. et al. "The Bronze Age Shipwreck at Ulu Burun: 1986 Campaign." *AJA* 93 (1989), 1-29.
Bassett, F. *Legends and Superstitions of the Sea and of Sailors.* 1885. Reprinted, Detroit: Singing Tree Press, 1971.
Baumgarten, A. I. *The Phoenician History of Philo of Byblos.* Leiden: E. J. Brill, 1981.
Ben-Dor, I. "A Middle Bronze-Age Temple at Nahariya." *QDAP* 14 (1950), 1-41.
Bertrandy, F. and M. Sznycer. *Les stèles puniques de Constantine.* Paris: Ministère de la Culture et de la Communication, 1987.
Betlyon, J. W. *The Coinage and Mints of Phoenicia.* Chico, CA: Scholars Press, 1980.
Bikai, P. M. "Black Athena and the Phoenicians." *Journal of Mediterranean Archaeology* 3/1 (1990), 67-75.
Binford, L. R. "Mortuary Practices: Their Study and their Potential." *Memoirs of the Society for American Archaeology* 25 (1971), 6-29.
Bintliff, J., ed. *The Annales School and Archaeology.* Leicester: Leicester University Press, 1991.
Bisi, A. M. "Le influenze puniche sulla religione libica: la gorfa di Kef el-Blida." *Studi e materiali di storia delle religioni* 37/1 (1966), 85-112.
Black, J. and A. Green. *Gods, Demons and Symbols of Ancient Mesopotamia.* London: British Museum Press, 1992.
Bleeker, C. J. "Quelques réflexions sur la signification religieuse de la mer." *Numen* 6 (1959), 234-40.
Boardman, J. "Al Mina and History." *Oxford Journal of Archaeology* 9/2 (1990), 169-90.
Bonnet, C. "Le culte de Melqart à Carthage: un cas de conservatisme religieux." In *StudPhoen*, vol. IV, *Religio Phoenicia*, eds. C. Bonnet et al. Namur: Société des études classiques, 1986, pp. 209-22.
—*Melqart*. Vol. VIII, *StudPhoen*. Leuven: Uitgeverij Peeters, 1988.
Bonnet-Tzavellas, C. "Le dieu Melqart en Phénicie et dans le bassin Méditerranéen: culte national et officiel." In *StudPhoen*, vol. I/II, *Sauvons Tyr/histoire phénicienne*, eds. E. Gubel et al. Leuven: Uitgeverij Peeters, 1983, pp. 195-207.
Bordreuil, P. *Catalogue des sceaux ouest-sémitiques inscrits.* Paris: Bibliothèque Nationale, 1986.
—"La citadelle sainte du Mont Nanou." *Syria* 66 (1989), 275-79.
Boreux, C. "Études de nautique égyptienne: l'art de la navigation en Égypte jusqu'à la fin de l'Ancien Empire." *Mémoires publiés par les membres de l'Institut français d'archéologie orientale du Caire.* Cairo: 1925.
—"La stèle C. 86 du Musée du Louvre et les stèles similaires." *Mélanges syriens offerts a Monsieur René Dussaud.* Vol. 2. Paris: Librarie orientaliste Paul Geuthner, 1939, pp. 673-87.
Borger, R. "Die Inschriften Asarhaddons Königs von Assyrien." *Archiv für Orientforschung*, Beiheft 9 (1956), 107-9.
—"Der Vertrag Asarhaddons mit Baal von Tyrus." In *Texte aus der Umwelt des Alten Testaments*, vol. I/2, eds. R. Borger et al. Gütersloh: G. Mohn, 1983, pp. 158-59.

Boulotis, C. "La déesse minoenne a la rame-gouvernail." In *Tropis*, vol. I, *1st International Symposium on Ship Construction in Antiquities*, ed. H. Tzalas. Piraeus: Hellenic Institute for the Preservation of Nautical Tradition, 1985, pp. 55-73.

Braidwood, R. J. "The Date of the Byblos Temples Buildings II, XVIII, and XL." *American Journal of Semitic Languages and Literatures* 58 (1941), 254-58.

Braudel, F. *The Mediterranean and the Mediterranean World in the Age of Philip II.* Trans. S. Reynolds. 2 vols. New York: Harper & Row, 1972.

Brown, F., S. R. Driver, and C. A. Briggs. *A Hebrew and English Lexicon of the Old Testament.* Oxford: Clarendon, 1907.

Brown, S. *Late Carthaginian Child Sacrifice and Sacrificial Monuments in their Mediterranean Context.* Sheffield: Sheffield Academic Press, 1991.

Bruneau, P. *Recherches sur les cultes de Délos à l'époque hellénistique et à l'époque impériale.* Paris: E. de Boccard, 1970.

Brunner, H. "Gebet." In *Lexikon der Ägyptologie*, vol. II, eds. W. Helck and W. Westendorf. Wiesbaden: Otto Harrassowitz, 1977, cols. 452-59.

Buck, A. de. *The Egyptian Coffin Texts.* Vol. I, *Texts of Spells 1-75.* Chicago: The University of Chicago Press, 1935.

Buhl, M. -L. *Sūkās.* Vol. VII, *The Near Eastern Pottery and Objects of Other Materials from the Upper Strata.* Copenhagen: Munksgaard, 1983.

Burkert, W. "Funerary Ritual." In *Homo Necans: The Anthropology of Ancient Greek Sacrificial Ritual and Myth.* Trans. P. Bing. Berkeley: University of California Press, 1983, pp. 48-58.

—*Greek Religion.* Cambridge, MA: Harvard University Press, 1985.

Bunnens, G. *L'expansion phénicienne en Mediterranée.* Vol. 17, *Études de philologie d'archéologie et d'histoire anciennes.* Brussels: Intitut historique belge de Rome, 1979.

—"Aspects religieux de l'expansion phénicienne." In *StudPhoen*, vol. IV, *Religio Phoenicia*, eds. C. Bonnet *et al.* Namur: Société des études classiques, 1986, pp. 119-25.

Callot, O. "Les huileries du Bronze Récent a Ougarit." In *Ras Shamra- Ougarit*, vol. III, *Le centre de la ville*, ed. M. Yon. Paris: Éditions recherche sur les civilizations, 1987, pp. 197-212.

Campbell, D. T. "Convergent and Discriminant Validation by the Multitrait-Multimethod Matrix." In *Methodology and Epistemology for Social Science.* Chicago: University of Chicago Press, 1988, pp. 37-61.

Caminos, R. A. *Late-Egyptian Miscellanies.* London: Oxford University Press, 1954.

Canney, M. A. "Boats and Ships in Temples and Tombs." In *Occident and Orient: Gaster Anniversary Volume*, eds. B. Schindler & A. Marmorstein. London: Taylor's Foreign Press, 1936, pp. 50-57.

Cantineau, J. "Un Poseidôn palmyrénien." *Syria* 19 (1938), 78-79.

Caquot, A., *et al. Textes Ougaritiques.* Vol. 1, *Mythes et Légendes.* Paris: Les éditions du Cerf, 1974.

Carrazé, F. "L'ancre de misericorde dans la marine antique." *Archéologia* 61 (1973), 13-19.

Casson, L. *Ships and Seamanship in the Ancient World.* Princeton: Princeton University Press, 1971.

Caubet, A. "Le sanctuaire Chypro-archaïque de Kition-Bamboula." In *Travaux de la Maison de l'Orient*, vol. 7, *Temples et sanctuaires*, ed. G. Roux. Lyon: GIS-Maison de l'Orient, 1984, pp. 107-18.

—"Les sanctuaires de Kition à l'époque de la dynastie phénicienne." In *StudPhoen*, vol. IV, *Religio Phoenicia*, ed. C. Bonnet *et al.* Namur: Société des études classiques, 1986, pp. 153-68.
Černy, J. *Ancient Egyptian Religion*. London: Hutchinson House, 1952.
Chang, K. C. *Early Chinese Civilization: Anthropological Perspectives*. Vol. 23, *Harvard-Yenching Institute Monograph Series*. Cambridge, MA: Harvard University Press, 1976.
Chase, D. "*Ba^{c}l Šamêm*: A Study of the Early Epigraphic Sources." Diss. Harvard University, 1994.
Cheyne, T. K. and J. S. Black, eds. "Castor and Pollux." *Encyclopaedia Biblica*. New York: Macmillan, 1899, pp. 708-9.
Cintas, P. "Le sanctuaire punique de Sousse." *Revue africaine* 91 (1947), 1-80.
—*Manuel d'archéologie punique*. Vol. I. Paris: A. et J. Picard, 1970.
Clamer, C. and D. Ussishkin. "A Canaanite Temple at Tell Lachish." *BA* 40 (1977), 71-76.
Clapham, L. R. "Sanchuniathon: The First Two Cycles." Diss. Harvard University, 1969.
Clifford, R. J. *The Cosmic Mountain in Canaan and the Old Testament*. Cambridge, MA: Harvard University Press, 1972.
—"The Temple in the Ugaritic Myth of Baal." In *Symposia Celebrating the Seventy-Fifth Anniversary of the Founding of the American Schools of Oriental Research (1900-1975)*, ed. F. M. Cross. Cambridge, MA: American Schools of Oriental Research, 1979, pp. 137-45.
Cook, A. B. *Zeus, a Study in Ancient Religion*. Vol. II, *Zeus God of the Dark Sky (Thunder and Lightning)*. New York: Biblo and Tannen, 1965.
Cook, S. A. *The Religion of Ancient Palestine in the Light of Archaeology*. London: Oxford University Press, 1930.
Cornelius, I. "Anat and Qudshu as the 'Mistress of Animals,' Aspects of the Iconography of the Canaanite Goddesses." *Studi epigrafici e linguistici* 10 (1993), 21-45.
—*The Iconography of the Canaanite Gods Reshef and Ba^{c}al*. Orbis Biblicus et Orientalis, vol. 140. Fribourg, Switzerland: University Press, 1994.
Couchoud, P. L. and J. Svoronos. "Le monument des 'taureaux' à Délos et le culte du navire sacré." *BCH* 45 (1921), 270-94.
Courbaud, E. "La navigation d'Hercule." *Mélanges d'archéologie et d'histoire, École Française de Rome* 12 (1892), 274-88.
Courtois, J. -C. "Ugarit Grid, Strata, and Find-Localizations: A Re-assessment." *Zeitschrift des deutschen Palästina-Vereins* 90 (1974), 97-114.
—"Ras Shamra: Archéologie." In *Supplément au Dictionnaire de la Bible*, vol. 9, ed. L. Pirot *et al.* Paris: Letouzey & Ané, 1979, cols. 1126-1295.
Cross, F. M. "The Origin and Early Evolution of the Alphabet." *EI* 8 (1967), 8*-24*.
—*Canaanite Myth and Hebrew Epic*. Cambridge, MA: Harvard University Press, 1973.
—"The 'Olden Gods' in Ancient Near Eastern Creation Myths." In *Magnalia Dei: The Mighty Acts of God*, eds. F. M. Cross *et al.* New York: Doubleday, 1976, pp. 329-38.
Culican, W. "Melqart Representations on Phoenician Seals." *Abr-Nahrain* 2 (1960-61), 41-54.
—*The First Merchant Venturers: the Ancient Levant in History and Commerce*. New York: McGraw-Hill, 1966.

—"A Votive Model from the Sea." *PEQ* 108 (1976), 119-23.
Daressy, G. "Une flotille phénicienne." *Revue archéologique* 27 (1895), 286-92.
Davaras, C. "Une ancre minoenne sacrée?" *BCH* 104 (1980), 47-71.
Davies, N. de G. and R. O. Faulkner. "A Syrian Trading Venture to Egypt." *Journal of Egyptian Archaeology* 33 (1947), 40-46.
Dever, W. G. "The Contribution of Archaeology to the Study of Canaanite and Early Israelite Religion." In *Ancient Israelite Religion*, eds. P. D. Miller *et al.* Philadelphia: Fortress, 1987, pp. 209-48.
Diakonoff, I. M. "The Naval Power and Trade of Tyre." *IEJ* 42 (1992), 168-93.
Dietrich, M., O. Loretz, and J. Sanmartin, eds. *Die keilalphabetischen Texte aus Ugarit.* Vol. 24, *Alter Orient und Altes Testament.* Germany: Neukirchener, 1976.
Dijkstra, M. "The Weather-God on Two Mountains." *UF* 23 (1991), 127-40.
Donner, H. and W. Röllig. *Kanaanäische und Aramäische Inschriften.* 3 vols. Wiesbaden: O. Harrassowitz, 1962-64.
Dothan, M. "Sanctuaries Along the Coast of Canaan in the MB Period: Nahariyah." In *Temples and High Places in Biblical Times.* Jerusalem: The Nelson Glueck School of Biblical Archaeology of Hebrew Union College - Jewish Institute of Religion, 1981, pp. 74-81.
Dowden, K. "Io." In *The Oxford Classical Dictionary*, 3rd ed., eds. S. Hornblower and A. Spawforth. Oxford: Oxford University Press, 1996, pp. 762-63.
Driver, G. R. "Isaiah I-XXXIX: Textual and Linguistic Problems." *Journal of Semitic Studies* 13 (1968),36-57.
Du Mesnil du Buisson, R. "Origine et évolution du panthéon de Tyr." *Revue de l'histoire des religions* 164 (1963), 133-63.
—*Nouvelles études sur les dieux et les mythes de Canaan.* Leiden: E. J. Brill, 1973.
Du Mesnil du Buisson, R. and R. Mouterde. "Inscriptions Grecques de Beyrouth." *MUSJ* 7 (1914-21), 382-94.
Dunand, M. *Fouilles de Byblos.* Vol. I, *Atlas.* Paris: Librairie orientaliste Paul Geuthner, 1937.
—*Fouilles de Byblos.* Vol. I, *Texte.* Paris: Librairie orientaliste Paul Geuthner, 1939.
—*Fouilles de Byblos.* Vol. II, *Atlas.* Paris: Librairie d'Amérique et d'Orient Adrien Maisonneuve, 1950.
—*Fouilles de Byblos.* Vol. II:1, *Texte.* Paris: Librairie d'Amérique et d'Orient Adrien Maisonneuve, 1954.
—*Fouilles de Byblos.* Vol. II:2, *Texte.* Paris: Librairie d'Amérique et d'Orient Adrien Maisonneuve, 1958.
—"Histoire d'une source." *MUSJ* 37 (1960-61), 39-53.
—"Le temple d'Echmoun a Sidon: essai de chronologie." *Bulletin du musée de Beyrouth* 26 (1973), 7-25.
—"Byblos et ses temples après la pénétration amorite." *Berliner Beiträge zum Vorderen Orient* 1/1 (1982), 195-201.
Dunand, M. and R. Duru. *Oumm el-ᶜAmed: une ville de l'époque hellénistique aux échelles de Tyr.* Paris: Libraireie d'Amérique et d'Orient Adrien Maisonneuve, 1962.
Dunand, M. and N. Saliby. "Rapport préliminaire sur les fouilles d'Amrith en 1955." *Les annales archéologique de Syrie* 6 (1956), 3-10.
—"Le sanctuaire d'Amrith." *Les annales archéologique de Syrie* 11-12 (1961-62), 3-12.

Durrbach, F. et al., eds. *Inscriptions de Délos*. Paris: H. Champion, 1926-72.
Dussaud, R. "Deux stèles de Ras Shamra portant une dédicace au dieu Dagon." *Syria* 16 (1935), 177-80.
—*Les découvertes de Ras Shamra (Ugarit) et l'Ancien Testament*. Paris: Librairie Orientaliste Paul Geuthner, 1941.
—"Melqart." *Syria* 25 (1946-48), 205-30.
—"Astarté, Pontos et Ba‹al." *Comptes rendus de l'Académie des inscriptions et belles-lettres* (1947), 201-224.
Edwards, I. E. S. "A Relief of Qudshu-Astarte-Anath in the Winchester Colledge Collection." *JNES* 14 (1955), 49-51.
Eisenberg, E. "The Temples at Tell Kittan." *BA* 40 (1977), 77-81.
Eissfeldt, O. *Baal Zaphon, Zeus Kasios und der Durchzug der Israeliten durchs Meer*. Halle: Max Niemeyer, 1932.
Eitam, D. and A. Shomroni. "Research of the Oil Industry During the Iron Age at Tel Miqne: A Preliminary Report." In *Olive Oil in Antiquity*, eds. M. Heltzer and D. Eitam. Haifa: University of Haifa, 1987, pp. 37-56.
Elat, M. "Tarshish and the Problem of Phoenician Colonization in the Western Mediterranean." *Orientalia lovaniensia periodica* 13 (1982), 55-69.
Elworthy, F. T. *The Evil Eye*. 1895. Reprinted, New York: Julian, 1958.
Engelken, K. "Ba‹alšamem: Eine Auseinandersetzung mit der Monographie von H. Niehr." Parts I and II. *Zeitschrift für die alttestamentiche Wissenschaft* 108, no. 2 (1996), 233-48; no. 3 (1996), 391-407.
Fantar, M. *Eschatologie phénicienne-punique*. Tunis: Ministère des affaires culturelles, 1970.
—"Le dieu de la mer chez les Phéniciens et les Puniques." *Studi semitici* 48 (1977), 1-133.
—"Le temple de Ras ed-Drek." In *Prospezione archeologica al Capo Bon*. Vol. II, eds. F. Barreca and M. Fantar. Rome: Consiglio nazionale delle ricerche, 1983, pp. 43-63.
Farnell, L. R. *The Cults of the Greek States*. 5 vols. Oxford: Clarendon, 1896-1909.
Faulkner, R. O. *The Ancient Egyptian Coffin Texts*. Vol. 1, *Spells 1-354*. Warminster, England: Aris & Phillips, 1973.
Fauth, W. "Das Kasion-Gebirge und Zeus Kasios." *UF* 22 (1990), 105-18.
Ferron, J. "Le mythe solaire de la resurrection des ames d'apres la peinture funeraire de Kef-el-Blida." *Archéologia* 20 (1968), 52-55.
Février, J. -G. *La religion des palmyréniens*. Paris: Librairie philosophique J. Vrin, 1931.
—"Les inscriptions puniques de Sousse." *Bulletin archéologique du comité des travaux historiques et scientifiques* (1946-49), 560-63.
—"L'ancienne marine phénicienne et les découvertes récentes." *La nouvelle Clio* 1-2 (1949-50), 128-43.
Fitzgerald, G. M. *The Four Canaanite Temples of Beth-Shan*. Vol. 2, *The Pottery*. Philadelphia: University of Pennsylvania, 1930.
Flusser, D. "Gods, Personification and Sea-Monsters." *Sefunim* 3 (1969-71), 22-46.
—"Isis, the Lady of the Seas." *Sefunim* 4 (1972-7), 9-14.
Follis, E. R. "Israel and the Sea: A Test Case in Hellenosemitic Studies." In *Society of Biblical Literature 1978 Seminar Papers*, vol. I, ed. P. J. Achtemeier. Missoula: Scholars Press, 1978, pp. 407-15.

Foucart, G. "Storm, Storm-Gods." *The Encyclopaedia of Religion and Ethics.* Vol. XI. Eds. J. Hastings *et al.* New York: Charles Scribner's Sons, 1921, pp. 882-3.
Fricke, P. H., ed. *Seafarer & Community: Towards a Social Understanding of Seafaring.* London: Croom Helm, 1973.
Frost, H. "The Stone-Anchors of Byblos." *MUSJ* 45 (1969a), 425-42.
—"The Stone-Anchors of Ugarit." *Ugaritica* VI (1969b), 235-45.
—"Egypt and Stone Anchor: Some Recent Discoveries." *Mariner's Mirror* 65 (1979), 137-61.
—"On a Sacred Cypriot Anchor." In *Archéologie au Levant, Recueil à la Mémoire de Roger Saidah.* Lyon: Collection de la maison de l'Orient méditerranéen 12, série archéologique 9 , 1982, pp. 161-66.
—"The Kition Anchors." In *Excavations at Kition,* vol. V, *The Pre-Phoenician Levels,* eds. V. Karageorghis and M. Demas. Nicosia: Cyprus Department of Antiquities, 1981, pp. 282-320.
—"The Birth of the Stocked Anchor and the Maximum Size of Early Ships." *Mariner's Mirror* 68 (1982), 263-73.
—"Anchors Sacred and Profane: Ugarit-Ras Shamra, 1986; the Stone Anchors Revised and Compared." In *Ras Shamra-Ougarit,* vol. VI, *Arts et Industries de la Pierre,* ed. M. Yon. Paris: ERC, 1991, pp. 355-410.
Frost, H., ed. "Lilybaeum (Marsala)-The Punic Ship: Final Excavation Report." *Notizie degli scavi di antichità,* Supplement, 30 (1976).
Gaidoz, H. "Un sacrifice humain à Carthage." *Revue archéologique* 7 (1886), 192-93.
Galling, K. "Beschriftete Bildsiegel des ersten Jahrtausends v. Chr. vornehmlich aus Syrien und Palästina." *Zeitschrift des deutschen Palästina-Vereins* 64 (1941), 121-202.
Gardiner, A. H. *Late Egyptian Miscellanies.* Vol. VII, *Bibliotheca Aegyptiaca.* Leiden: E. J. Brill, 1937.
Garland, R. *The Piraeus.* Ithaca, NY: Cornell University Press, 1987.
Garwood, P. et al., eds. *Sacred and Profane: Proceedings of a Conference on Archaeology, Ritual and Religion.* Vol. 32, *Oxford University Committee for Archaeology Monograph.* Oxford: Oxford University Committee for Archaeology, 1991.
Gaster, T. H. "The Battle of the Rain and the Sea: An Ancient Semitic Nature-Myth." *Iraq* 4 (1937), 21-32.
—"Groupings of Deities in the Ritual Tariffs from Ras Shamra-Ugarit." *Archiv für Orientforschung* 12 (1937-39), 148-50.
—"A Phoenician Naval Gazette." *PEQ* 70 (1938), 105-112.
—"The Egyptian 'Story of Astarte' and the Ugaritic Poem of Baal." *Biblioteca Orientalis* 9 (1952), 82-85.
Gates, M. -H. "Archaeology in Turkey." *AJA* 98 (1994), 249-78.
Gauckler, P. *Nécroples puniques.* 2 vols. Paris: A. Picard, 1915.
Gelb,I. J. et al., eds. *The Assyrian Dictionary.* B vol. 2. Chicago: Oriental Institute, 1965.
Gianfrotta, P. A. "First Elements for the Dating of Stone Anchor Stocks." *The International Journal of Nautical Archaeology and Underwater Exploration* 6/4 (1977), 285-92.
Gibson, J. C. L. "The Theology of the Ugaritic Baal Cycle." *Orientalia* 53/2 (1984), 183-201.

Ginsberg, H. L. "The Victory of the Land-God Over the Sea-God." *Journal of the Palestine Oriental Society* 15 (1935), 327-33.
—"Two Religious Borrowings in Ugaritic Literature." *Orientalia* 9 (1940), 39-44.
—"The Legend of King Keret, a Canaanite Epic of the Bronze Age." *BASOR Supplementary Studies* 2-3 (1946).
—"Ugaritic Myths, Epics, and Legends." In *Ancient Near Eastern Texts Relating to the Old Testament*, ed. J. B. Pritchard. 3rd ed. Princeton: Princeton University Press, 1969, pp. 129-55.
Gjerstad, E., et al. *The Swedish Cyprus Expedition*. Vol. III. Stockholm: The Swedish Cyprus Expedition, 1937.
Glanville, S. R. K. "Records of a Royal Dockyard of the Time of Tuthmosis III: Papyrus British Museum 10056, part I." *Zeitschrift für Ägyptische Sprache und Altertumskunde* 66 (1931), 105-21.
—"Records of a Royal Dockyard of the Time of Tuthmosis III: Papyrus British Museum 10056, part II. Commentary." *Zeitschrift für Ägyptische Sprache und Altertumskunde* 68 (1932), 7-41.
Glynn, R. "Herakles, Nereus and Triton: A Study of Iconography in Sixth Century Athens." *AJA* 85 (1981), 121-32.
Gonen, R. *Burial Patterns and Cultural Diversity in Late Bronze Age Canaan*. Winona Lake, IN: Eisenbrauns, 1992.
Gordon, C.H. *Ugaritic Literature*. Rome: Pontificium Institutum Biblicum, 1949.
Göttlicher, A. *Materialien für ein Corpus der Schiffsmodelle im Altertum*. Mainz am Rhein: Philipp von Zabern, 1978.
—*Kultschiffe und Schiffskulte im Altertum*. Berlin: Gebr. Mann, 1992.
Gras, M., P. Rouillard, and J. Teixidor. "The Phoenicians and Death." *Berytus* 39 (1991), 127-76.
Grave, C. "The Etymology of Northwest Semitic ṣapānu." *UF* 12 (1980), 221-29.
Gray, J. *The KRT Text in the Literature of Ras Shamra*. Leiden: E. J. Brill, 1964.
Gsell, S. *Histoire ancienne de l'Afrique du nord*. Vol. IV, *La civilization carthaginoise*. Paris: Librairie Hachette, 1920.
Gubel, E. "The Iconography of Inscribed Phoenician Glyptic." In *Studies in the Iconography of Northwest Semitic Inscribed Seals*, vol. 125, *Orbis Biblicus et Orientalis*, eds. B. Sass and C. Uehlinger. Fribourg, Switzerland: University Press, 1993, pp. 101-29.
Haldane, D. "At the Crossroads of History: Nautical Archaeology in Syria." *Institute of Nautical Archaeology Quarterly* 20.3, 1993, 7-11.
Haines,R. C. *Excavations in the Plain of Antioch*. Vol. II, *The Structural Remains of the Later Phases*. Chicago, IL: The University of Chicago Press, 1971.
Hallote, R. S. "Mortuary Archaeology and the Middle Bronze Age Southern Levant." *Journal of Mediterranean Archaeology* 8/1 (1995), 93-122.
Hamburger, H. "A Hoard of Syrian Tetradrachms and Tyrian Bronze Coins from Gush Halav." *IEJ* 4 (1954), 201-26.
Hamilton, R. W. "Excavations at Tell Abu Hawam." *QDAP* 4 (1935), 1-69.
Hanson, D. P. "Some Remarks on the Chronology and Style of Objects from Byblos." *AJA* 73 (1969), 281-84.
Harden, D. *The Phoenicians*. Harmondsworth, England: Penguin Books, 1971.
Harris, Z. S. *A Grammar of the Phoenician Language*. New Haven, CT: American Oriental Society, 1936.

Hassan, S. "The Causeway of *Wnis* at Sakkara." *Zeitschrift für Ägyptische Sprache und Altertumskunde* 80 (1955), 136-39.
Hasslöf, O., et al. *Ships and Shipyards, Sailors and Fishermen: Introduction to Maritime Ethnology.* Copenhagen: Copenhagen University Press, 1972.
Hatch, E. and H. Redpath. *A Concordance to the Septuagint.* Vol. II. Oxford: Clarendon, 1897.
Helck, W. "Zum Auftreten Fremder Götter in Ägytpen." *Oriens antiquus* 5 (1966), 1-14.
—"Ein Indiz Früher Handelsfahrten Syrischer Kaufleute." *UF* 2 (1970), 35-37.
Heltzer, M. *The Rural Community in Ancient Ugarit.* Wiesbaden: Dr. Ludwig Reichert, 1976.
—*Goods, Prices and the Organization of Trade in Ugarit.* Wiesbaden: Dr. Ludwig Reichert, 1978.
—*The Internal Organization of the Kingdom of Ugarit.* Wiesbaden: Dr. Ludwig Reichert, 1982.
Herdner, A. *Corpus des tablettes en cunéiformes alphabétiques.* Paris: Imprimerie Nationale, 1963.
Hertz, R. "A Contribution to the Study of the Collective Representation of Death." In *Death and the Right Hand.* Trans. R. and C. Needham. Glencoe, IL: The Free Press, 1960, pp. 27-86.
Herzog, Z., G. Rapp, and O. Negbi, eds. *Excavations at Tel Michal, Israel.* Minneapolis: The University of Minnesota Press, 1989.
Hess, R. S. "Divine Names in the Amarna Texts." *UF* 18 (1986), 140-68.
Hestrin, R. "The Lachish Ewer and the ʾAsherah." *IEJ* 37 (1987), 212-23.
—"The Cult Stand from Taʿanach and its Religious Background." In *StudPhoen*, vol. V, *Phoenicia and the Eastern Mediterranean in the First Millennium B.C.*, ed. E. Lepinski. Leuven: Uitgeverij Peeters, 1987, pp. 60-77.
Hill, G. F. *Catalogue of the Greek Coins of Phoenicia.* London: British Museum, 1910.
Hirschfeld, Y. "The Anchor Church at the Summit of Mt. Berenice, Tiberias." *BA* 57/3 (1994), 122-33.
Hodder, I. "The Contribution of the Long Term." In *Archaeology as Long-Term History*, ed. I. Hodder. Cambridge: Cambridge University Press, 1987, pp. 1-8.
—*Reading the Past: Current Approaches to Interpretation in Archaeology.* Cambridge: Cambridge University Press, 1991.
Hoftijzer, J. and W. H. van Soldt. "Texts from Ugarit Pertaining to Seafaring." Appendix to *Seagoing Ships and Seamanship in the Bronze Age Levant*, by S. Wachsmann. College Station, TX: Texas A & M University Press, 1998, pp. 333-44.
Hopfer, T. "Astragalomanteia." In *Real-Encyclopädie der classischen Altertumswissenschaft*, Supplement vol. 4, eds. A. Pauly et al. Stuttgart: J. B. Metzler, 1924, cols. 51-56.
Hornell, J. "The Prow of the Ship: Sanctuary of the Tutelary Deity." *Man* 43 (1943), 121-28.
—*Water Transport: Origins & Early Evolution.* Cambridge: Cambridge University Press, 1946.
Hours-Miedan, M. "Les représentations figurées sur les stèles de Carthage." *Cahiers de Byrsa* 1 (1950), 15-160.
Hunt, P. N. "Mount Saphon in Myth and Fact." In *StudPhoen*, vol.XI, *Phoenicia and the Bible*, ed. E. Lipinski. Leuven: Uitgeverij Peeters, 1991, pp. 103-15.

Huntington, R. and P. Metcalf. *Celebrations of Death: The Anthropology of Mortuary Ritual*. Cambridge: Cambridge University Press, 1979.
Hvidberg-Hansen, O. "Baʿal-Malagê dans le traité entre Asarhaddon et le roi de Tyr." *Acta orientalia* 35 (1973), 57-81.
—"Uni-Ashtarte and Tanit-Iuno Caelestis: Two Phoenician Goddesses of Fertility Reconsidered from Recent Archaeological Discoveries." In *Archaeology and Fertility Cult in the Ancient Mediterranean*. Ed. A. Bonanno. Amsterdam: B.R. Grüner Publishing, 1986.
Jidejian, N. *Byblos Through the Ages*. Beirut: Dar el-Machreq Publishers, 1971.
Johansen, Ø. "Religion and Archaeology: Revelation or Empirical Research?" In *Words and Objects: Towards a Dialogue Between Archaeology and History of Religion*, ed. G. Steinsland. Oslo, Denmark: Norwegian University Press, 1986, pp. 67-77.
Johnston, A. W. "Graffiti on Attic Vases." In *Excavations at Kition*, vol. IV, *The Non-Cypriote Pottery*, V. Karageorghis, et al. Nicosia: Cyprus Department of Antiquities, 1981, pp. 45-49.
Johnston, P. F. *Ship and Boat Models in Ancient Greece*. Annapolis, MD: Naval Institute Press, 1985.
Jones, D. *A Glossary of Ancient Egyptian Nautical Titles and Terms*. London: Kegan Paul International, 1988.
Jones, S. *The Archaeology of Ethnicity: Constructing Identities in the Past and Present*. London: Routledge, 1997.
Kaiser, O. *Die Mythische Bedeutung des Meeres in Agypten, Ugarit und Israel*. Berlin, 1959.
Kamp, K. A. and N. Yoffee. "Ethnicity in Ancient Western Asia During the Early Second Millennium B.C.: Archaeological and Ethnoarchaeological Perspectives." *BASOR* 237 (1980), 85-104.
Kapitän, G. "Ancient Anchors--Technology and Classification." *The International Journal of Nautical Archaeology and Underwater Exploration* 13/1 (1984), 33-44.
—"Archaeological Evidence for Rituals and Customs on Ancient Ships." In *Tropis*, vol. I, 1st International Symposium on Ship Construction in Antiquities, ed. H. Tzalas. Piraeus: Hellenic Institute for the Preservation of Nautical Tradition, 1985, pp. 147-62.
Karageorghis, V. *A View from the Bronze Age*. New York: E.P. Dutton, 1976.
Karageorghis, V. and M. Demas, eds. *Excavations at Kition*. Vol. V, *The Pre-Phoenician Levels*. Nicosia: Cyprus Department of Antiquities, 1985.
Katzenstein, H. J. *The History of Tyre*. Jerusalem: The Schocken Institute for Jewish Research, 1973.
—"Tyre in the Early Persian Period (539-486 B.C.E.)." *BA* 42/1 (1979), 23-34.
—"Some Reflections on the Phoenician Deities Mentioned in the Treaty Between Esarhaddon King of Assyria and Baal King of Tyre." *Atti del II congresso internazionale di studi fenici e punici*. Vol. I. Rome: Consiglio Nazionale delle Ricerche, 1991, pp. 373-77.
Keel, O. and C. Uehlinger. *Göttinnen, Götter und Gottessymbole*. Vol. 134, *Quaestiones disputatae*. Freiburg: Herder, 1992.
Kelly, M. C. S. and R. E. Kelly. "Approaches to Ethnic Identification in Historical Archaeology." In *Archaeological Perspectives on Ethnicity in America*, vol. 1, *Baywood Monographs in Archaeology*, ed. R. L. Schuyler. Farmingdale, NY: Baywood Publishing, 1980, pp. 133-43.
Kennedy, C. A. "Early Christians and the Anchor." *BA* 38/3-4 (1975), 115-24.

Knapp, A. B. *Society and Polity at Bronze Age Pella: An Annales Perspective*, vol. 6, *JSOT/ASOR Monograph Series*. Sheffield: Sheffield Academic Press, 1993.

Knapp, A. B., ed. *Archaeology, Annales, and Ethnohistory*. Cambridge: Cambridge University Press, 1992.

Knudsen, E. E. "Spirantization of Velars in Akkadian." In *lišān mithurti: Festschrift Wolfram Freiherr von Soden*, vol. 1, *Alter Orient und Altes Testament*, eds. M. Dietrich and W. Röllig. Neukirchen-Vluyn: Butzon & Bercker Kevelaer, 1969, pp. 147-55.

Lacroix, L. "Héraclès, héros voyageur et civilisateur." *Bulletin de la Classe des Lettres et des Sciences morales et politiques de l'Academie royale de Belgique* 60 (1974), 34-59.

Lambdin, T. O. "Egyptian Loan Words in the Old Testament." *JAOS* 73 (1953), 145-55.

Lamer, H. "Hippokampus." In *Real-Encyclopädie der classischen Altertumswissenschaft*, vol. 8, eds. A. Pauly *et al.* Stuttgart: J. B. Metzler, 1913, cols. 1748-72.

Lange, H. "Zur Sakralkultur der Schiffahrt." *Volk und Volkstum* 3 (1938), 371-73.

Laroche, E. "Le dieu anatolien Sarrumma." *Syria* 40 (1963), 277-302.

—"Glossaire de la langue hourrite," *Revue hittite et asianique* 34 (1976), 13-161.

Lethbridge, T. C. *Boats and Boatmen*. London: Thames and Hudson, 1952.

Levine, B. "Ugaritic Descriptive Rituals." *Journal of Cuneiform Studies* 17 (1963), 105-11.

Levy, T. E., and A. F. C. Holl. "Social Change and the Archaeology of the Holy Land." In *The Archaeology of Society in the Holy Land*, ed. T. E. Levy. New York: Facts on File, 1995, pp. 2-8.

Liddell, H. G., R. Scott, and H. S. Jones. *A Greek-English Lexicon (with Supplement)*. Oxford: Clarendon, 1968.

Linder, E. "The Maritime Texts of Ugarit: A Study in Late Bronze Age Shipping." Diss. Brandeis University, 1970.

—"A Cargo of Phoenicio-Punic Figurines." *Archaeology* 26/3 (1973), 182-87.

—"Ugarit: a Canaanite Thalassocracy." In *Ugarit in Retrospect*, ed. G. D. Young. Winona Lake, IN: Eisenbrauns, 1981, pp. 31-42.

—"The Ma'agan Mikhael Shipwreck Excavations." *Qadmoniot* 24/1-2 (1991), 39-46 (Hebrew).

Lipinski, E. "Note de topographie historique: Ba'li-Ra'ši et Ra'šu Qudšu," *Revue biblique* 78 (1971), 84-92.

—"The Goddess Aṯirat in Ancient Arabia, in Babylon, and in Ugarit." *Orientalia lovaniensia periodica* 3 (1972), 101-19.

—"Products and Brokers of Tyre According to Ezekiel 27." In *StudPhoen*, vol. III, *Phoenicia and its Neighbours*. Leuven: Uitgeverij Peeters, 1985, pp. 213-20.

—"Carthage et Tarshish." *Biblioteca Orientalis* 45 (1988), 59-81.

—*Dieux et déesses de l'univers phénicien et punique*. Vol. XIV, *StudPhoen*. Leuven: Uitgeverij Peeters & Departement Oosterse Studies, 1995.

Littauer, M. A. and J. H. Crouwel. *Wheeled Vehicles and Ridden Animals in the Ancient Near East*. Leiden: E. J. Brill, 1979.

Liverani, M. "Ras Shamra: Histoire." In *Supplément au Dictionnaire de la Bible*, vol. 9, ed. L. Pirot *et al.* Paris: Letouzey & Ané, 1979, cols. 1298-1347.

—"The Trade Network of Tyre According to Ezek. 27." In *Ah, Assyria*, vol. 33, *Scripta Hierosolymitana*, ed. M. Cogan and I. Eph‘al. Jerusalem: Magnes, 1991, pp. 65-79.
Logan, D. "The Known and Unknown Wind." *Parabola* 20/1 (1995), 34-39.
Luce, S. B. "Heracles and the Old Man of the Sea." *AJA* 26 (1922), 174-92.
MacAdams, H. I. Review of *Sūkās VIII: The Habitation Quarters*, by J. Lund. *JNES* 50/2 (1991), 153-55.
Maier, W. A. *ʾAšerah: Extrabiblical Evidence*. Atlanta, GA: Scholars Press, 1986.
Malamat, A. "The Divine Nature of the Mediterranean Sea in the Foundation Inscription of Yaḫdulim." In *Mari in Retrospect: Fifty Years of Mari and Mari Studies*, ed. G. D. Young. Winona Lake, IN: Eisenbrauns, 1992, pp. 211-15.
Maloney, C. "Don't Say 'Pretty Baby' Lest you Zap it with Your Eye--The Evil Eye in South Asia." In *The Evil Eye*, ed. C. Maloney. New York: Columbia University Press, 1976, pp. 102-48.
Maloney, C., ed. *The Evil Eye*. New York: Columbia University Press, 1976.
Marcus, J. and K. V. Flannery. "Ancient Zapotec Ritual and Religion: An Application of the Direct Historical Approach." In *The Ancient Mind: Elements of Cognitive Archaeology*, eds. C. Renfrew and E. B. W. Zubrow. Cambridge: Cambridge University Press, 1994, pp. 55-74.
Margalit, B. "Studia Ugaritica II: Studies in *Krt* and *Aqht*." *UF* 8 (1976), 137-92.
—"Death and Dying in the Ugaritic Epics." In *Death in Mesopotamia*, vol. 8, *Mesopotamia*, ed. B. Alster. Copenhagen: Akademish Forlag, 1980, pp. 243-54.
Margueron, J. "Rapport preliminaire sur les 3e, 4e, 5e et 6e campagnes de fouilles a Meskene-Emar." *Les annales archéologique arabes syriennes* 32 (1982), 233-49.
—"Emar." *Les annales archéologique arabes syriennes* 33/2 (1983), 175-85.
—"A propos des temples de Syrie du nord." In *Sanctuaires et clergés*, eds. M. Philonenko and M. Simon. Paris: Paul Geuthner, 1985, pp. 11-38.
Matthiae, P. "Unité et dévelopement du temple dans la Syrie du Bronze Moyen." In *Uitgaven van Het Nederlands Historisch-Archaeologisch Instituut te Istanbul*. Vol. 37, *Le Temple et le Culte*. Istanbul: Nederlands Historisch-Archaeologisch Instituut, 1975, pp. 43-72.
—*Ebla: An Empire Rediscovered*. Trans. C. Holme. London: Hodder and Stoughton, 1977.
Maxwell-Hyslop, K. R. *Western Asiatic Jewellery*. London: Methuen, 1971.
May, H. G. and R. Engberg, eds. *Material Remains of the Megiddo Cult*. Chicago: University of Chicago Press, 1935.
Mazar, A. "Temples of the Middle and Late Bronze Ages and the Iron Age." In *The Architecture of Ancient Israel*, eds. A. Kempinski and R. Reich. Jerusalem: Israel Exploration Society, 1992, pp. 161-87.
Mazar, B. *The Early Biblical Period*. Jerusalem: Israel Exploration Society, 1986.
McCaslin, D. E. *Stone Anchors in Antiquity: Coastal Settlements and Maritime Trade-Routes in the Eastern Mediterranean ca. 1600-1050 B.C.* Vol. 61, *Studies in Mediterranean Archaeology*. Göteborg: Paul Åström, 1980.
McGovern, P. *Late Bronze Palestinian Pendants: Innovation in a Cosmopolitan Age*. Sheffield, England: JSOT, 1985.
McGuire, R. H. "The Study of Ethnicity in Historical Archaeology." *Journal of Anthropological Archaeology* 1 (1982), 159-78.
Meier, S. "Baal's Fight With Yam (KTU 1.2.I,IV)." *UF* 18 (1986), 241-54.

Metzger, M. "Über die spätbronzezeitlichen Tempel." In *Frühe Phöniker im Libanon* , ed. R. Hachmann. Mainz am Rhein: Philipp von Zabern, 1983, pp. 66-78.
Moll, F. "The History of the Anchor." *Mariner's Mirror* 13 (1927), 293-332.
Montgomery, J.A. "Ras Shamra Notes IV: The Conflict of Baal and the Waters." *JAOS* 55 (1935), 268-77.
Moore, A. "A Ship at Carthage." *Mariner's Mirror* 1 (1911), 280-81.
Moran, W. L. *The Amarna Letters*. Baltimore: The Johns Hopkins University Press, 1992.
Morris, I. *Burial and Ancient Society*. Cambridge: Cambridge University Press, 1987.
Moscati, S. *The World of the Phoenicians*. Trans. A. Hamilton. New York: Frederick A. Praeger, 1968.
Moscati, S. ed. *The Phoenicians*. Milan: Bompiani, 1988.
Moss, L. W. and S. C. Cappannari. "Mal'occhio, Ayin ha ra, Oculus fascinus, Judenblick: The Evil Eye Hovers Above." In *The Evil Eye*, ed. C. Maloney. New York: Columbia University Press, 1976, pp. 1-15.
Müller, C. *Geographici Graeci Minores*. Vol. I. Paris: 1855.
Müller, L. *Numismatique de l'ancienne Afrique*. Vol. 2. Copenhagen: F. S. Mule, 1861.
Negbi, O. *Canaanite Gods in Metal*. Tel Aviv: Tel Aviv University Institute of Archaeology, 1976.
Negbi, O. and S. Moskowitz. "The 'Foundation Deposits' or 'Offering Deposits' of Byblos." *BASOR* 184 (1966), 21-26.
Nelson, H. H. "The Naval Battle Pictured at Medinet Habu." *JNES* 2 (1943), 40-55.
Nicolaou, K. *The Historical Topography of Kition*. Vol. 43, *Studies in Mediterranean Archaeology*. Göteborg: Paul Åström, 1976.
Niehr, H. *Der höchste Gott: Alttestamentlicher JHWH-Glaube in Kontext syrisch-kanaanäischer Religion des 1. Jahrtausend v. Chr*. Beihefte zur Zeitschrift für die alttestamentiche Wissenschaft, vol. 190. Berlin & New York: Walter de Gruyter, 1990.
Ninck, M. "Das Wasser in Mythologie, Religion und Volkskunde." *Ciba Zeitschrift* 9/107 (1947), 3933-39.
North, R. "Ugarit Grid, Strata, and Find-Localizations." *Zeitschrift des deutschen Palästina-Vereins* 89 (1973), 113-60.
Obermann, J. "Votive Inscriptions from Ras Shamra." *JAOS* 61 (1941), 31-45.
—"How Baal Destroyed a Rival, a Mythological Incantation Scene." *JAOS* 67 (1947), 195-208.
Oden, R. A. *Studies in Lucian's 'De Syria Dea.'* Missoula: Scholars Press, 1977.
—"Philo of Byblos and Hellenistic Historiography." *PEQ* (1979), 115-26.
Olyan, S. M. *Asherah and the Cult of Yahweh in Israel*. Vol. 34, *Society of Biblical Literature Monograph Series*. Atlanta, GA: Scholars Press, 1988.
Pader, E. -J. "Death and Ritual: Anthropological and Archaeological Perspectives." In *Symbolism, Social Relations and the Interpretation of Mortuary Remains*, vol. 130, B. A. R. International Series. Oxford: B. A. R. , 1982, pp. 36-68.
Parker, R. C. T. "Selene." In *The Oxford Classical Dictionary*, 3rd ed., eds. S. Hornblower and A. Spawforth. Oxford: Oxford University Press, 1996, pp. 1379-80.

Parpola, S. and K.Watanabe. *Neo-Assyrian Treaties and Loyalty Oaths.* Helsinki: Helsinki University Press, 1988.
Peckham, B. "Phoenicia and the Religion of Israel: The Epigraphic Evidence." In *Ancient Israelite Religion*, eds. P. D. Miller et al. Philadelphia: Fortress, 1987, pp. 79-100.
Picard, C. "Le dauphin au trident sur le sarcophage sidonien 'au navire'." *Syria* 14 (1933), 318-21.
—*Catalogue du musée Alaoui.* Vol. I. Tunis: 1957.
—"Les représentations de sacrifice molk sur les ex-voto de Carthage." *Karthago* 17 (1976), 67-138.
—"Les représentations de sacrifice molk sur les stèles de Carthage." *Karthago* 18 (1978), 5-116.
Picard, G. C. and C. Picard. *Daily Life in Carthage.* New York: Macmillan, 1961.
—*The Life and Death of Carthage.* London: Sidgwick & Jackson, 1968.
Polanyi, K. "Ports of Trade in Early Societies." *The Journal of Economic History* 23/1 (1963), 30-45.
Pope, M. *El in the Ugaritic Texts.* Vol. 2, Vetus Testamentum Supplement. Leiden: E. J. Brill, 1955.
—"Jamm." In *Wörterbuch der Mythologie*, vol. I, *Götter und Mythen im Vorderen Orient*, ed. H. W. Haussig. Stuttgart: Ernst Klett, 1965, pp. 289-91.
—"Marginalia to M. Dahood's Ugaritic-Hebrew Philology." *Journal of Biblical Literature* 85 (1966), 455-66.
Porada, E. "The Cylinder Seal from Tell el-Dabʿa." *AJA* 88 (1984), 485-88.
Prausnitz, M. W. "Achzib." In *The New Encyclopedia of Archaeological Excavations in the Holy Land*, vol. 1, ed. E. Stern. New York: Simon and Schuster, 1993, pp. 32-35.
Pritchard, J. B. *The Ancient Near East in Pictures Relating to the Old Testament.* 2nd ed. Princeton, NJ: Princeton University Press, 1969.
—*Ancient Near Eastern Texts Relating to the Old Testament.* 3rd ed. Princeton, NJ: Princeton University Press, 1969.
—*Recovering Sarepta, A Phoenician City.* Princeton, NJ: Princeton University Press, 1978.
Pritchard, J. B., et al. *Sarepta: A Preliminary Report on the Iron Age.* Philadelphia: University of Pennsylvania, 1975.
Pulak, C. M. "A Late Bronze Age Shipwreck at Ulu Burun: Preliminary Analysis." M. A. Thesis Texas A & M University, 1987.
Queyrel, F. "Aphrodite et les marins." In *Tropis*, vol. II, *2nd International Symposium on Ship Construction in Antiquities*, ed. H. Tzalas. Delphi: Hellenic Institute for the Preservation of Nautical Tradition, 1987, pp. 283-85.
Quirini, B . Z. "L'interpretatio graeca dell'ugaritico Yam." *Atti del II Congresso Internazionale di Studi Fenici e Punici.* Vol. I. Rome: Consiglio Nazionale delle Ricerche, 1991, pp. 431-37.
Rainey, A. F. "Organized Religion at Ugarit." *Christian News from Israel* 15/1 (1964), 16-24.
—Review of *Canaanite Toponyms in Ancient Egyptian Documents*, by S. Ahituv. *JAOS* 107 (1987), 534-38.
—"The 'Lord of Heaven' at Tel Michal." In *Excavations at Tel Michal, Israel*, eds. Z. Herzog, G. Rapp, and O. Negbi. Minneapolis: The University of Minnesota Press, 1989, pp. 381-82.
Rawlinson, G. "Ships, Navigation, and Commerce." In *History of Phoenicia.* London: Longmans, Green, 1889, pp. 271-308.

Redford, D. B. "The Sea and the Goddess." In *Studies in Egyptology Presented to Miriam Lichtheim*, vol. 2, ed. S. Israelit-Groll. Jerusalem: Magnes, 1990, pp. 824-35.
Reiner, E. "Akkadian Treaties from Syria and Assyria." In *Ancient Near Eastern Texts Relating to the Old Testament*, ed. J. B. Pritchard. 3rd ed. Princeton: Princeton University Press, 1969, pp. 531-41.
Renfrew, C. *The Archaeology of Cult: The Sanctuary at Phylakopi*. London: The British School of Archaeology at Athens, 1985.
—"The Archaeology of Religion." In *The Ancient Mind: Elements of Cognitive Archaeology*, eds. C. Renfrew and E. B. W. Zubrow. Cambridge: Cambridge University Press, 1994, pp. 47-54.
Revere, R. B. "'No Man's Coast': Ports of Trade in the Eastern Mediterranean." In *Trade and Market in the Early Empires*, eds. K. Polanyi *et al*. Glencoe, IL: The Free Press, 1957.
Ribichini, S. "Beliefs and Religious Life." In *The Phoenicians*, ed. S. Moscati. Milan: Bompiani, 1988, pp. 104-25.
Richard, F. "Les dieux des Phares." *Sefunim* 6 (1981), 37-45.
Riis, P. J. *Sūkās*. Vol. I, *The North-East Sanctuary and the First Settling of Greeks in Syria and Palestine*. Copenhagen: Munksgaard, 1970.
—*Sūkās* Vol. VI, *The Graeco-Phoenician Cemetery and Sanctuary at the Southern Harbour*. Copenhagen: Munksgaard, 1979.
Ringels, J. "The Harbour God of Caesarea Maritima." *Sefunim* 4 (1972-75), 22-27.
Rivers, W. H. R. "Ships and Boats." *The Encyclopaedia of Religion and Ethics*. Vol. XI, eds. J. Hastings *et al*. New York: Charles Scribner's Sons, 1921, pp. 471-74.
Rougé, J. *La marine dans l'Antiquité*. Vendome: Presses universitaires de France, 1975.
Rouse, W. H. D. *Greek Votive Offerings*. Cambridge: Cambridge University Press, 1902.
Rowe, A. *The Four Canaanite Temples of Beth-Shan*. Philadelphia: University of Pennsylvania, 1940.
Rudolph, R. C. "Boat-Models From Early Chinese Tombs." *AJA* 78 (1974), 65-68.
Rudolph, W. *Harbor and Town: A Maritime Cultural History*. German Democratic Republic: Edition Leipzig, 1980.
Saadé, G. "Légendes et histoire d'une montagne syrienne." *Levante* 15 (1968), 5-22.
—*Ougarit: Métropole cananéenne*. Beirut: Imprimerie catholique, 1979.
Sader, H. "Phoenician Stelae from Tyre." *Berytus* 39 (1991), 101-26.
Safar, F. "A Further Text of Shalmaneser III from Assur." *Sumer* 7 (1951), 3-21.
Saghieh, M. *Byblos in the Third Millennium B.C.* England: Aris & Phillips, 1983.
Salač, A. "ΖΕΥΣ ΚΑΣΙΟΣ." *BCH*, 46 (1922), 160-89.
Salles, J. -F. *La nécropole "K" de Byblos*. Boulogne: Maison de l'Orient, 1980.
Sasson, J. M. "Canaanite Maritime Involvement in the Second Millennium B.C." *JAOS* 86 (1966), 126-38.
—*Jonah*. New York: Doubleday, 1990.
Säve-Söderbergh, T. *The Navy of the Eighteenth Egyptian Dynasty*. Uppsala: A. B. Lundequistska Bokhandeln, 1946.
Savignac, J. de. "Le sens du terme Ṣâphôn." *UF* 16 (1984), 273-78.

Schaeffer, C. F. A. "Les fouilles de Minet-el-Beida et de Ras-Shamra, deuxième campagne (printemps 1930)." *Syria* 12 (1931), 1-14.
—"Les fouilles de Minet-el-Beida et de Ras-Shamra, quatrième campagne (printemps 1932)." *Syria* 14 (1933), 91-127.
—"Les fouilles de Ras Shamra, cinquième campagne (printemps 1933)." *Syria* 15 (1934), 105-31.
—"Les fouilles de Ras Shamra-Ugarit, sixième campagne (printemps 1934)." *Syria* 16 (1935), 141-76.
—"Fouilles sur le sommet du Djebel Akra et aux ruines du couvent de Saint-Barlaam." *Syria* 19 (1938), 323-26.
—"Ras Shamra-Ugarit et le monde egéen." *Ugaritica* 1 (1939), 53-60.
—"La grande stele du Baal au foudre de Ras Shamra." *Ugaritica* 2 (1949), 121-30.
—"Remarques sur les ancres en pierre d'Ugarit." *Ugaritica* 7 (1978), 371-81.
Schaeffer-Forrer, C. F. A. *Corpus des cylindres-sceaux de Ras Shamra-Ugarit et d'Enkomi-Alasia*. Vol. 1, *Mission archéologique de Ras Shamra-Ugarit et d'Enkomi-Alasia*. Paris, Éditions recherche sur les civilizations, 1983.
Schmidt, B. B. *Israel's Beneficent Dead*. Vol. 11, *Forschungen zum Alten Testament*. Tübingen: J. C. B. Mohr, 1994.
Sébillot, P. *Le folk-lore des pêcheurs*. Paris: G. -P. Maisonneuve & Larose, 1968.
Seeden, H. "A Tophet in Tyre?" *Berytus* 39 (1991), 39-82.
Semple, E. C. "The Templed Promontories of the Ancient Mediterranean." *The Geographical Review* 17/3 (1927), 353-86.
Shaw, J. W. "Excavations at Kommos (Crete) During 1979." *Hesperia* 49/3 (1980), 207-50.
—"Phoenicians in Southern Crete." *AJA* 93/2 (1989), 165-83.
—"Two Three-holed Stone Anchors from Kommos, Crete: Their Context, Type, and Origin." *The International Journal of Nautical Archaeology* 24/4 (1995), 279-91.
Shepard, K. *The Fish-Tailed Monster in Greek and Etruscan Art*. New York: Privately printed, 1940.
Shennan, S., ed. *Archaeological Approaches to Cultural Identity*. London: Unwin Hyman, 1989.
Simons, J. *Handbook for the Study of Egyptian Topographical Lists Relating to Western Asia*. Leiden: E. J. Brill, 1937.
Smith, S. "The Ship Tyre," *PEQ* (1953), 97-110.
Soden, W. von. *Grundriss der Akkadischen Grammatik*. Vol. 33/47, *Analecta orientalia*. Rome: Pontificium Institutum Biblicum, 1969.
Staatliche Museen zu Berlin, Vorderasiatische Abteilung. *Keilschrifturkunden aus Boghazköi*. Berlin: 1921-.
Stadelmann, R. *Syrisch-Palästinensische Gottheiten in Ägypten*. Leiden, 1967.
Stager, L. E. "The Rite of Child Sacrifice at Carthage." In *New Light on Ancient Carthage*, ed. J. Pedley. Ann Arbor: University of Michigan Press, 1980, pp. 1-11.
—"Carthage: A View from the Tophet." In *Phönizier im Westen*, ed. H. G. Niemeyer. Mainz am Rhein: Philipp von Zabern, 1982, pp. 155-66.
—*Ashkelon Discovered*. Washington, DC: Biblical Archaeological Society, 1991.
—"Ashkelon." In *The New Encyclopedia of Archaeological Excavations in the Holy Land*, vol. 1, ed. E. Stern. New York: Simon and Schuster, 1993, pp. 103-112.

Stager, L. E. and S. R. Wolff. "Production and Commerce in Temple Courtyards: An Olive Press in the Sacred Precinct at Tel Dan." *BASOR* 243 (1981), 95-102.
Stern, E. "A Late Bronze Temple at Tell Mevorakh." *BA* 40 (1977), 89-91.
—*Material Culture of the Land of the Bible in the Persian Period 538-332 B.C.* Warminster: Aris & Phillips, 1982.
—*Excavations at Tel Mevorakh, Part Two: The Bronze Age.* Vol. 18, *Qedem.* Jerusalem: The Institute of Archaeology, the Hebrew University of Jerusalem, 1984.
—"A Phoenician-Cypriote Votive Scapula from Tel Dor: A Maritime Scene." *IEJ* 44 (1994), 1-11.
Svoronos, J. N. "Stylides, ancres hierae, aphlasta, stoloi, ackrostolia, embola, proembola et totems marins." *Journal international d'archéologie numismatique* 16 (1914), 81-152.
Tarragon, J. M. de. *La culte à Ugarit.* Vol. 19, *Cahiers de la Revue biblique.* Paris: Gabalda, 1980.
Teissier, B. *Egyptian Iconography on Syro-Palestinian Cylinder Seals of the Middle Bronze Age.* Vol. 11, *Orbis Biblicus et Orientalis, Series Archaeologica.* Fribourg, Switzerland: University Press, 1996.
Teixidor, J. *The Pagan God.* Princeton, NJ: Princeton University Press, 1977.
—*The Pantheon of Palmyra.* Leiden: E. J. Brill, 1979.
Thierry, G. de. "Schiffahrt der Phöniker." *Technik Geschichte* 27 (1938), 123-28.
Thomas, L. -V. "Funeral Rites." Trans. K. Anderson. In *The Encyclopedia of Religion*, vol. 5, ed M. Eliade. New York: Macmillan, 1987, pp. 450-59.
Tomback, R. S. *A Comparative Semitic Lexicon of the Phoenician and Punic Languages.* Missoula, MT: Scholars Press, 1978.
Toombs, L. E. "Baal, Lord of the Earth: The Ugaritic Baal Epic." In *The Word of the Lord Shall Go Forth*, eds. C. L. Meyers and M. O'Connor. Winona Lake, IN: Eisenbrauns, 1983, pp. 613-23.
Torr, C. *Ancient Ships.* 1895. Reprinted, with additional material edited by A. J. Podlecki, Chicago: Argonaut, 1964.
Tuffnell, O., C. H. Inge, and L. Harding. *Lachish.* Vol. II, *The Fosse Temple.* London: Oxford University Press, 1940.
Turner, V. W. *The Ritual Process.* Chicago: Aldine Publishing, 1969.
Ussishkin, D. "Excavations at Tel Lachish--1973-1977, Preliminary Report." *Tel Aviv* 5 (1978), 1-97.
—"Lachish." In *The New Encyclopedia of Archaeological Excavations in the Holy Land*, vol. 3, ed. E. Stern. New York: Simon and Schuster, 1993, pp. 897-911.
Van Berchem, D. "Sanctuaires d'Hercule-Melqart contribution a l'étude de l'expansion phénicienne en Méditerranée." *Syria* 44 (1967), 73-109, 307-38.
Vandenabeele, F. "Le monde marin dans les sanctuaires minoens." In *Thalassa: L'Égée préhistorique et la mer*, eds. R. Laffineur and L. Basch. Liège: Université de Liège, 1991, pp. 239-52.
Van Dijk, H. J. *Ezekiel's Prophecy on Tyre.* Vol. 20, *Biblica et orientalia.* Rome: Pontifical Biblical Institute, 1968.
Vanel, A. *L'iconographie du dieu de l'orage.* Vol. 3, *Cahiers de la Revue biblique.* Paris: Gabalda, 1965.
Van Gennep, A. *The Rites of Passage.* Trans. M. B. Vizedom and G. L. Caffee. Chicago: The University of Chicago Press, 1960.
Van Nouhuys, J. W. "The Anchor." *Mariner's Mirror* 37 (1951), 17-47.

Vaux, R. de. *Ancient Israel: Its Life and Institutions.* Trans. J. McHugh. London: Darton, Longman, and Todd, 1961.
Virolleaud, C. *La légende phénicienne de Danel.* Vol. I, *Mission de Ras-Shamra.* Paris: Librairie orientaliste Paul Geuthner, 1936.
—"Le dieu de la mer dans la mythologie de Ras Shamra." *Comptes rendus de l'Académie des inscriptions et belles-lettres* (1946), 498-509.
Wachsmann, S. *Seagoing Ships and Seamanship in the Bronze Age Levant.* College Station, TX: Texas A & M University Press, 1998.
Wachsmuth, D. ΠΟΜΠΙΜΟΣ Ο ΔΑΙΜΩΝ: *Untersuchung zu den Antiken Sakralhandlungen bei Seereisen.* Berlin: Ernst-Reuter-Gesellschaft, 1967.
Warmington, B. H. *Carthage.* New York: Frederick A. Praeger, 1969.
Wensinck, A. J. *The Ocean in the Literature of the Western Semites.* Amsterdam: Johannes Müller, 1918.
Westerberg, K. *Cypriote Ships from the Bronze Age to c. 500 BC.* Göteborg: Paul Åströms Förlag, 1983.
White, L. *Medieval Technology and Social Change.* London: Oxford University Press, 1962.
Whitaker, R. E. *A Concordance of the Ugaritic Literature.* Cambridge, MA: Harvard University Press, 1972.
Wiggins, S.A. "The Myth of Asherah: Lion Lady and Serpent Goddess." *UF* 23 (1991), 383-94.
Will, E. "Au sanctuaire d'Héraclès a Tyr: L'olivier enflammé, les stèles et les roches ambrosiennes." *Berytus* 10 (1952-53), 1-12.
Woolley, L. *Alalakh, an Account of the Excavations at Tell Atchana in the Hatay, 1937-1949.* Oxford: The Society of Antiquaries, 1955.
Wright, G. E. *Shechem.* New York: McGraw-Hill, 1964.
Wright, G. R. H. "Pre-Israelite Temples in the Land of Canaan." *PEQ* 103 (1971), 17-32.
—*Ancient Building in South Syria and Palestine.* 2 vols. Leiden: E. J. Brill, 1985.
Xella, P. *Baal Hammon.* Vol. 32, *Collezione di studi fenici.* Rome: Consiglio nazionale delle ricerche, 1991.
Yadin, Y. "Symbols of Deities at Zinjirli, Carthage and Hazor." In *Near Eastern Archaeology in the Twentieth Century,* ed. J. A. Sanders. Garden City, NY: Doubleday, 1970, pp. 199-231.
—*Hazor.* London: Oxford University Press, 1972.
—"New Gleanings on Reshef from Ugarit." In *Biblical and Related Studies Presented to Samuel Iwry,* eds. A. Kort and S. Morschauser. Winona Lake, IN: Eisenbrauns, 1985, pp. 259-74.
Yon, M. "Sanctuaires d'Ougarit." In *Travaux de la Maison de l'Orient,* vol. 7, *Temples et sanctuaires,* ed. G. Roux. Lyon: GIS-Maison de l'Orient, 1984, pp. 37-50.
—"Cultes phéniciens à Chypre: L'interprétation chypriote." In *StudPhoen,* vol. IV, *Religio Phoenicia.* Namur: Société des études classiques, 1986, pp. 127-52.
—"Stèles de pierre." In *Ras Shamra-Ougarit,* vol. VI, *Arts et industries de la pierre,* ed. M. Yon. Paris: ERC, 1991, pp. 273-344.
—"Ougarit et ses relations avec les regions maritimes voisines." In *Ugarit and the Bible.* Vol. 11, *Ugaritish-Biblische Literatur,* eds. G. J. Brooke, A. H. W. Curtis, and J. F. Healey. Münster: Ugarit-Verlag, 1994, pp. 421-39.
Zimmerli, W. *Ezekiel 2.* Trans. J. D. Martin. Philadelphia: Fortress, 1983.

LIST OF FIGURES

1. Goddess riding on crescent, gold pendant, Minet el-Beida (after Negbi, 1976, fig. 117).
2. Goddess with crescents in headdress, riding on lioness, gold pendant, Minet el-Beida (after Negbi, 1976, fig. 118).
3. Goddess riding on lioness, gold pendant, Minet el-Beida (after Negbi, 1976, fig. 119).
4. *Qudšu* stela, Egypt (after *ANEP*, fig. 471).
5. *Qudšu* stela, Egypt (after *ANEP*, fig. 472).
6. *Qudšu* stela, Egypt (after *ANEP*, fig. 473).
7. Head of goddess over rudders of opposed ships, cylinder seal (after Teissier, 1996, fig. 206).
8. Goddess riding on lionesses, god sitting on bull calf, cylinder seal, Minet el-Beida (after Schaeffer-Forrer, 1983, p. 16).
9. Palm tree flanked by goats, riding on lioness, painted pithos, Kuntillet ʿAjrûd (after Keel, 1992, fig. 219).
10. Ship with storm god and totem animals, cylinder seal, Tell el-Dabʿa (after Porada, 1984, ill. 1).
11. Goddess symbols on coins, Carthage (after L. Müller, 1861, nos. 32 & 284).
12. Sign of Tinnit on clay pellet (after Gubel, 1993, fig. 27).
13. Crescent-and-disk motif combined with the sign of Tinnit, three sacrificial stelae, Carthage (after Hours-Miedan, 1950, pl. VI.e,h,j).
14. Tinnit on a dolphin, sacrificial stela, Constantine (after Bertrandy, 1987, no. 2).
15. Tinnit and fish, sacrificial stela, Carthage (after Hours-Miedan, 1950, pl. XXIII.e).
16. Signs of Tinnit and caduceus on ship's standards, sacrificial stela, Carthage (after Bartoloni, 1979, pl. LXI.a).
17. Sign of Tinnit and anchor, sacrificial stela (after Bertrandy, 1987, no. 92).
18. Caduceus on ship's prow, sacrificial stela, Carthage (after Hours-Miedan, 1950, pl. XXXIX.d).
19. Ship's stern with enshrined figurine, sacrificial stela, Carthage (after Hours-Miedan, 1950, pl. XXXIX.c).
20. Ship's rudder, dolphin, and sign of Tinnit, sacrificial stela, Carthage (after Hours-Miedan, 1950, pl. XXXVIII.f).
21. Warship with lioness headed prow, riding on hippokamp, coin, Byblos (after Moscati, 1988, p. 72).
22. Warship with horse headed prow, riding on hippokamp, coin, Byblos (after Babelon, 1910, no. 858).
23. "Marine god" on his hippokamp, coin, Tyre (after Dussaud, 1946-48, fig. 3).
24. Smiting god on prow of Phoenician warship, tomb painting, Kef el-Blida (after Ferron, 1968, p. 52).
25. Milqart on metal bowl, and on razor from the necropolis of Saint Monica (after Barnett, 1969, fig. 1; Bonnet, 1988, pl. IV, fig. 11).
26. Milqart on seals (after Culican, 1960-61, figs. 1.a,b).
27. Milqart on inscribed stela, Aleppo (after Cornelius, fig. 31c).
28. Greek Herakles on a raft, seal (after Courbaud, 1892, p. 274).
29. Phoenician fishtailed creature, seal (after Bordreuil, 1986, no. 28).

30. Greek Herakles battles fishtailed creature, Attic red-figured vase (after Shepard, 1940, fig. 55).
31. Phoenician fishtailed creature, coin, Aradus (after Dussaud, 1946-48, fig. 1).
32. Greek Herakles battles fishtailed creature, Attic red-figured vase (after Shepard, 1940, fig. 54).
33. Byblos, architectural overview (after Saghieh, 1983, plan II).
34. Byblos, stone anchors from Tower Temple (after Frost, 1969a, figs. 23-28).
35. Byblos, stone anchors from Temple of Obelisks (after Frost, 1969a, figs. 1-4).
36. Byblos, stone anchors from the Sacred Enclosure (after Frost, 1969a, figs. 17-22).
37. Byblos, bronze model ship with rudder from votive cache, Field of Offerings (after Dunand, 1937-58, pl. LXIX, no. 10089).
38. Byblos, two bronze model ships from votive cache, Field of Offerings (after Dunand, 1937-58, pl. LXXIV, nos. 10642 & 10643).
39. Byblos, two of ten bronze model ships from votive cache, Temple of Obelisks (after Dunand, 1937-58, fig. 874, nos. 15069 & 15070).
40. Byblos, stone anchor from Necropolis "K" (after Salles, 1980, pl. 28.1).
41. Ugarit, plan showing distribution of anchors on the tell and concentration around the Temple of Baʿl (after Frost, 1991, pl. I.a).
42. Ugarit, stone anchors from Temple of Baʿl (after Frost, 1991, pl. III.1-6).
43. Ugarit, plan showing the find spots of anchors from the Temple of Baʿl (after Frost, 1991, pl. I.b).
44. Ugarit, stone anchors from Temple of Baʿl (after Frost, 1991, pl. IV.7-9, 11-16).
45. Ugarit, plan of Temple of Baʿl (1) and Temple of Dagnu (2) on the acropolis of the site (after Yon, 1984, fig. 2).
46. Stone anchors from graves at Ugarit (22) and Minet el-Beida (36 &37) (after Frost, 1991, pl. VII, no. 22 & pl. X, nos. 36 & 37).
47. Anchor 36 in situ in grave, Minet el-Beida (after Frost, 1991, pl. X, no. 36a).
48. Kition-Bamboula, second phase of Cypro-Archaic sanctuary with votive weight anchor (after Caubet, 1984, fig. 2).
49. Kition-Bamboula, third phase of Cypro-Archaic sanctuary with votive stone anchor stock (after Caubet, 1984, fig. 5).
50. Kition-Bamboula, find spots of weight anchor (K80) and anchor stock (K81), and details of both anchors (after Frost, 1982, figs. 1, 3, & 5).
51. Tell Sūkās, tripartite sanctuary with anchor in "holy of holies" (after Riis, 1970, fig. 23).
52. Tell Taʿyinat, tripartite temple (after Haines, 1971, pl. 103).
53. ʿAin Dara, tripartite temple (after Abou-Assaf, 1990, Ab. 14).
54. Nahariyah, site plan showing isolated nature of sanctuary and proximity to the sea and freshwater spring at water's edge; detailed plan of shrine (after Ben-Dor, 1950, figs. 2 & 3).
55. Ashkelon, artist's rendition of shrine outside city rampart showing proximity to the northern gate and the sea (after Stager, 1991, p. 4).
56. Tel Mevorakh, map of site and possible Late Bronze Age roadways, detail of temple (after Stern, 1984, figs. II & V).
57. Makmish ("Northeastern Hillock"), site plan showing distance from Tel Michal ("Northern Hill" & "High Tell"), the sea, and nearby rivulet (after Herzog, 1989, fig. 1.2).
58. Tell Sūkās, plan of sanctuary isolated from settlement (after Riis, 1979, fig. 220).
59. Kommos, plan of isolated shrine near coast (after Shaw, 1989, fig. 3).

List of Figures 127

60. Capo San Marco, plan of promontory temple (after Barreca, 1958, fig. 1).
61. Capo San Marco, map showing location of promontory temple (marked as "Archaic temple") away from the main features of the city of Tharros (after Moscati, 1988, p. 220).
62. Ras ed-Drek, map showimg location of temple on promontory and a detailed plan of the sacred building (after Fantar, 1983, figs. 3 & 7).
63. Phoenician horseheaded vessels, wall reliefs, Khorsabad (after Moscati, 1988, p. 40).
64. Phoenician horseheaded vessels, bronze gate bands, Balawat (after Moscati, 1988, p. 559).
65. Phoenician ships with anthropomorphic figures and apotropaic eyes at their prows, coins (after Basch, 1969, figs. 18, 19, 22, 23-25).
66. Phoenician ships with crescent-and-disk standards at their stern, coins (after Basch, 1969, figs. 13, 14) and a detail of crescent and crescent and disk stern standards, coins (after Svoronos, 1914, fig. A.11-13).
67. Symbols of boats, anchors, and rudders on sacrificial stelae, Carthage (after Hours-Miedan, 1950, pls. XXXVIII. a,b,c,e,g & XXXIX.a,e).
68. Canaanite figurine of a goddess, bronze with gold foil, Uluburun shipwreck (after Haldane, 1993).
69. Detail of figurine in shrine at the stern of a vessel, sacrificial stela, Carthage (after Bartoloni, 1977, fig. 4.c).
70. Detail of figure and apotropaic eye at prow, sacrificial stela, Carthage (after Bartoloni, 1977, fig. 4.a).
71. Stone anchor used as sacrificial stela in probable tophet, Tyre (after Seeden, 1991, fig. 19).
72. Two terra-cotta model ships from graves, Achziv (after Göttlicher, 1978, figs. 102 & 103).
73. Nautical relief from the mortuary complex of Sahu-Re, Abusir (after Basch, 1987, fig. 70).
74. Nautical scene depicted on a funerary causeway of the Pharaoh Ounas, Sakkara (after Basch, 1985, fig. 2).
75. Maritime scene carved on scapula, Tel Dor (after Stern, 1994, fig. 8).
76. Canaanite ships docking in Egypt, painting from tomb of Kenamun, Thebes (after Davies, 1947, pl. 8).
77. Kition, map showing location of promontory temple in relation to the ancient settlement (after Caubet, 1986, fig. 1).
78. Stone anchor from Middle Bronze IIB burial, Tel Akko, scale 1:5.
79. Stone anchor from Middle Bronze IIB-IIC structural tomb, Tel Ashkelon.

FIGURES

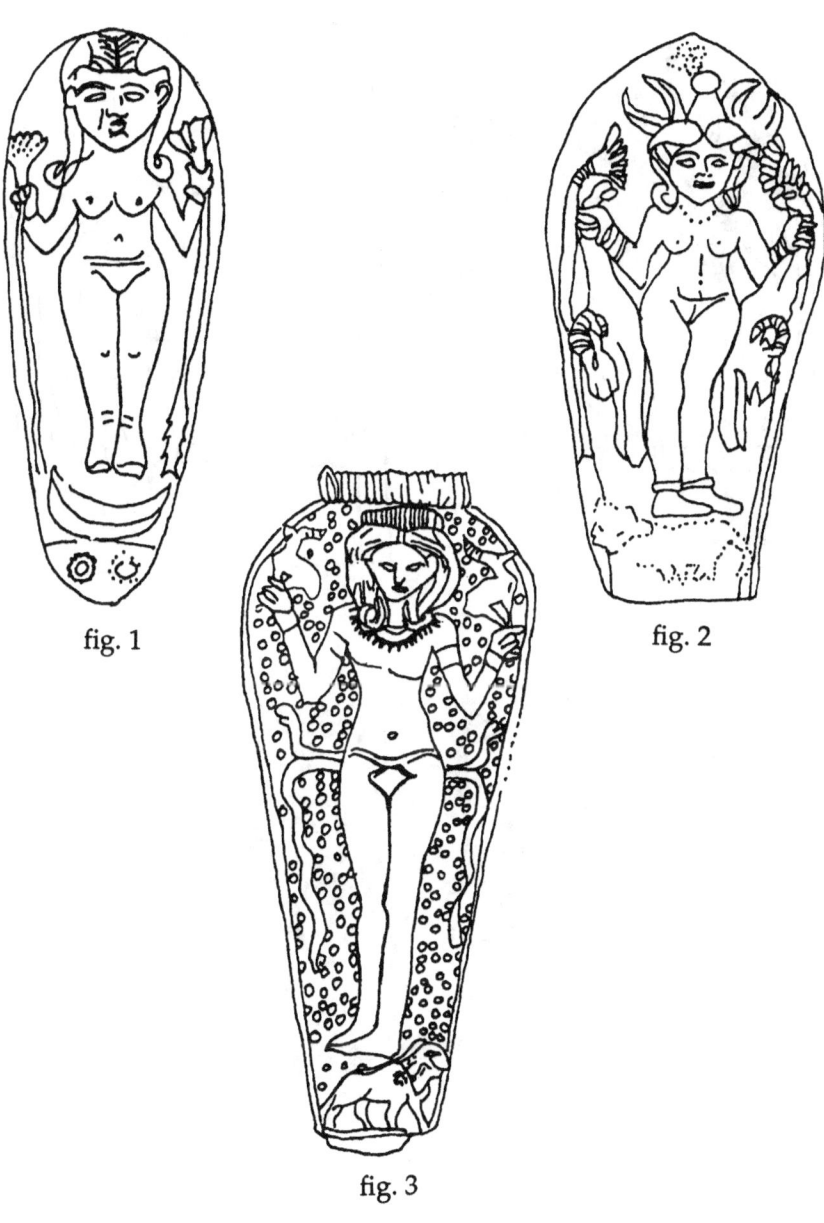

fig. 1

fig. 2

fig. 3

130   Each Man Cried Out to His God

fig. 4

fig. 5

fig. 6

Figures

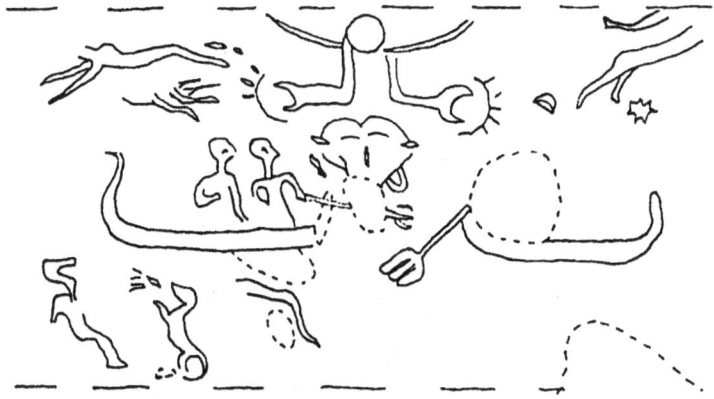

fig. 7

fig. 8

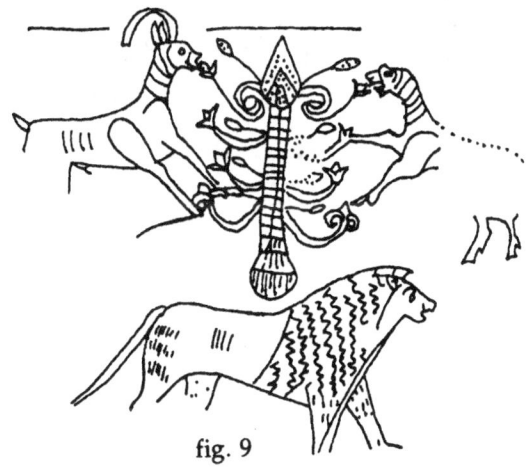

fig. 9

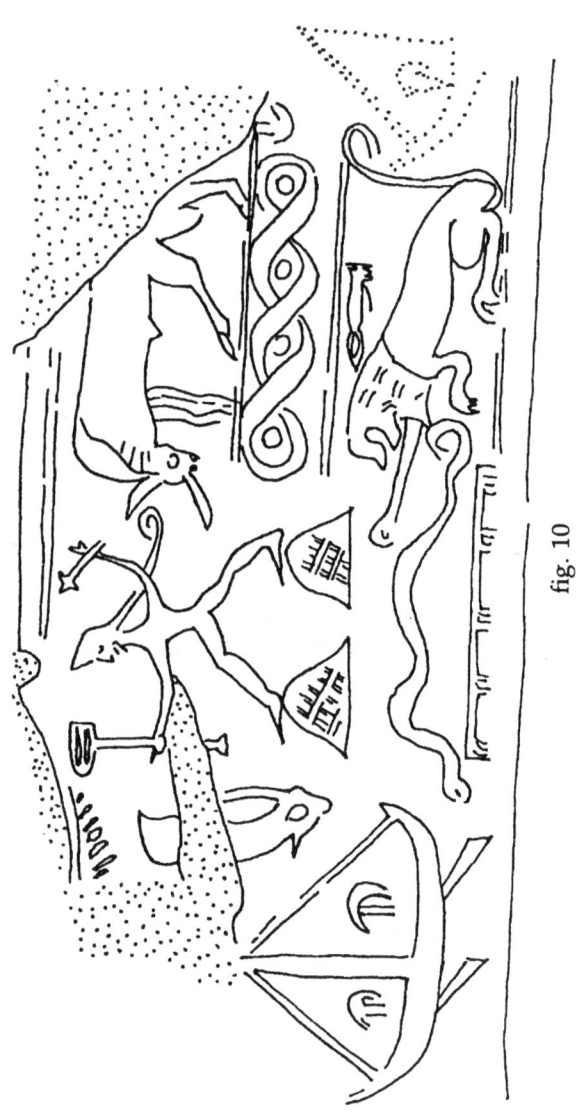

fig. 10

Figures

fig. 11

fig. 12

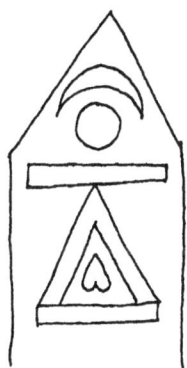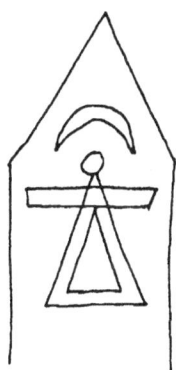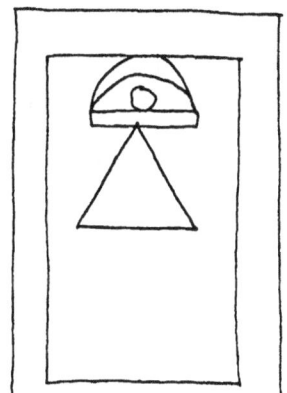

fig. 13

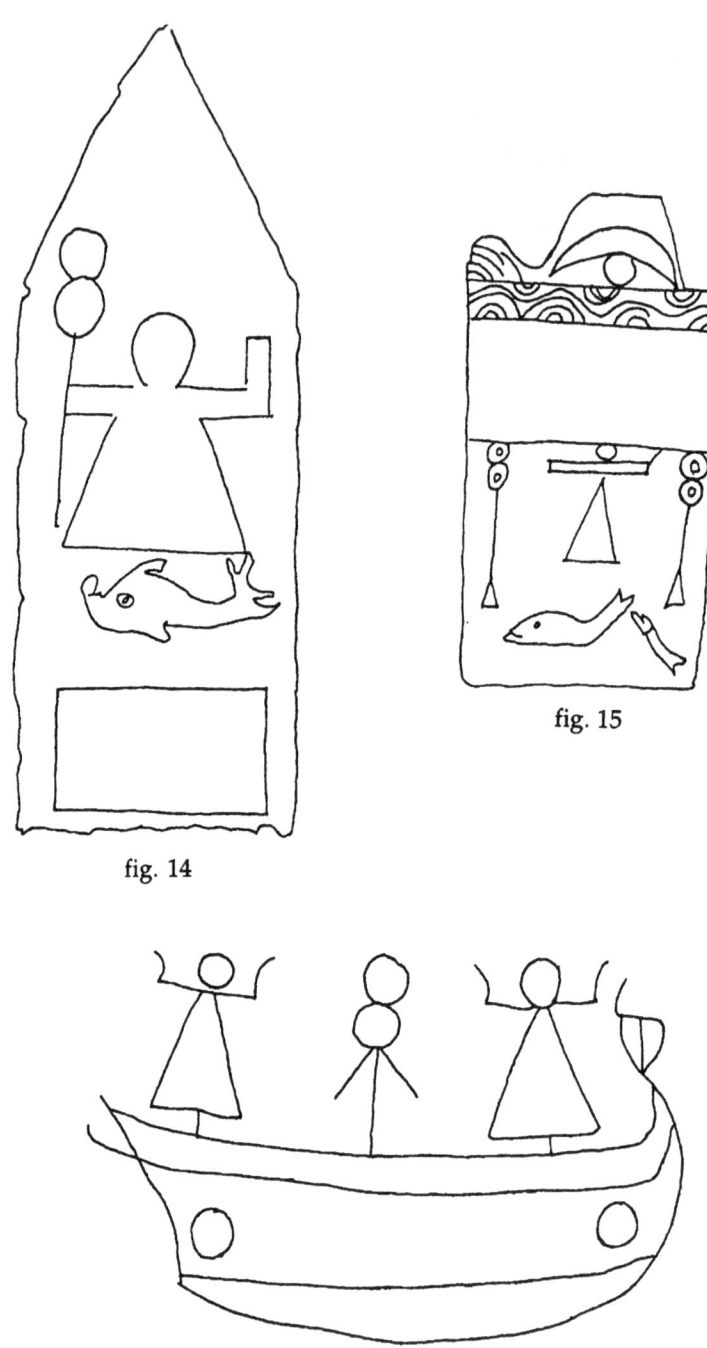

fig. 14

fig. 15

fig. 16

Figures

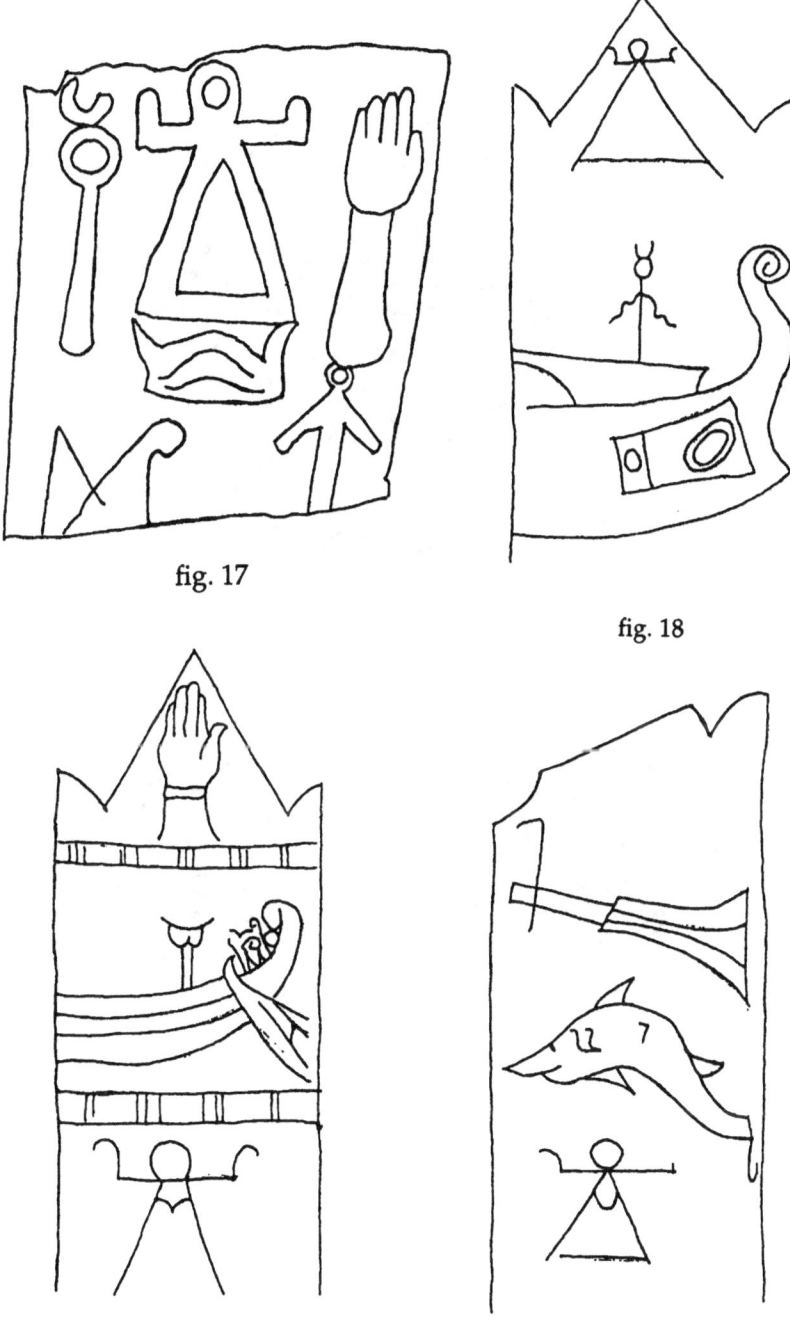

fig. 17

fig. 18

fig. 19

fig. 20

fig. 21

fig. 22

fig. 23

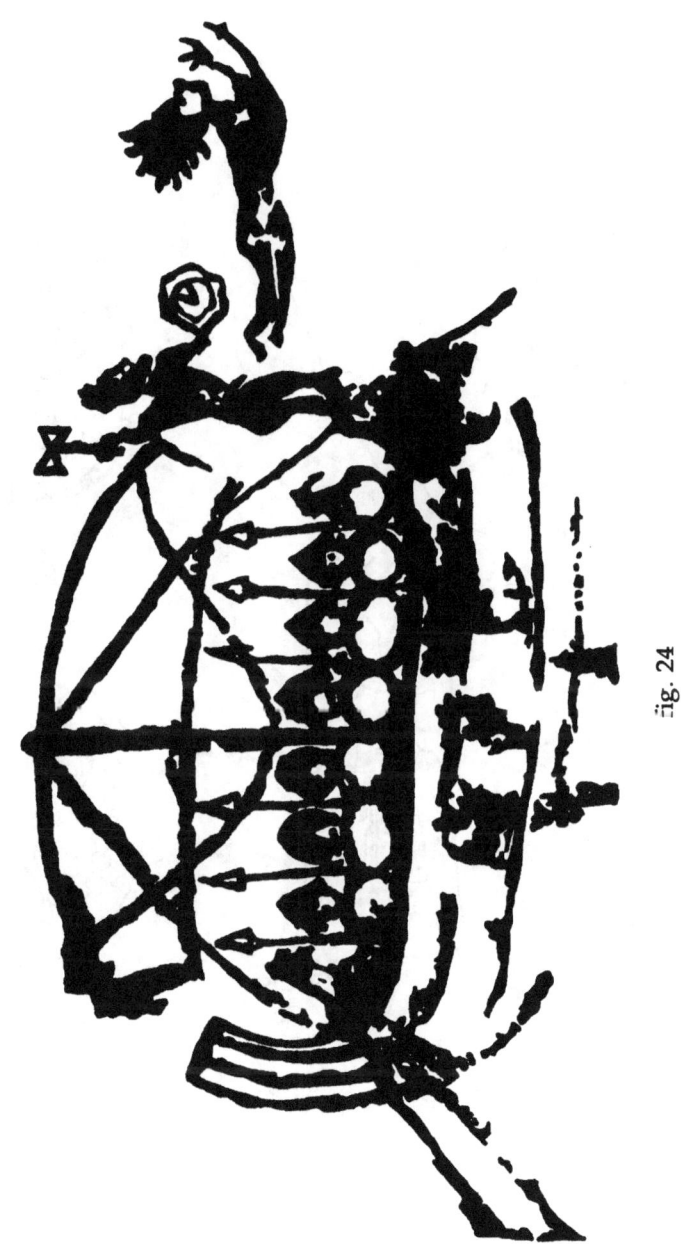

Fig. 24

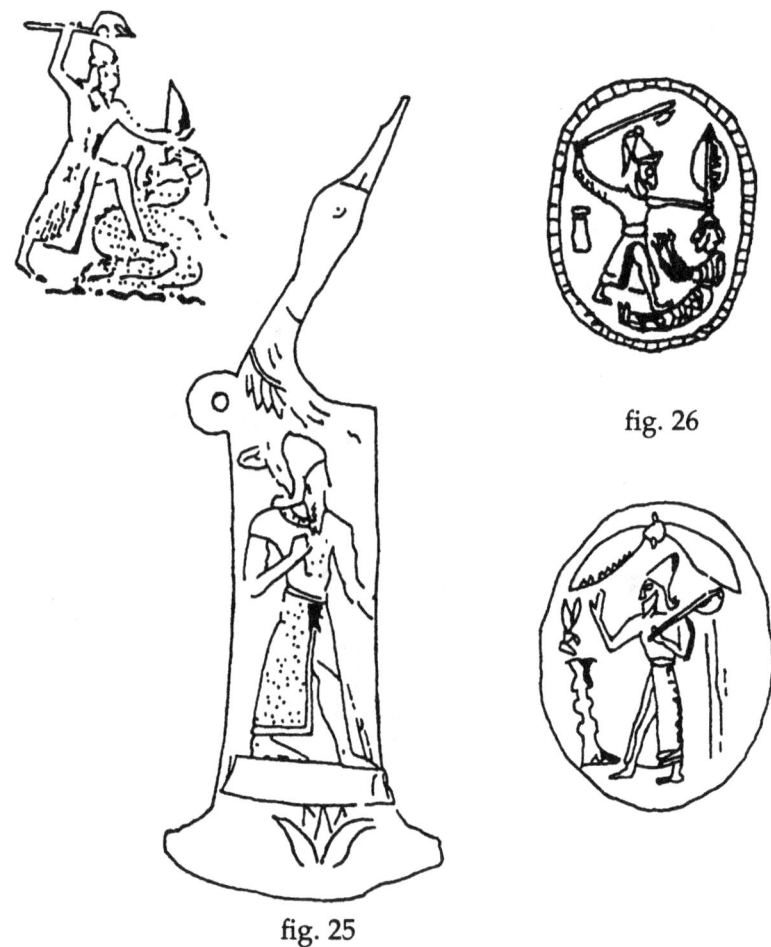

fig. 25

fig. 26

Figures

fig. 27

fig. 28

fig. 29

fig. 30

fig. 31

fig. 32

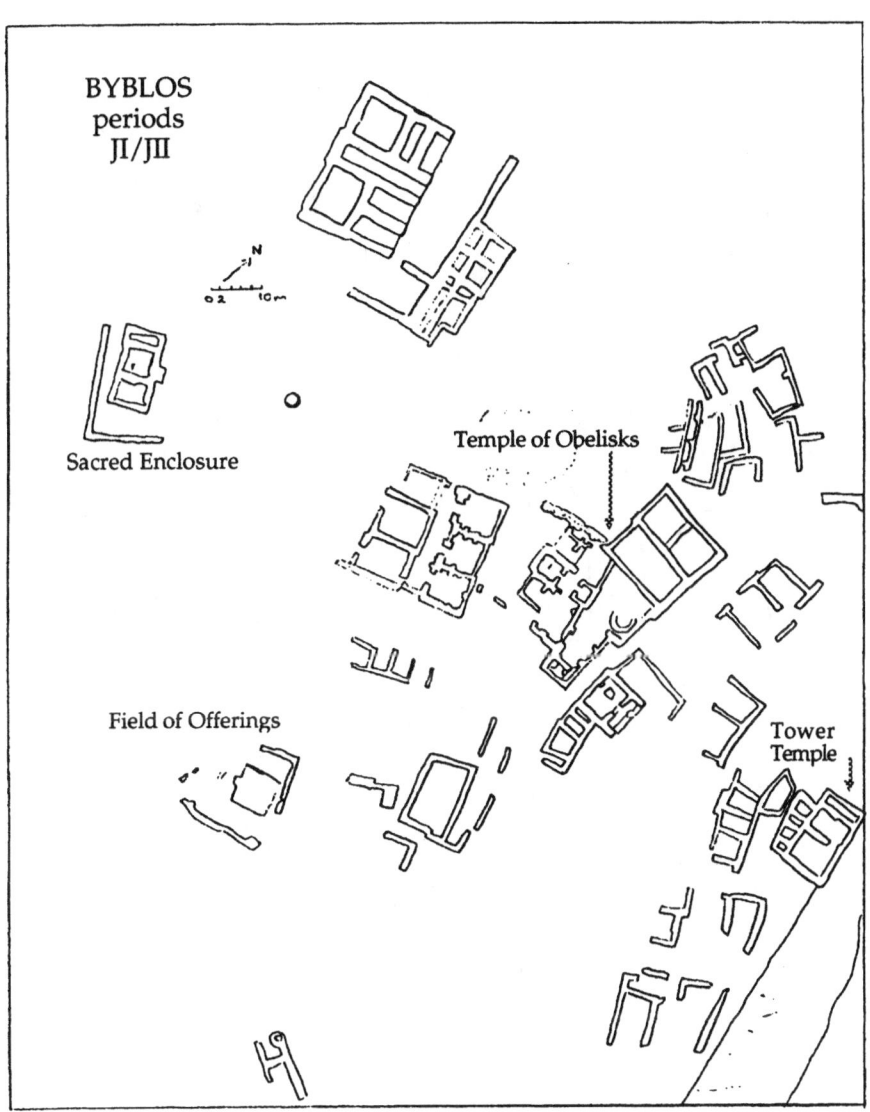

fig. 33

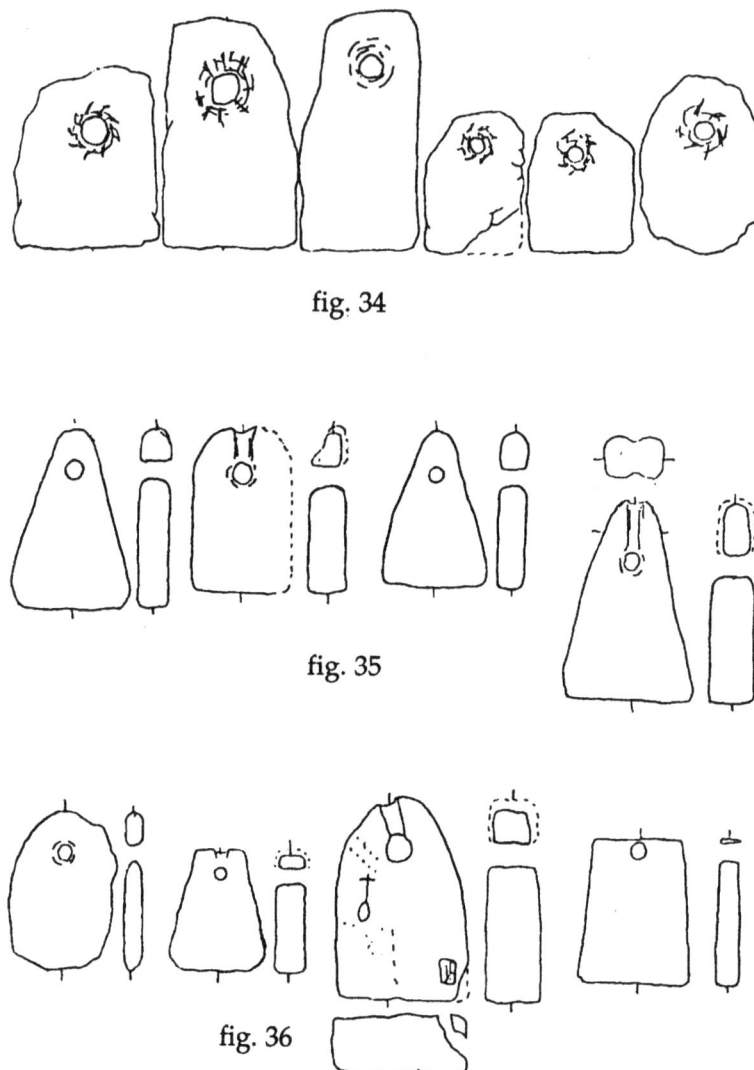

fig. 34

fig. 35

fig. 36

Figures

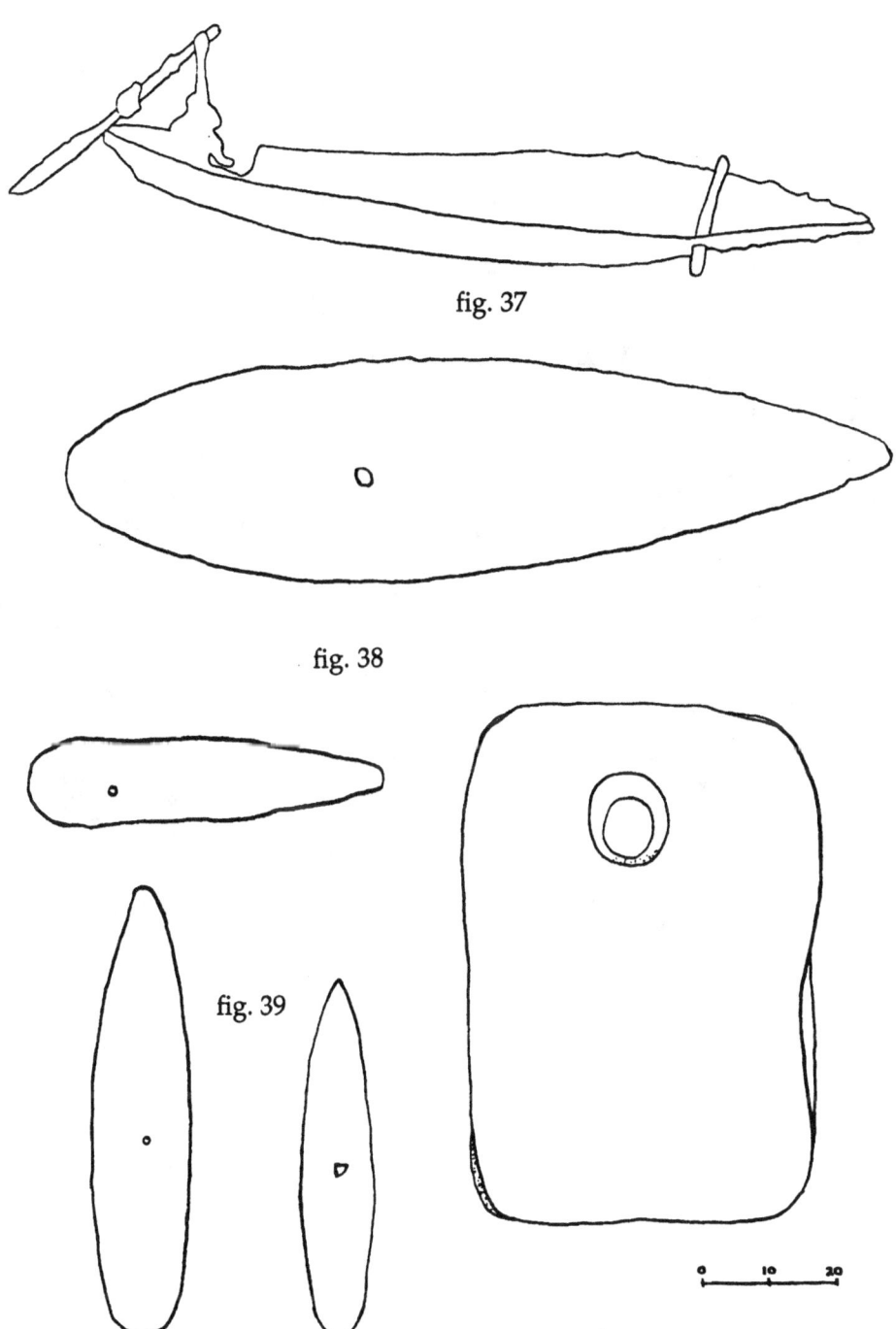

fig. 37

fig. 38

fig. 39

fig. 40

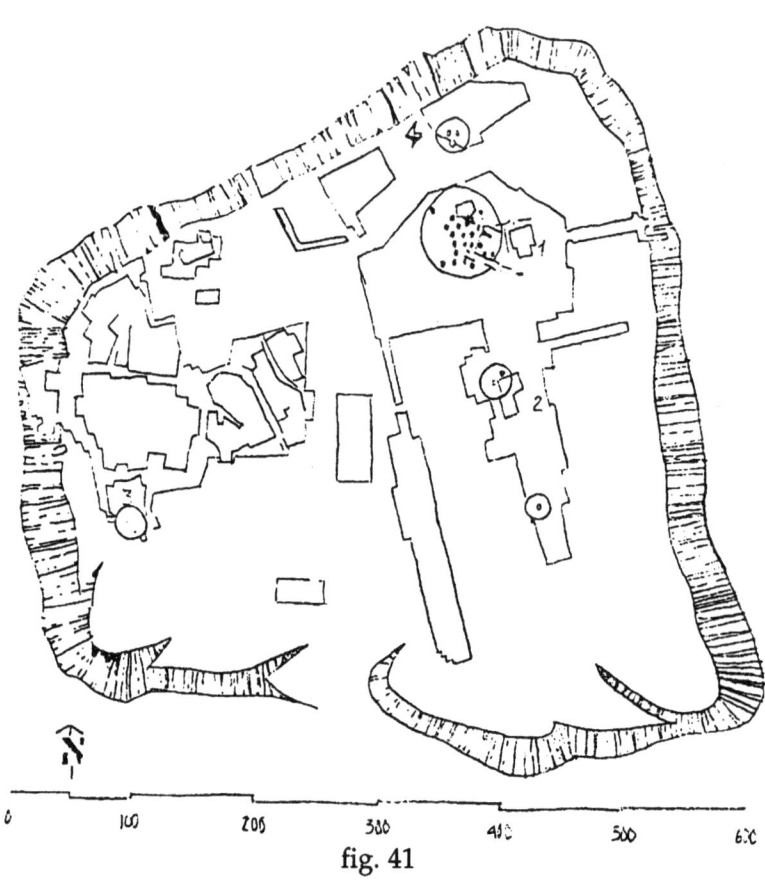
fig. 41

Figures

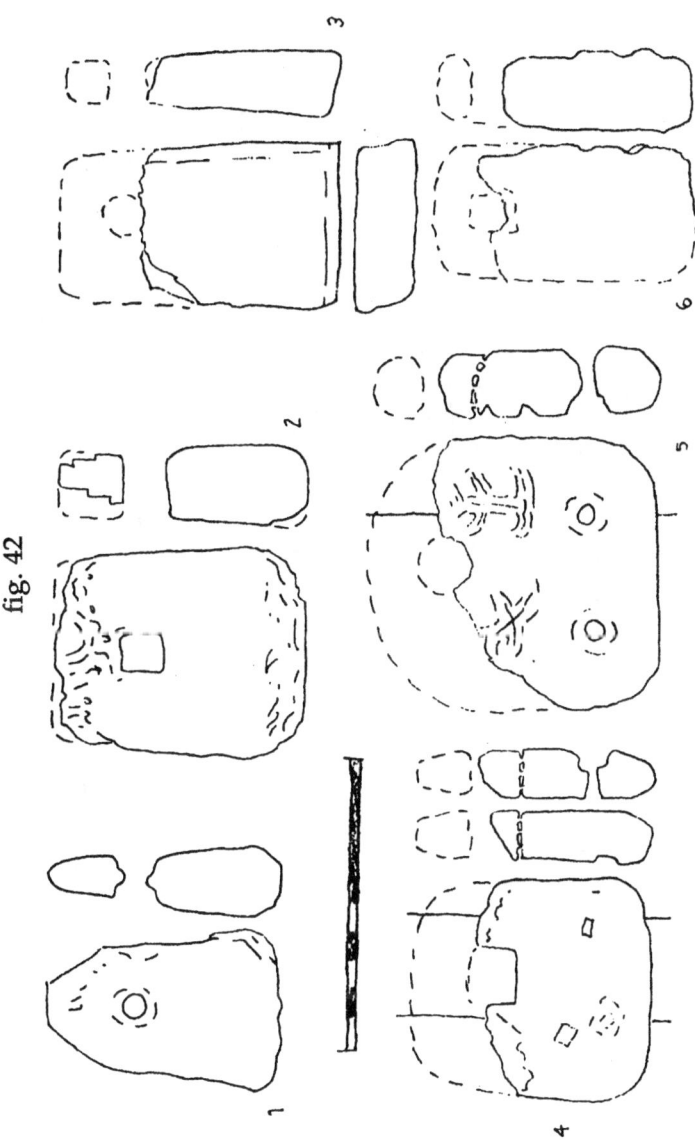

fig. 42

146   Each Man Cried Out to His God

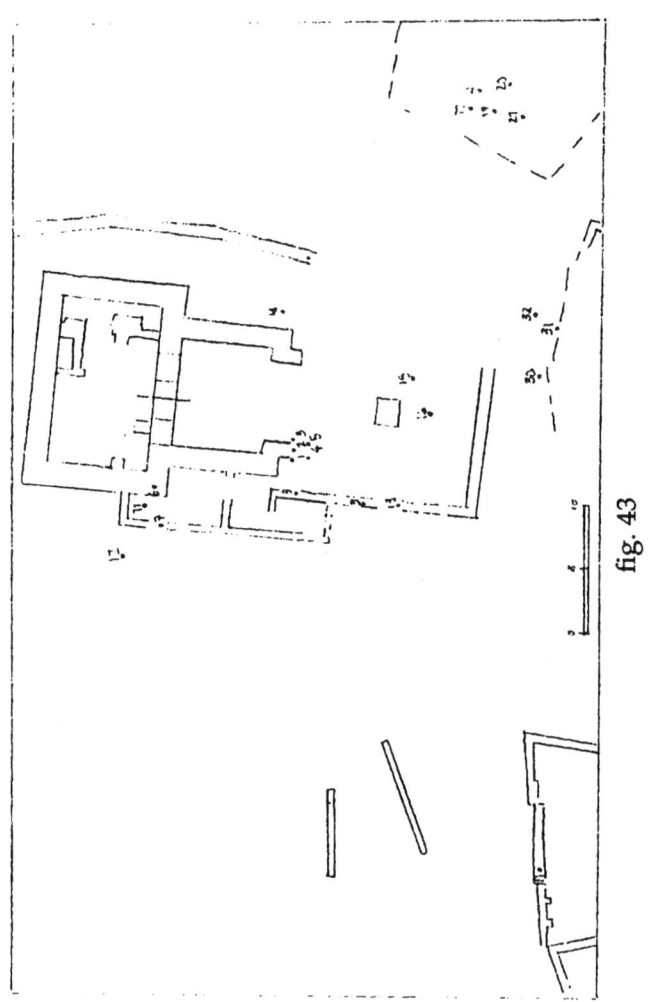

fig. 43

Figures

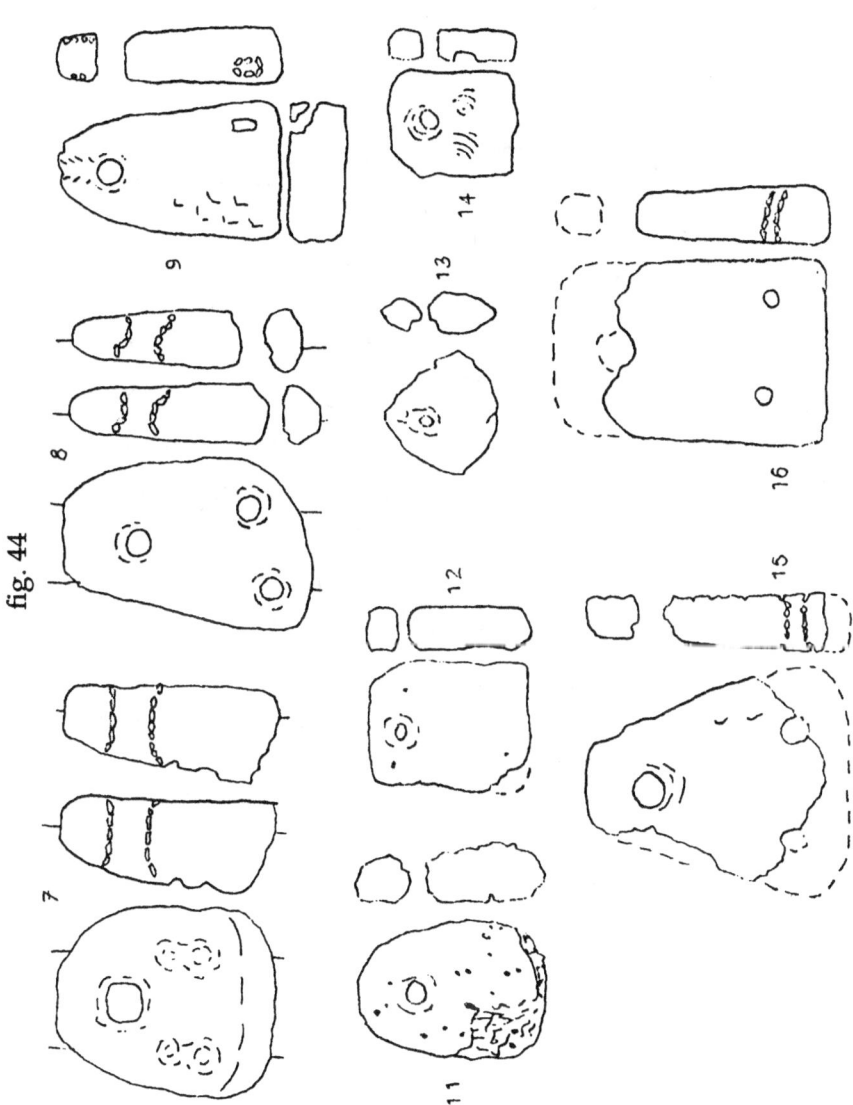

fig. 44

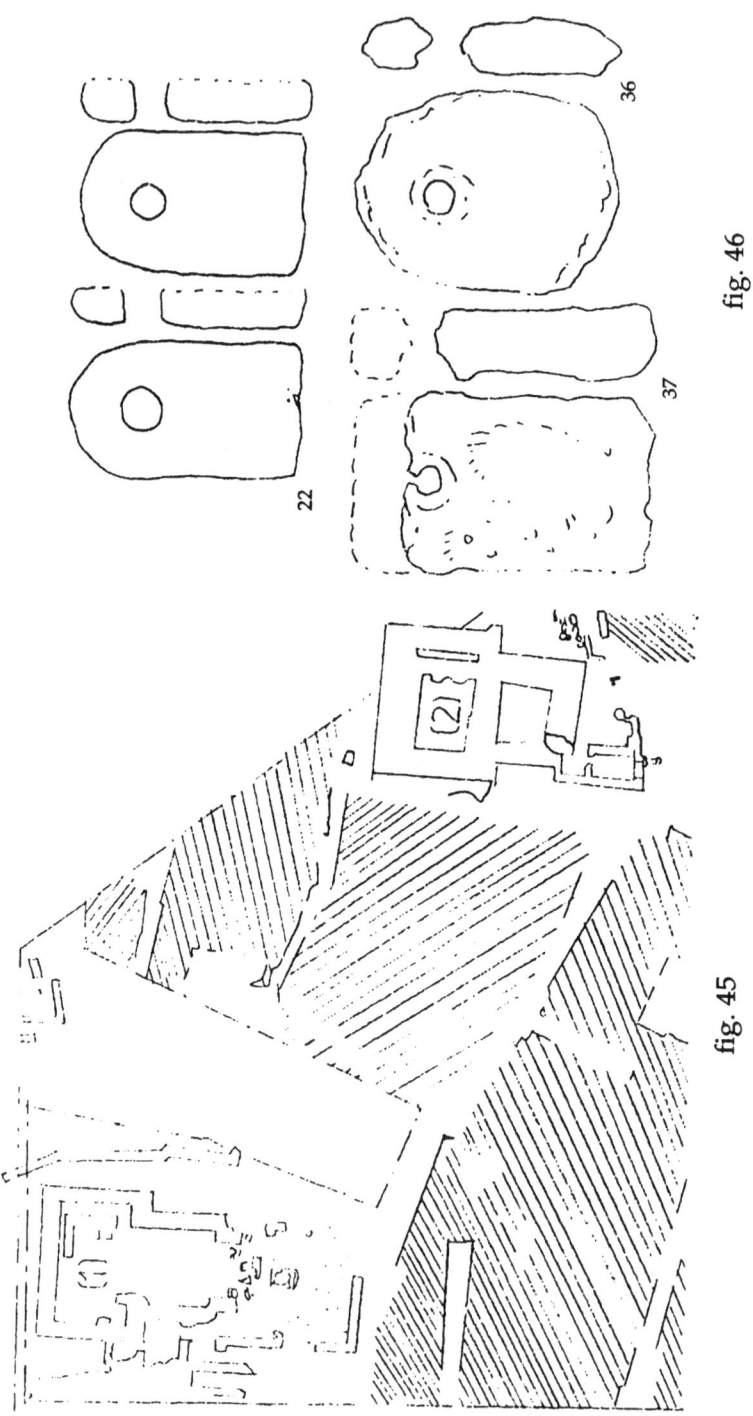

fig. 46

fig. 45

Figures

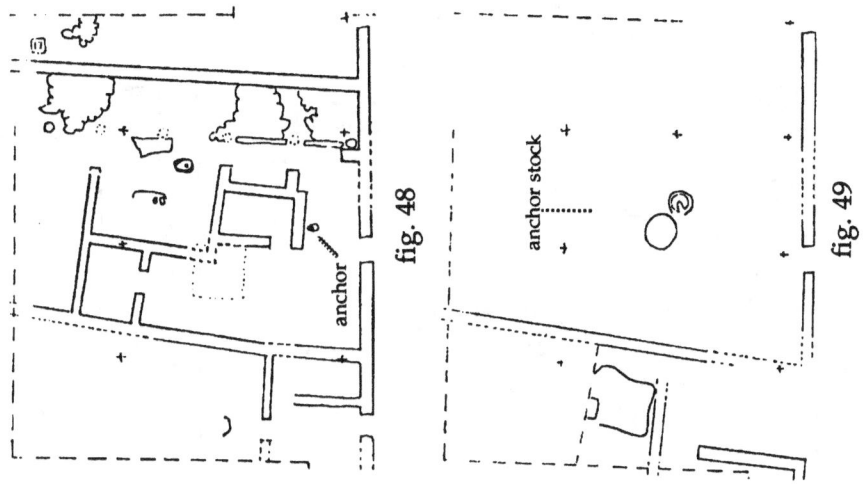

fig. 48

fig. 49

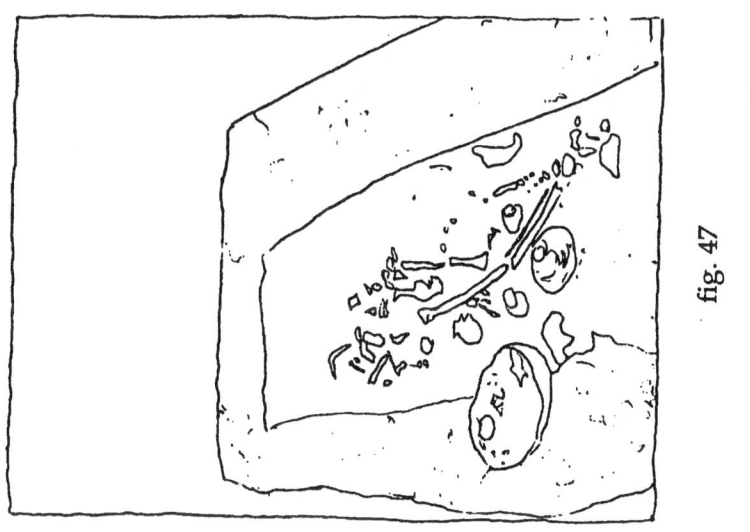

fig. 47

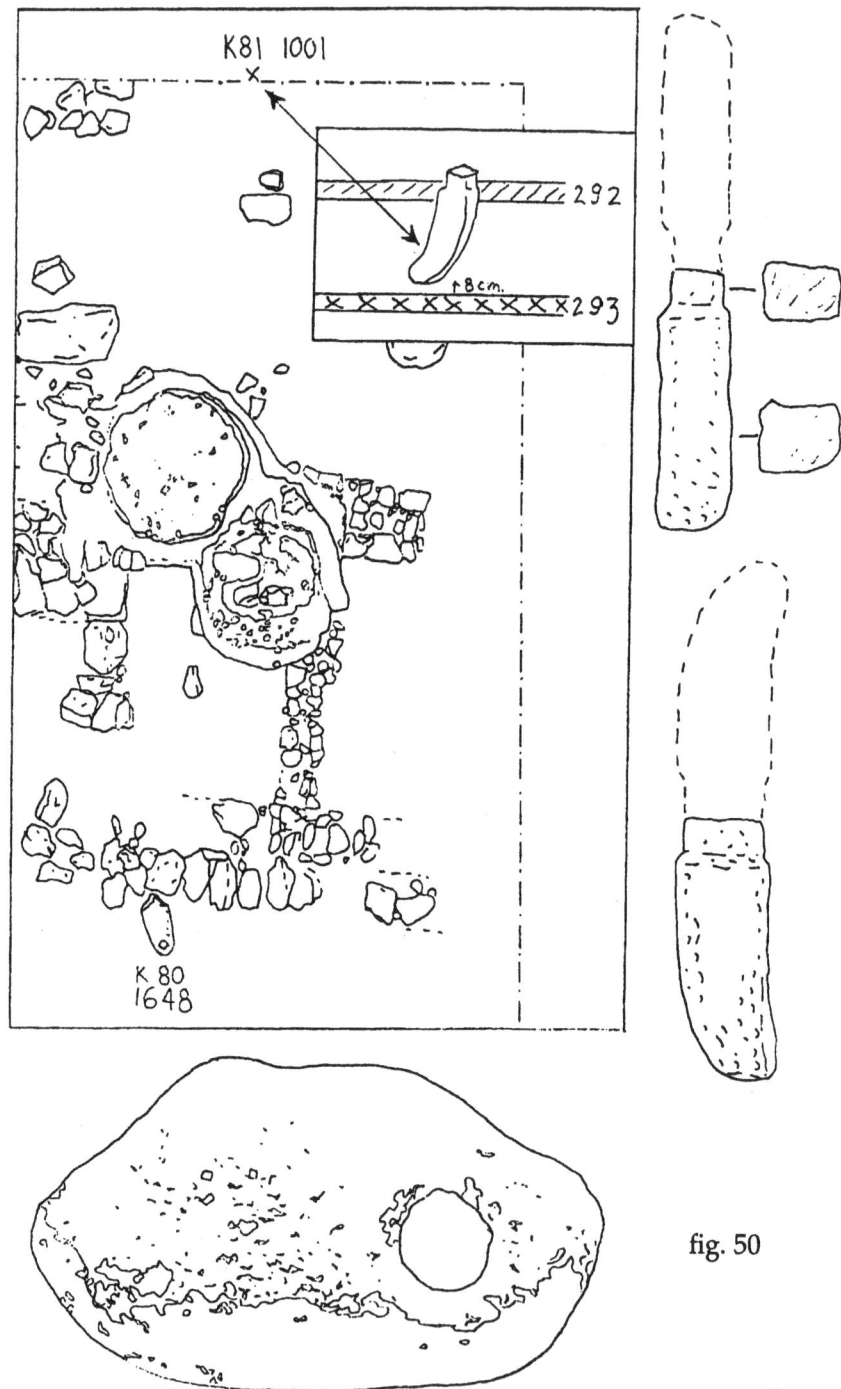

fig. 50

Figures

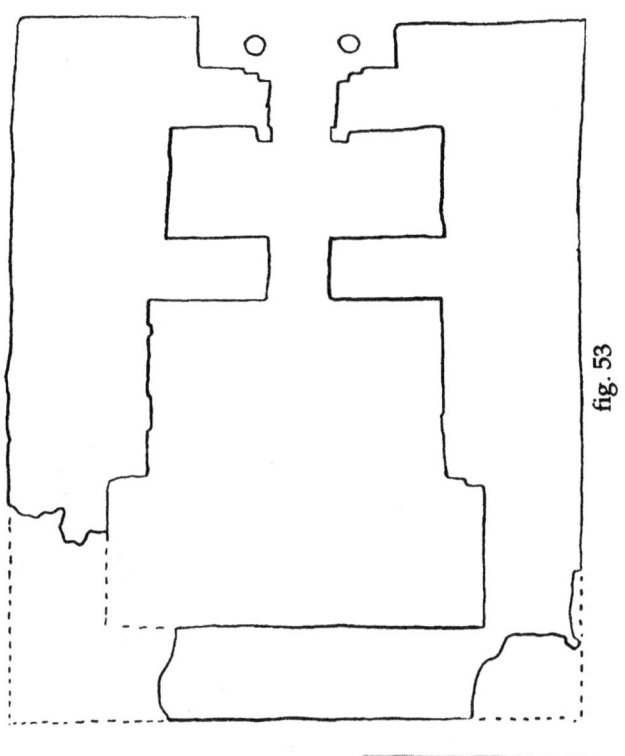

fig. 53

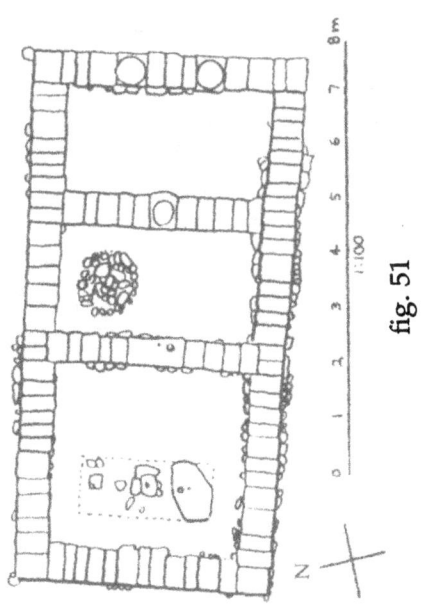

fig. 51

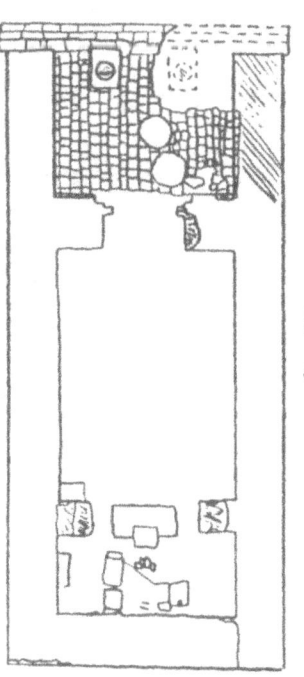

fig. 52

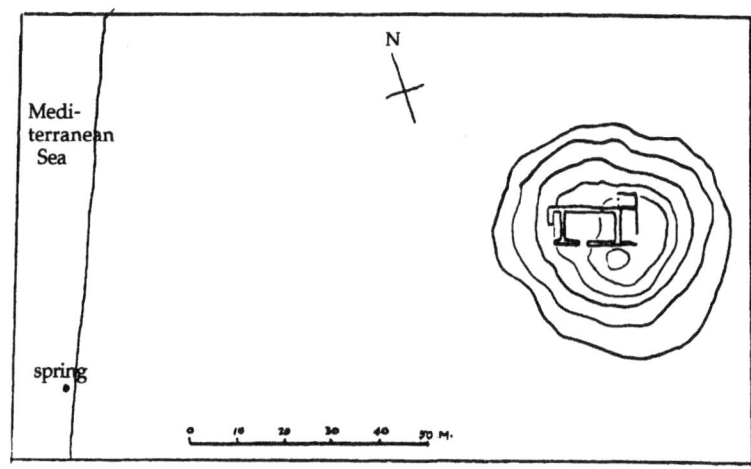

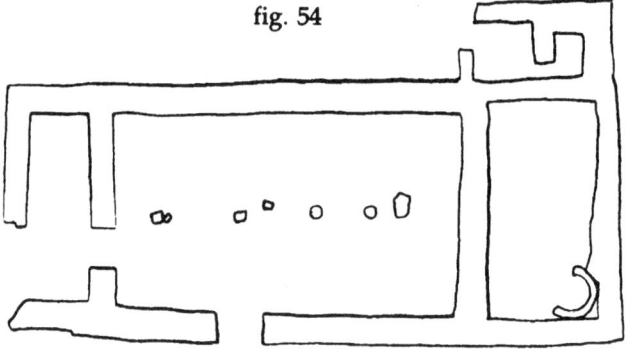

fig. 54

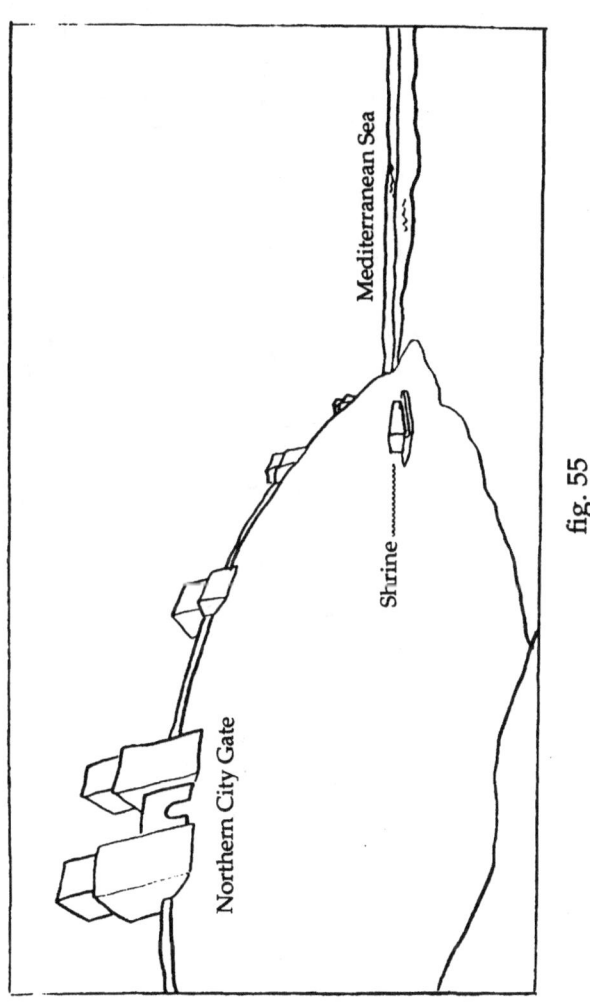

fig. 55

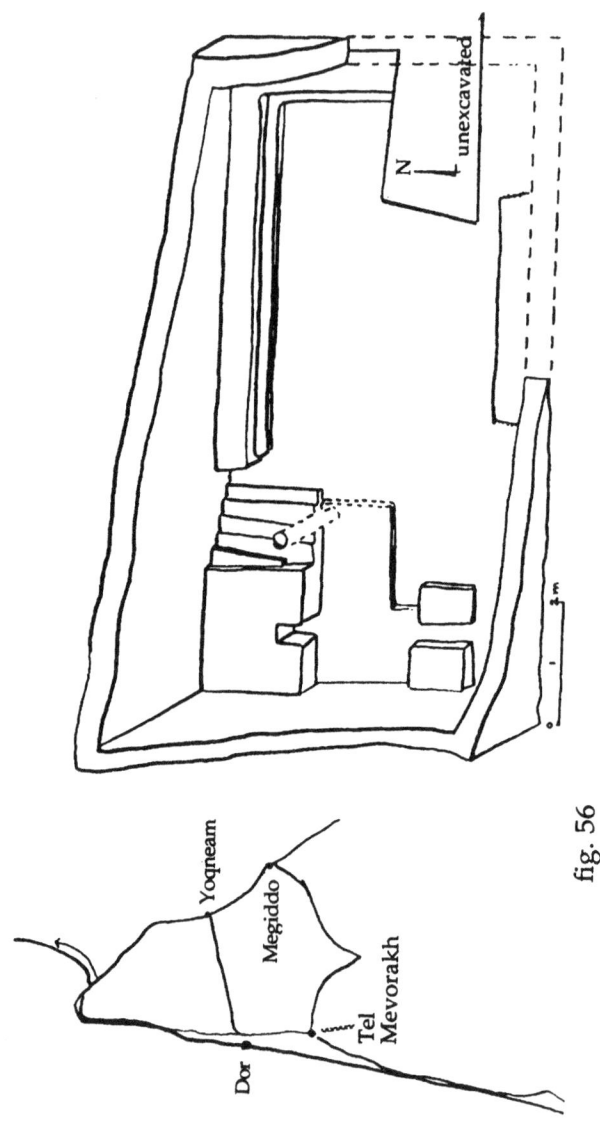

fig. 56

Figures 155

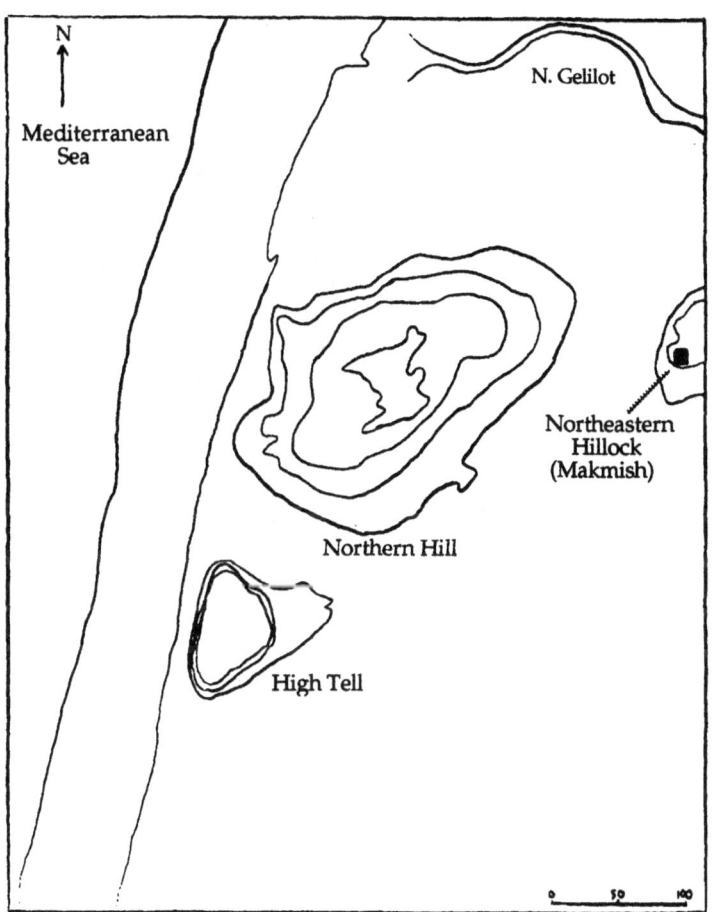

fig. 57

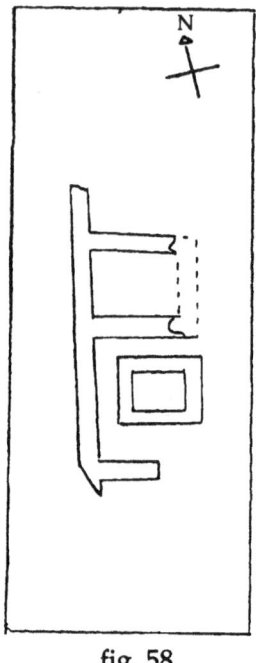

fig. 58

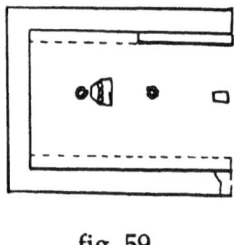

fig. 59

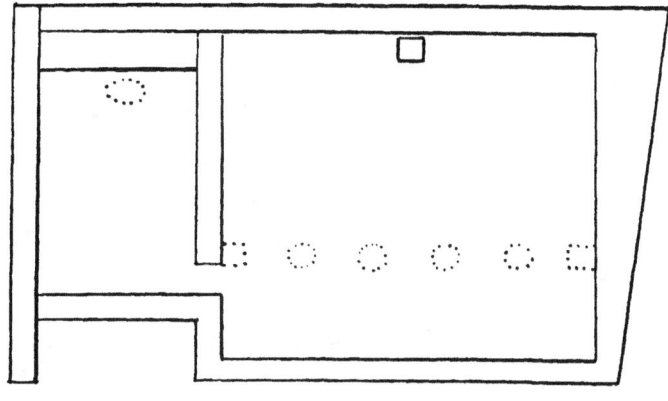

fig. 60

fig. 61

158 Each Man Cried Out to His God

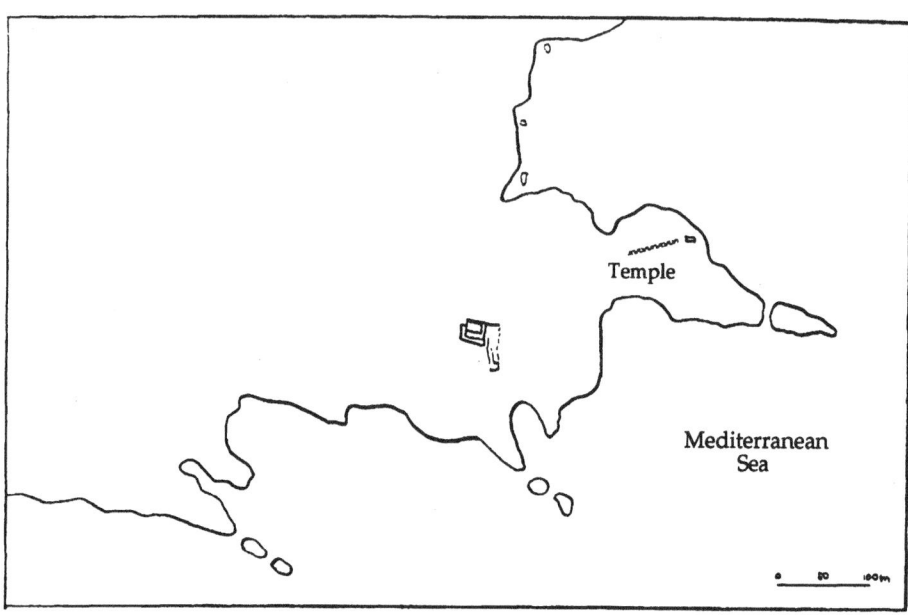

fig. 62

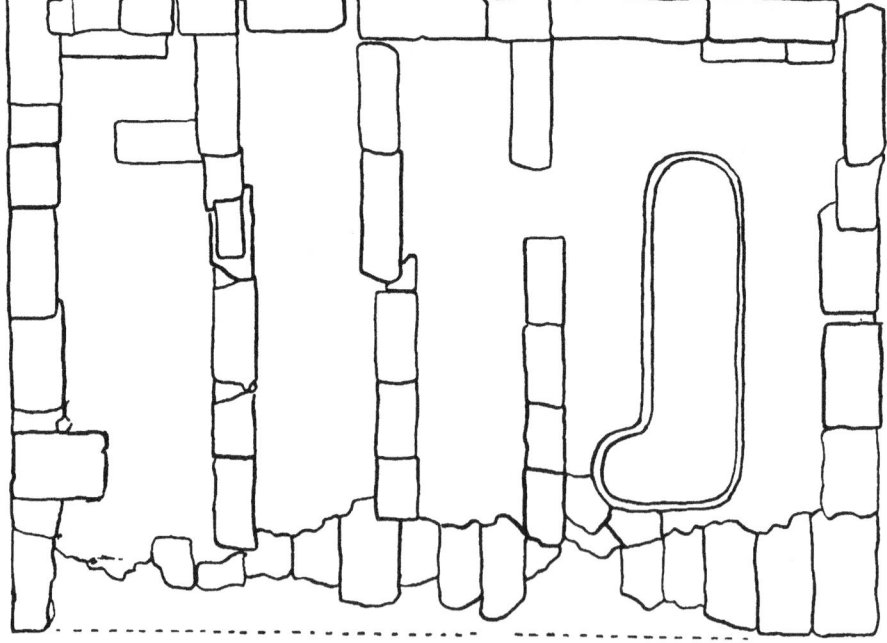

Figures

fig. 63

fig. 64

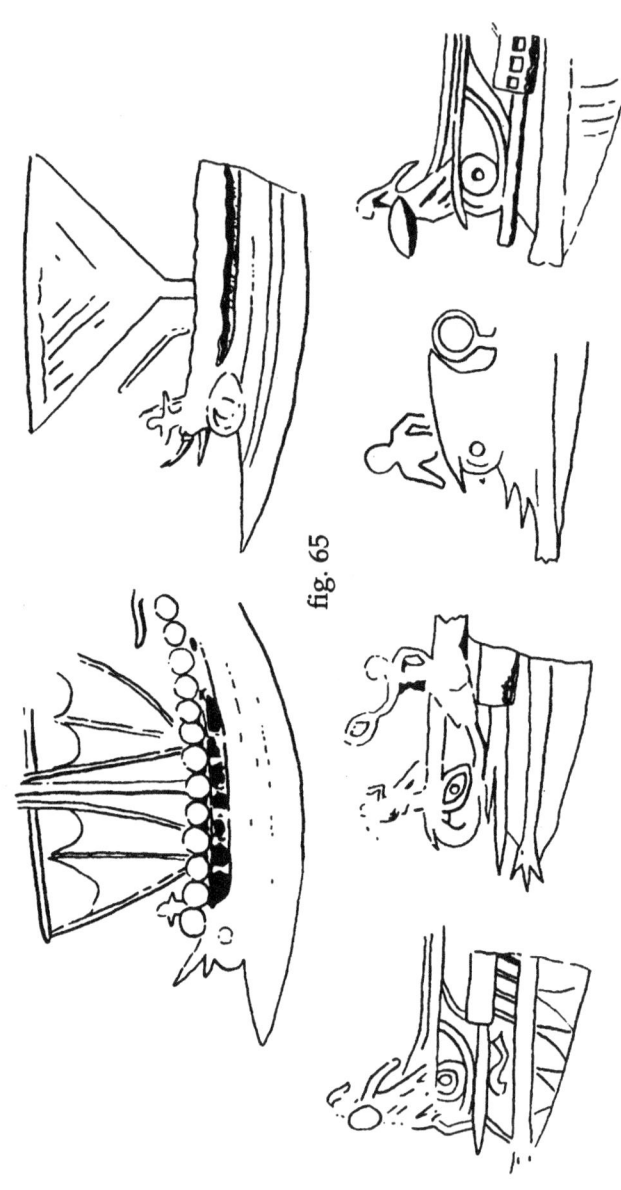

fig. 65

Figures

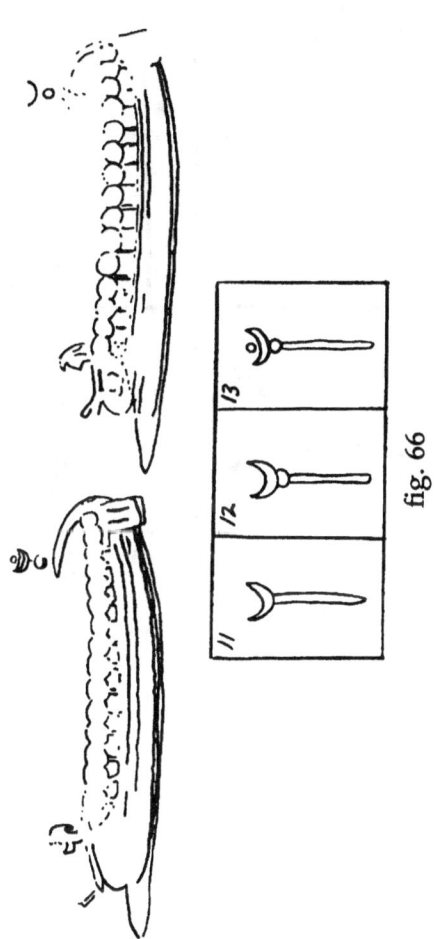

fig. 66

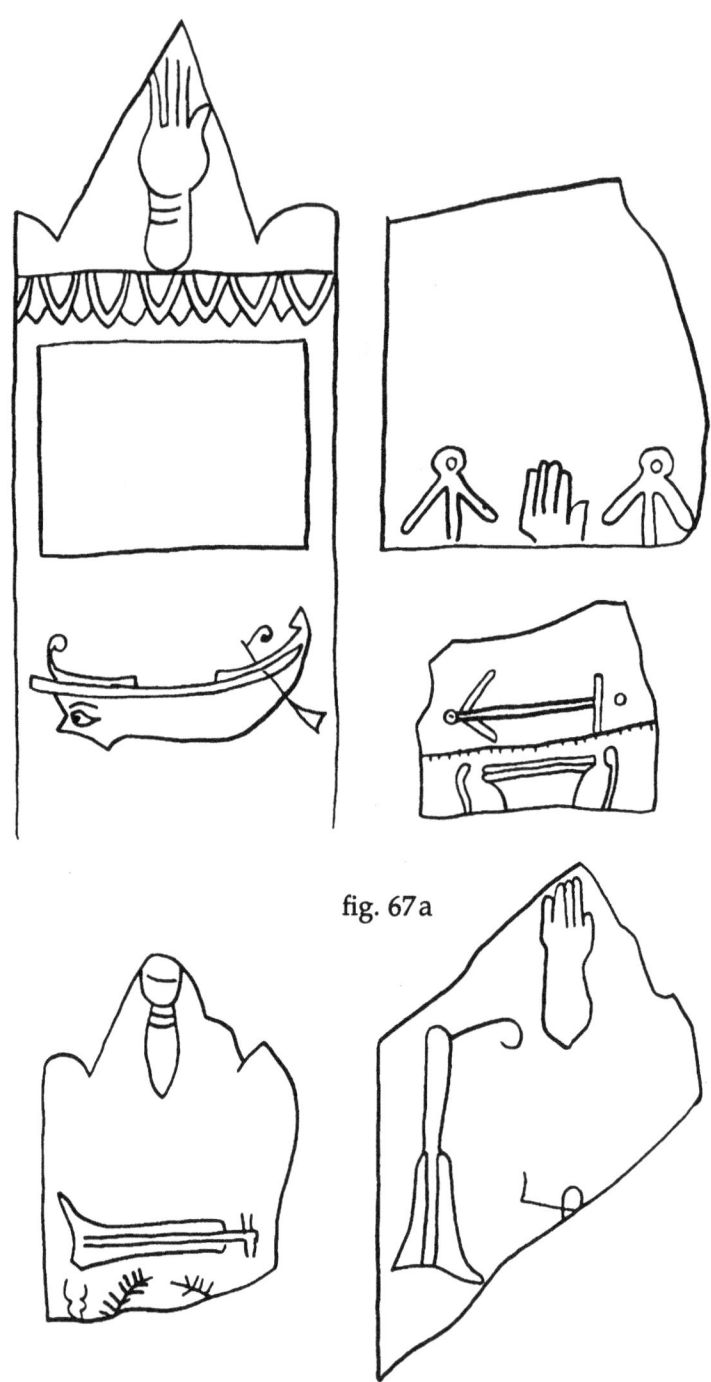

fig. 67a

fig. 67 b

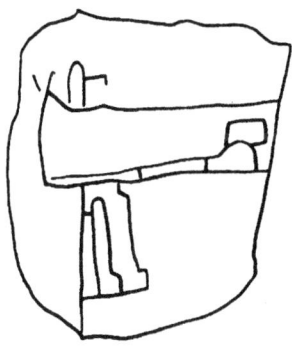

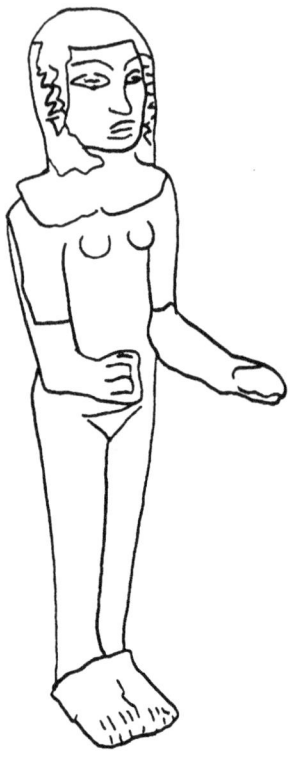

fig. 68

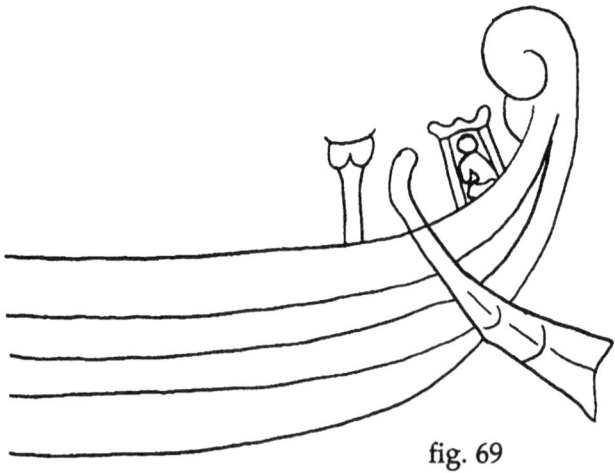

fig. 69

fig. 70

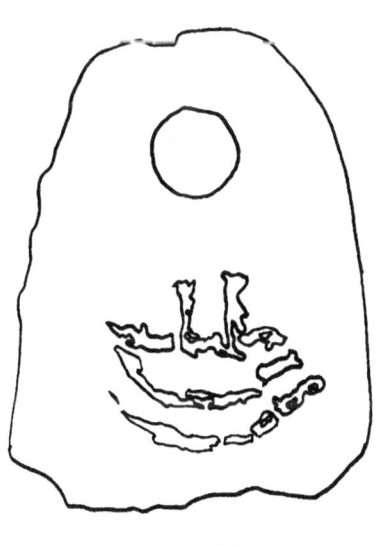

fig. 71

166 Each Man Cried Out to His God

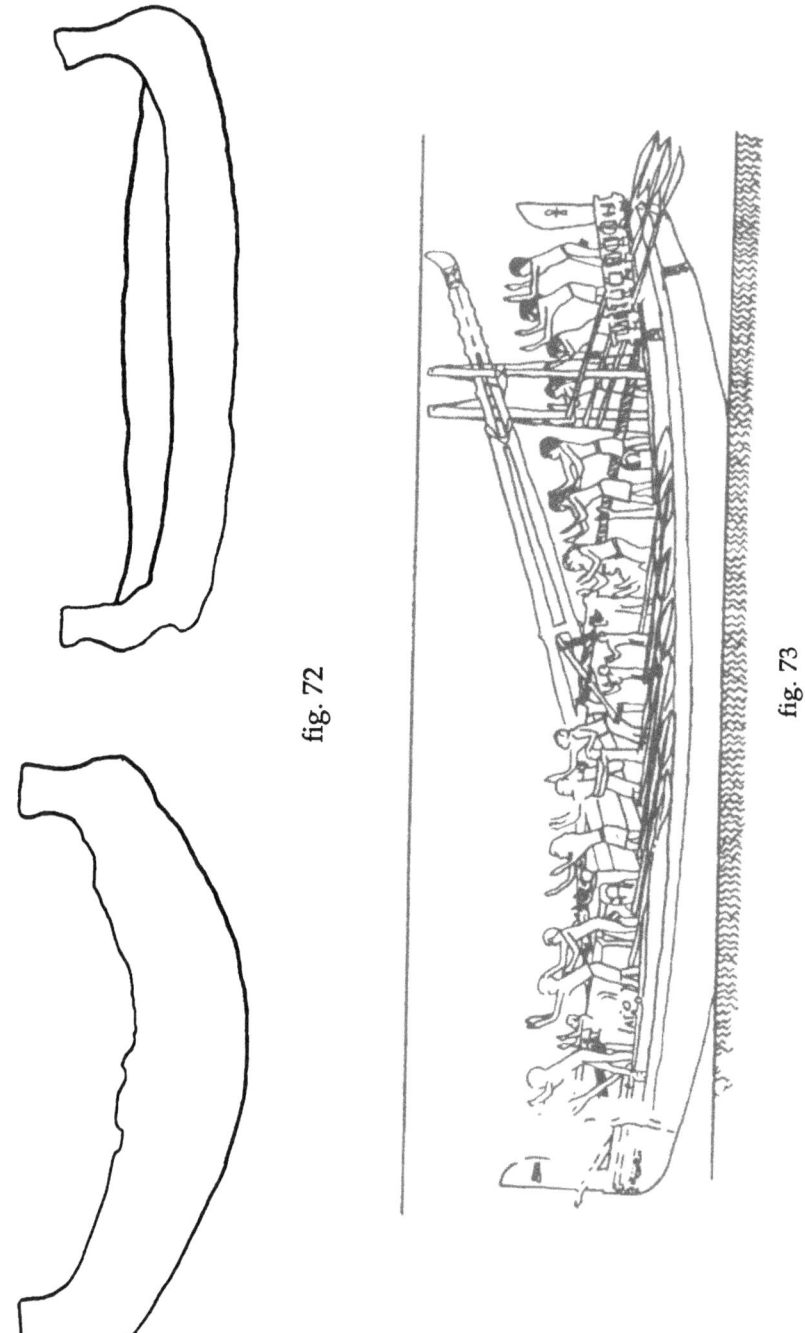

fig. 72

fig. 73

Figures

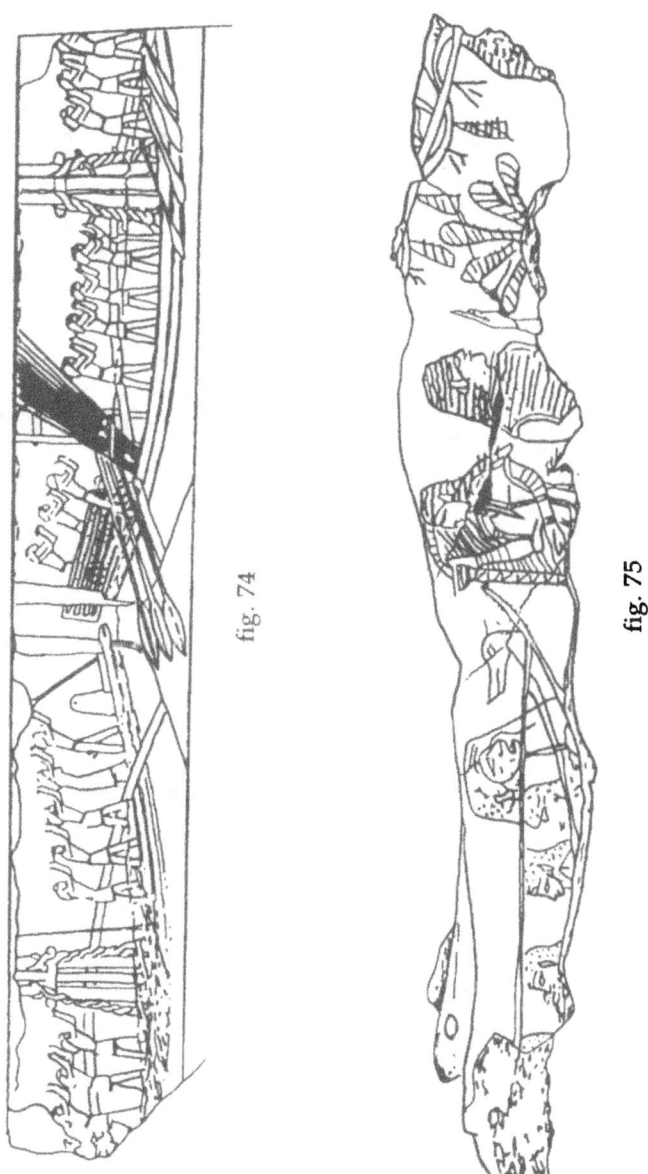

fig. 74

fig. 75

168　Each Man Cried Out to His God

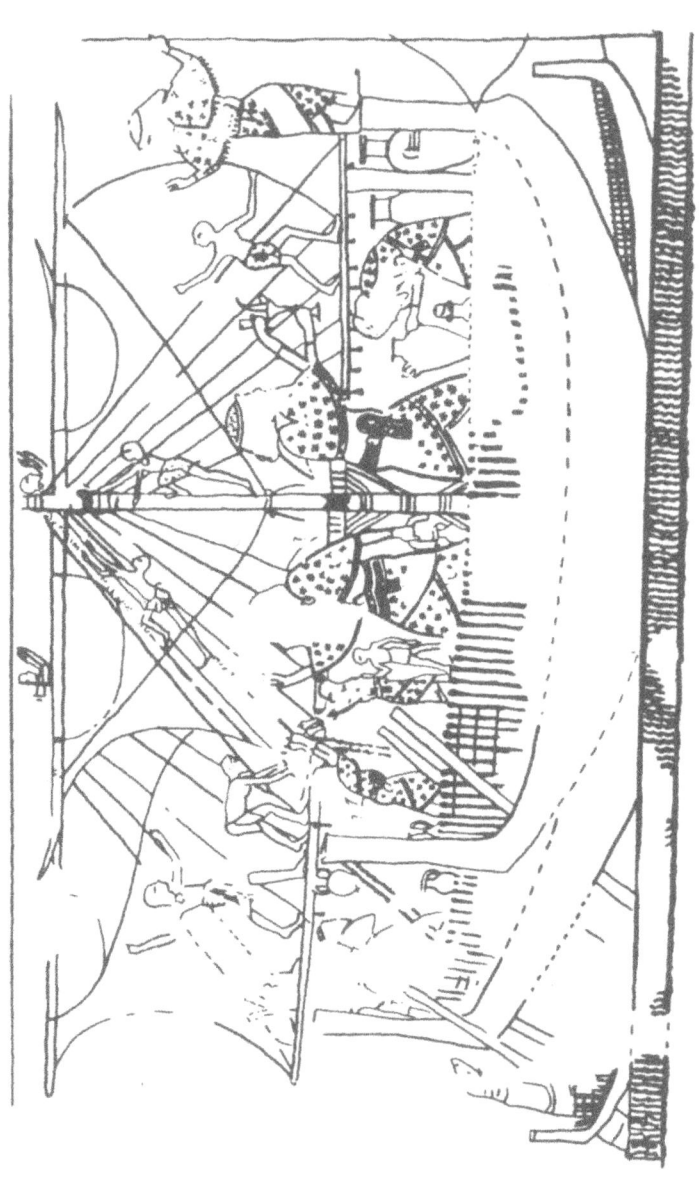

fig. 76a

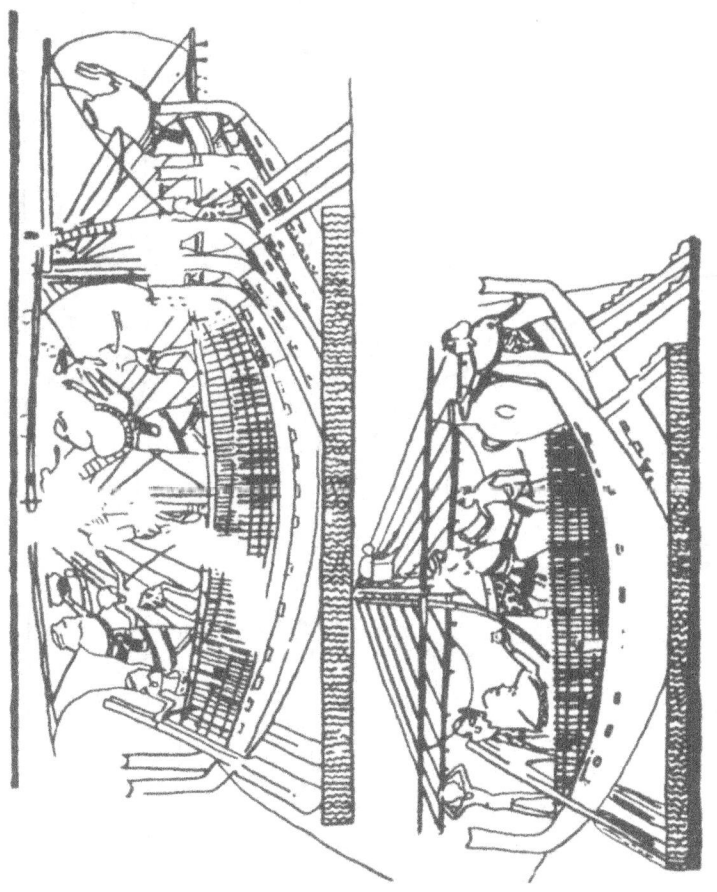

fig. 76b

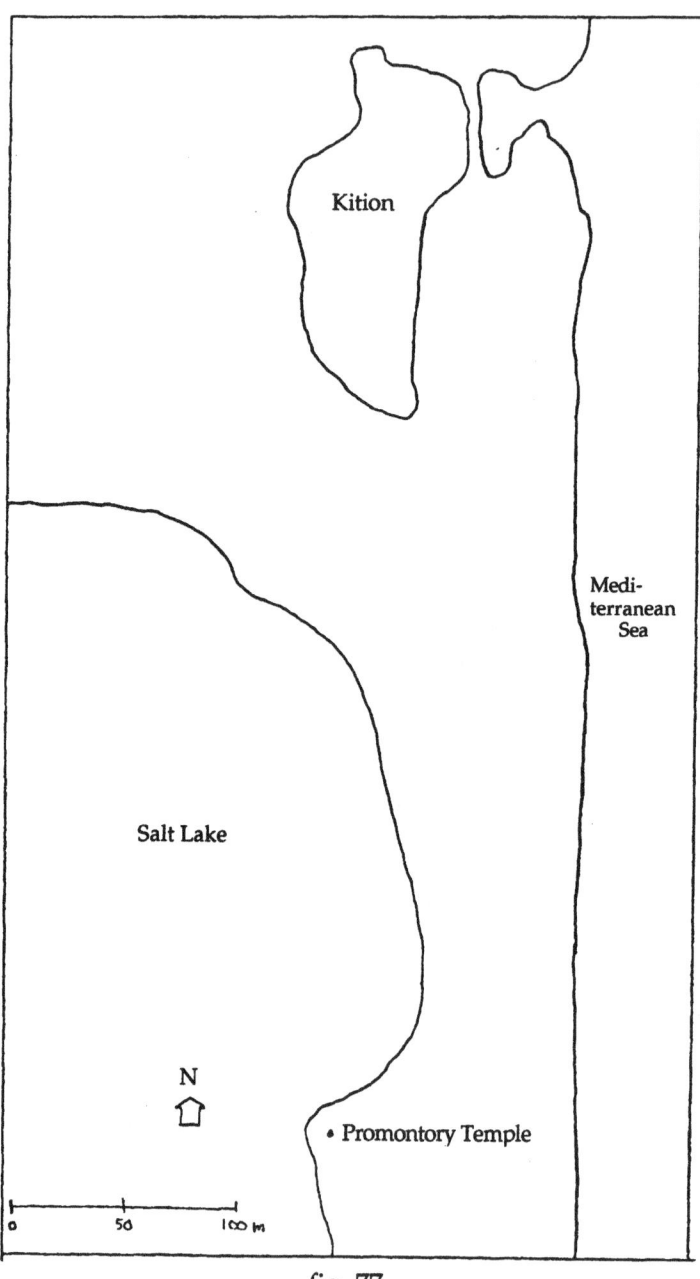

fig. 77

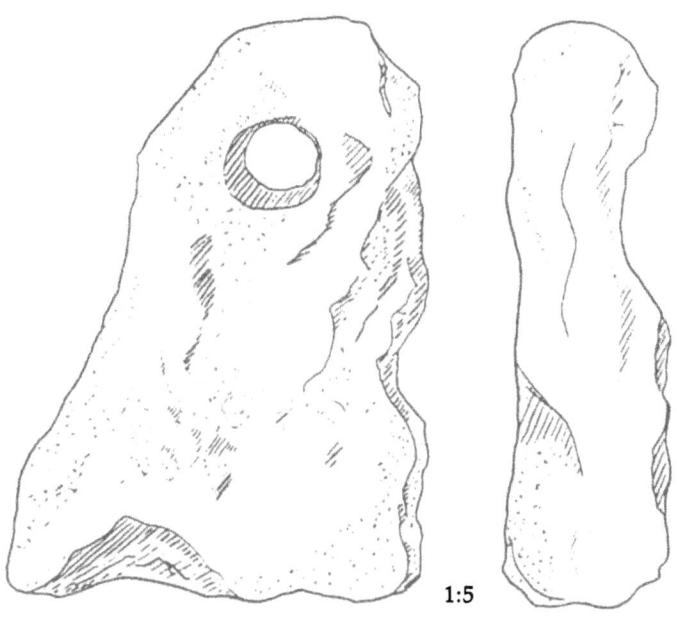

fig. 78

fig. 79

INDEX

anchors. *See* ship equipment and decorations
ancient Near Eastern texts
    Annals of Shalmaneser III, 21
    CIS I.264, 34n. 119, 81n. 42
    CTA 5.1.14, 29n. 94, 70n. 39
    Emar 373:74′, 378:10, 37, 37n. 131
    Esarhaddon/Ba'l of Tyre treaty, 10, 11, 13, 35, 95
    KAI 10, 45n. 27; 26 AIII.18, 23n. 65; 47, 33n. 111; 47.1, 35n. 120; 53, 31n. 99; 86, 35n. 119, 81n. 42; 129.1, 23n. 65; 244.3, 23n. 65
    KTU 1.1, 19n. 45; 1.2, 19n. 45; 1.2.19, .35, .37, 13n. 17; 1.3.III. 44, 56n. 95; 1.3. V.10, .13, .35, 56n. 95; 1.4.V.51-57, 19n. 46; 1.5.I.14, 29n. 94, 70n. 39; 1.6.II.7-9, .28-30, 56n. 95; 1.14.II.25, 13n. 17; 1.4.IV.7, 13n. 17; 1.14.IV.35, .39, 29n. 91; 1.16.I.6-9, 15; 1.16.I.8, 15n. 26, 16n. 30; 1.16.II. 44-47, 15; 1.16.II.46, 15n. 26, 16n. 30; 1.39.14, 27n. 85; 1.43.14, 27n. 85; 1.108.12, 56n. 95; 2.38, 65n. 11; 2.38. 13-14, 66n. 12
    KUB XXVII I rev ii.23, XXXIV.102, ii.13, 37, 37n. 130
    Middle Kingdom coffin text no. 61, 28, 45n. 28, 97
    Papyrus Sallier IV, 17-18, 65
Annales archaeology, 7n. 26
archaeology and religion, 7, 7n. 27, 8
astragali, 84
Ba'l cycle, 19
biblical references
    Exodus 14:2, 9, 18n. 38; 32, 56n. 95
    Numbers 33:7, 18n. 38
    Deuteronomy 2:8, 29n. 91; 33:26-29, 82n. 53
    I Samuel 4:12, 89n. 7
    II Samuel 3:31, 89n. 7
    I Kings 5-8, 54n. 79; 12:28, 32, 56n. 95
    II Kings 14:22, 29n. 91; 16:6, 29n. 91
    Isaiah 2:16, 18:1, 2, 16n. 33; 26:21, 16n. 31
    Jeremiah 16:6-7, 89n. 7
    Ezekiel 27, 88, 102; 27:3, 27:10, 27:11, 16n. 31; 27:26-36, 87, 87n. 2; 27:27-36, 89
    Amos 8:10, 89n. 7
    Jonah 1, 82n. 53; 1:3, 82; 1:5, 82; 1:7, 84; 1:8, 82, 82n. 50; 1:9, 11n. 7; 1:16, 82
    Micah 1:8-10, 89n. 7
    Nahum 3:8, 16n. 31
    Habakkuk 3:8-15, 25n. 76
    Psalms 18:8-16, 65:8, 77:17-20, 89:10, 107:23-30, 148:7-8, 82n. 53
    Job 40:25-32, 40:26b, 40:31, 40:31a, 40:31b, 17n. 33
    Lamentations 2:8, 16n. 31
bowls, 34, 34n. 116, 60, 69, 73, 79, 80
burial practices, 89-94
ceremonies and rituals, 73-85
    See also mortuary rituals, sacrifices
classical references
    Apollonius Rhodius, *The Argonautica* I.570-72, 9; I.955-60, 40n. 5, 55n. 85, 76, 76n. 12; IV. 1592-1602, 64n. 5, 71n. 45, 74n. 3; IV.1693, 41n. 7; IV.1701-4, 82n. 47
    Apuleius, *The Golden Ass* XI.1-7, 28n. 88; XI.16, 64, 74n. 3
    Arrian, *Annabasis of Alexander* II. 24.6, 33, 67; VI.3.1, 74n. 3; *Periplus Maris Euxini* XI, 76n. 12
    Artemidorus Daldianus, *Onirocritica* I.16, 32n. 105
    Diodorus V.58.2, 23n. 64, 25n. 72, 48n. 44, 82n. 48; XI.21.1, 24n. 71; XI.21.4, 23n. 64, 24; XIII.86.3, 23n. 64; XVII.104.1, 74n. 3
    Diogenianus I.10.11, 71n. 47, 78n. 23
    GGM, Periplus of Hanno, 22n. 62, 23n. 64, 24, 24n. 67, 59, 81n. 43; XIV, 84; Periplus of Pseudo-Scylax, 23n. 64, 24
    Heliodorus of Emesa, *Aethiopica* IV.16.8, 34n. 117, 75

Herodotus, *The Persian Wars* VII. 167, 24n. 71; VII.180, 64n. 5, 71n. 45, 74n. 3; VII.192, 24n. 66; VIII. 121-22, 40n. 3, 64n. 5, 71n. 45
Homer, *Iliad* VIII.238-40, 39, 55n. 87, 81n. 44; *Odyssey* II.430-34, 74n. 3; III.176-79, 39, 55n. 87, 81n. 45; III.287-90, 9-10; XII.345-49, 39n. 2; XII.345-51, 22
ID 1519-20, 1720-96, 2323-27, 2611, 23n. 64
Isidorus, *Origines* XVII.6, .11, 32n. 105
Livy XXIV.3.3-7, 41n. 7; XXIX.27.1-4, 82n. 47; XL.52.5-7, 39n. 2
Lucan, *The Civil War* V.552-60, 32
Lucretius, *De Rerum Natura* V.1226-32, 82n. 47
Pausanias, *Description of Greece* I.1.3, 9n. 1, 18n. 39, 22n. 61, 39n. 2; I.4.5, 76n. 12; I.40.5, 40n. 3; II.32.2, 39n. 2, 48n. 45, 76n. 15; III.24.7, 48n. 45, 76n. 15; IX.11.4, 76n. 15
Philo of Byblos, *Praep. Evang.* 1.10.11, 12-13; 1.10.16, .25, 13n. 17; 1.10.26, 67; 1.10.26-27, 23n. 63, 67; 1.10.27, 23n. 64, 33n. 111, 36n. 129; 1.10.28, 23n. 63, 36n. 129; 1.10.31, 24n. 65; 1.10.35, 23n. 63-64, 36n. 129
Polybius VII.9.2, 23n. 64, 24n. 65, 36n. 128
Procopius, *De Bello Gothico* IV:22, 19n. 43
Silius Italicus, *Punica* I.617-23, 74n. 3; II.580-83, 41n. 8, 55n. 86; III.6-11, 20n. 52; III.647-49, 20n. 53; III.663-65, 28n. 87; XII.605-22, 20; XIV.436-39, 20; XIV.436-40, 66, 68; XIV.436-41, 82; XIV.438, 20; XIV.440-41, 20n. 50; XIV.455-56, 83-84; XIV.457, 28n. 87; XIV.458-61, 20n. 51, 66, 68, 83; XIV.517-18, 66; XIV.572, 66; XIV.573, 66; XIV.580, 66; XV.158-62, 64n. 5, 71n. 45
Strabo, *Geography* II.3.4, 67; III.1.4, 33n. 112, III.5.5, 34, 58n. 109, 58n. 110, 75, 83n. 61; III.5.7, 59n. 111

Thucydides, *History of the Peloponnesian War* III.94.2, 41n. 7; VI.3.1-2, 22, 41n. 7; VI.32.1-2, 73; VI.44.2-3, 41; VII.26.2, 41n. 7
Valerius Maximus IX.2 ext. 1, 83
Virgil, *Aeneid* III.527-32, 64n. 5, 71n. 45, 73; V.775-78, 64n. 5, 71n. 45, 74; VI.149-51, 93n. 30; X.209-12, 63; *Georgics* I.424-37, 28
coins and coinage, 2, 5, 25-26, 29-30, 32, 34-36, 67-71, 93, 96-97, 100
companion animals. *See* symbols and companions of deities
cylinder seals, 18, 28-29, 56n. 95, 96-97
divination, 83-85
  cleromancy, 84
  soothsayers, 84
ethnicity, 1n. 1, 6n. 25
figurines, 32n. 106, 44, 45, 56, 58, 59, 66, 68, 68n. 36, 71-72, 83, 91, 100, 101
gems, 35
geographical names
  Achziv, 92
  Akko, 89, 90, 102
  Aradus (Arwad), 16n. 31, 26, 26n. 79, 36, 71
  Ashkelon, 23n. 64, 56, 89, 91, 99, 102
  Baʿal Ṣapôn, port, 18, 29, 96
  Byblos, 6, 21, 26, 43-46, 48, 55, 69, 71, 75, 89, 90, 99, 102
  ʾĒlat, port, 29, 97
  El-Khaḍr, 29n. 94
  Carthage, 5, 20, 24, 31n. 99, 32-34, 60, 66, 71, 75, 84, 98, 101
  Gader, 34, 58, 67, 69, 75, 83, 98, 101
  Karatepe, 69n. 36
  Kef el-Blida, 34, 69, 83, 93, 101
  Kition, 42n. 13, 49-52, 54, 60, 75, 99
  Kommos, 42n. 13
  Kuntillet ʿAjrûd, 29n. 94
  Minet el-Beida, 14, 46, 56n. 95, 91-92, 102
  Nahal Meʿarot, 57n. 96
  Rōʾšu Qudši, 21, 22, 81
  Rōš Milqart, 34, 81, 98
  Ṣapōn, Mount, 13-15, 19, 22, 65, 95-96
  Sarepta, 53, 59n. 117, 80
  Shave-Ziyyon, 32n. 106
  Sidon, 66-67, 69n. 36, 80

Taʿanach, 30n. 94
Tarshish, 82
Tel Dor, 57, 80
Tell el-Dabʿa, 18, 29, 96, 97
Tell Sūkās, 52-54, 58, 75, 99
Tharros, 59
Tyre, 10, 16n. 31, 21-22, 25, 26n. 79, 29, 32n. 106, 33, 35, 66, 67, 69, 69n. 36, 78, 88-89, 96, 98, 100
Ugarit, 5, 6, 14, 19, 22, 22n. 63, 27, 29, 33, 36n. 129, 42n. 11, 42n. 13, 46-49, 50, 56n. 95, 65-66, 75, 89, 91-92, 95, 99-100, 102
See also temples and shrines
gods and goddesses, 9-38
Adad, 57n. 95
ʿAglibōl, 56n. 95
ʿAnat, 56n. 95
Artemis, 9, 31n. 99, 41
ʾAšerah, 26-30, 31-32, 38, 51n. 61, 56n. 90, 66, 68, 70-72, 96-98, 100
ʿAštart (Astarte), 27n. 84, 53, 58n. 107
ʿAtik, 56n. 95
Baʿlat Gebal, 17, 28, 45, 45n. 28, 97
Baʿl-Haddu, 10, 15, 19, 22n. 63, 23n. 65, 35n. 120, 36n. 129, 37, 51n. 61, 56, 82n. 53
Baʿl Ḥamōn, 5, 20, 24n. 67, 31-33, 96
Baʿl Malagê, 10, 11-13, 35, 37, 95
Baʿl Rōʾš, 21-22, 37, 81, 96
Baʿl Šamêm, 10, 11, 23n. 65, 25n. 76, 35, 37, 58, 95
Baʿl Ṣapōn, 5-6, 10-11, 13-19, 22, 29, 35, 37, 48-49, 65, 95-97, 100
Baʿl Ṣur, 35
Daggay ʾAṯirati, 27
Dagnu (Dagan), 13n. 17, 36n. 128, 47
Demarous, 23n. 63, 24n. 65, 36n. 129
ʾĒl, 23n. 65, 56n. 95
ʾĒlat, 27n. 84, 29, 97
Fish-tailed god/monster, 26n. 79, 36
Hades, 22n. 63
Halios Gerōn, 36
Ḥathor, 28-29, 45n. 28, 51n. 61, 66, 97
Hekate, 31n. 99
Hephaistos, 13

Herakles and Herakles-Milqart, 33-36, 38, 51n. 61, 58, 67, 69, 75, 81, 83, 98, 100, 101
Iršappa, 35, 37, 38, 98
Išmun (Eshmun), 35, 60
Jove/Jupiter, 20, 96
Kôṯar, 13, 13n. 16
Kronos, 22n. 63
Lady of Byblos. *See Baʿlat Gebal*
Libyan Ammon, 20, 37, 66, 68, 83, 96
"Marine" deity/god, 25-26, 35, 38, 71, 96
Milqart, 5n. 19, 23n. 63, 25n. 76, 30n. 96, 33-37, 38, 45, 51n. 61, 58, 60, 67, 69, 70n. 40, 75, 81, 83, 98, 100, 101
Môt, 22n. 63
Nereus, 36
Nergal, 35, 37, 38, 98
Pontos, 23n. 63, 36n. 129, 67
Poseidon, 22, 23-25, 37-38, 39, 48, 59, 81, 82, 96, 101
Qudšu, 17, 27n. 83, 29n. 94, 30n. 95, 31, 51n. 61, 97
Rašp (Reshef), 37, 45n. 26
Šarruma, 57n. 95
Saturn, 20, 24n. 67, 31
Sekhmet, 30n. 95
Selene, 27n. 84, 31n. 99
Sidon, 67
Tešub, 57n. 95
Tinnit (Tanit), 5, 5n. 21, 26, 30-33, 38, 53, 66, 70, 72, 97, 98, 100
Triton, 36, 36n. 128, 63
Yahweh, 11n. 7, 25n. 76, 30n. 94, 56n. 95, 82, 82n. 53, 101
Yamm, 19, 19n. 47, 22, 22n. 63, 35n. 120, 36n. 129, 67, 96
Yariḫ, 27
Zeus, Zeus Kasios, Zeus Meilichios, Zeus Soter, 10, 12-13, 19, 19n. 44, 22n. 63, 24n. 65, 39, 51n. 61, 65
incense stands and braziers, 79
mortuary ritual, 88-89
See also burial practices
musical instruments, 79-80, 101
merchants, 19, 34, 56, 75
navigation, 9, 14, 22, 27, 28, 28n. 87, 33, 38, 41, 55, 70-71, 77, 95, 97, 99
pendants, 27, 80, 97

periploi, 41.
　See also Classical references,
　　GGM
razors, 34, 69
reliefs
　Assyrian, 16n. 31, 68-69, 100
　Egyptian, 78-79, 101
　Hurrian, 57n. 95
sacred anchors. See ship equipment
sacred promontories and headlands, 2,
　21, 22, 24, 33, 34, 38, 40-41, 55, 59-
　61, 73, 74-75, 81, 84-85, 87, 96, 98-
　101
sacrifices, 3, 20, 22, 24, 34, 38, 74-75, 77-
　78, 81-83, 85, 90, 93, 96, 98, 100-
　102
　See also ceremonies and rituals
sacrificial stelae, 5, 31-34, 38, 66, 68, 71-
　72, 74, 76-78, 85, 93n. 28, 97, 100
seals and seal stones, 30n. 96, 34, 36, 69
　See also cylinder seals
stelae, 14, 21, 24n. 67, 27, 30n. 96, 34, 44,
　45n. 26, 47, 51n. 61, 52, 69, 95, 97
　See also sacrificial stelae
ship equipment and decorations,
　anchors, 5, 19, 22, 34n. 116, 42-44, 48-
　　49, 51-52, 54, 71, 76-77, 88-92, 94,
　　98, 100, 102
　anchor stocks, 2, 19, 52, 54, 61, 75-76,
　　84
　holy steering rudders, 71n. 47, 78n.
　　23
　oars, 16, 17n. 33, 26n. 81, 40, 71
　oculi (apotropaic eyes), 4, 63, 69n.
　　36, 70, 72, 99-100
　poles, 27, 31, 72, 97
　prow figure (figurehead), 26, 29-30,
　　30n. 95, 30n. 96, 34, 63, 67, 69-70,
　　72, 93, 98-100
　sacred anchors (sheet anchors), 2,
　　33, 40, 71, 76-77
　sails, 17n. 33, 93
　shrines aboard ship, 71
　standards, 33, 38, 70, 72, 97, 100
　steering oars and rudders, 5, 16,
　　17n. 33, 26n. 81, 27, 28, 33, 40,
　　45n. 28, 71, 77, 93, 97-98, 100
　stone anchors, 6, 14, 33, 42-45, 47-52,
　　54, 61, 75, 78, 90-92, 95, 100, 102
　stylides, 2n. 5, 27n. 84, 69n. 36
　stylis, 70, 72

ship graffiti, 50, 57n. 96
ship models, 2, 4, 40-41, 44-45, 48, 55,
　61, 75-76, 90, 92, 94, 99-100, 102
ships and parts of ships, 63-72
　boats, 8, 11, 18, 32, 16n. 33, 57, 65, 67,
　　69, 72, 78, 94, 97
　deck, 79
　crow's nest, 79
　fishing boats, 17n. 33, 67
　galleys, 29, 31, 66, 70, 83, 97, 100
　hippoi, 26, 67, 69
　hull, 26n. 81, 32n. 106, 61, 65, 71, 76,
　　79, 83, 93
　keels, 83, 101
　Kenamun flotilla, 68n. 36, 79, 101
　merchant ships, 16n. 31, 17n. 33, 37
　prow, 4, 33, 40, 64, 65, 68, 70-72, 74,
　　77, 79, 83, 92, 93n. 28, 98-100
　rigging, 79
　stern, 20, 27, 31, 33, 38, 46n. 31, 64-
　　66, 68-73, 77, 83, 93, 96-100
　warships and war galleys, 16n. 31,
　　17n. 33, 20, 30, 30n. 95, 66-70, 82-
　　83, 93, 96-98, 100-101
ships' names, 63-64, 66-67, 72, 99
ship's crew, 26, 28, 38, 65, 72, 77, 79-82,
　84, 87, 89, 101-102
　captain, 24, 59, 79, 101
　pilot (navigator), 20, 27-29, 38, 70,
　　72, 77-78, 83, 97, 101-102
ship terminology
　Eg. *śk.ty* (ship), 17n. 33
　Heb. *kalê gōmeʾ* (reed vessels), 17n.
　　33; *ʾŏnîyāh* (ship), 16n. 31, 89;
　　ṣilṣal dāgîm (fishing boat), 17n.
　　33; *ṣilṣal kənāpāyīm* (oared boat),
　　17n. 33; *śukkôt* (ship), 17n. 33
　Ug. *any* (ship), 15, 16n. 31, 65, 66,
　　96; *ṯkt*(ship), 17n. 33
　West Semitic *ʾany* (ship), 17-18, 65
shipwrecks, 10, 41, 55, 61, 64-68, 87, 100
　El Barco de El Sec, 65n. 8, 68n. 29
　Cape Gelidonya, 64n. 8, 68n. 29, 79,
　　84, 102
　Lilybaeum, 65n. 8, 68n. 29
　Maʿagan Mikhael, 65n. 8, 68n. 29
　Uluburun, 42, 43n. 14, 65n. 8, 68,
　　68n. 29, 69n. 36, 79, 100, 101
statues, 20, 35-36, 51n. 61, 58, 66, 98

symbols and companions of deities
- bull and bull calf, 18, 29, 56, 56n. 95, 59, 91, 96
- caduceus, 31, 72, 100
- crescent-and-disk, 27-28, 31-32, 66, 70, 96-97, 100
- crescent moon, 27-28, 31, 31n. 99, 38, 66, 70, 96-97, 100
- dolphins, 32, 97
- fish, 32, 97
- hippokamp or winged seahorse, 22, 23n. 63, 25-26, 35, 37, 71, 96
- horse, 25-26, 67, 69-70, 70n. 43, 71, 96, 100
- lion or lioness, 18, 27n. 83, 29-30, 69-71, 97, 100
- Sign of Tinnit (Tanit), 31-33, 38, 72, 97, 100
- snake, 18, 29, 97

temples and shrines, 36-61, 74-76, 81
- ꜥAin Dara, 54
- Ashkelon, 56, 91, 99
- Byblos, 43-45, 48, 75, 90, 99
- Capo San Marco, 59-60, 99
- Kition, 49-52, 60, 75, 99
- Kommos, 59, 99
- Makmish (Tel Michal), 57-58, 99
- Nahariyah, 55-56, 99
- Ras ed-Drek, 60, 99
- Serepta, Tinnit/ ꜥAštart temple, 53
- Tell Sūkās, 52-54, 58, 75, 99
- Tell Taꜥyinat, 54
- Tel Mevorakh, 57
- Tel Nami, 57n. 96
- Temple of Herakles, Erythrae, 35
- Temple of Milqart, Gader, 34, 58, 98
- Temple of Poseidon, Cadmus myth, 25, 48, 82, 96
- Temple of Saturn (Baꜥl Ḥamōn), Carthage, 24n. 67
- Temple of Solomon, Jerusalem, 54
- Ugarit, 14, 22, 33, 46-49, 50, 75, 92, 95, 99

tomb paintings, 34, 68, 69, 79, 83, 93, 94, 98, 100-102

votive offerings, 2, 14, 32n. 106, 40-42, 45-46, 48-49, 51n. 61, 55, 58-61, 74-76, 80, 85, 95, 99, 102
- anchors, 2, 6, 14, 22, 40-41, 44, 47-52, 54-55, 61, 71, 75-77, 90, 92, 95, 99-100
- model ships, 2, 4, 40-41, 44, 48, 76, 99, 102
- rudders, 71-72

www.ingramcontent.com/pod-product-compliance
Lightning Source LLC
Chambersburg PA
CBHW070614300426
44113CB00010B/1529